REMINISCENCES

OF A

COUNTRY JOURNALIST.

REMINISCENCES

OF A

COUNTRY JOURNALIST.

BY

THOMAS FROST,

AUTHOR OF "FORTY YEARS' RECOLLECTIONS," "IN KENT WITH
CHARLES DICKENS," ETC.

London:

WARD AND DOWNEY,

12, YORK STREET, COVENT GARDEN.

1886.

[*All rights reserved.*]

PREFACE.

It has been remarked by more than one keen observer of human nature, that the life of the most obscure individual, if truthfully told, would be both interesting and instructive; and the observation applies with more than ordinary force to the lives of men who, like authors and actors, are known, and yet unknown, to a large proportion of the community of which they form a part. Few persons connect what they read with the man from whose brain it has emanated. The majority peruse a book without a thought of its genesis, or any idea as to the author. To them he is is an abstraction, and his life a mystery.

These remarks apply with the greatest force to authors who adopt literature as a profession, the plodders along its highways and byeways, who work as methodically and as regularly as artisans, and support themselves and their families by the products of their brains. The world little knows how much it is indebted to such men, without whom the gigantic, ever-teeming newspaper and periodical press of this country could have no existence. Sometimes it gets a glimpse of the indebtedness when one of the ablest of its teachers has passed away from this life, as unknown as the man whose light Dr. Mackay saw nightly gleaming from the window of a London garret; but during their lives it knows no more of them than the poet knew of that solitary brain-worker by the midnight lamp, and even when they have passed away it learns only that they were the authors of certain works by which it has been delighted and instructed. Of their lives it knows nothing.

In the instance of the humble individual who presents this transcript of his past life,—in which nothing has been exaggerated or over-coloured, nothing distorted or concealed,—whatever interest the record may have for his readers may be supposed to be enhanced by the circumstance that, while his footfalls along the path of life have been too noiseless to attract public attention, the literary labours of his later years have differed so widely in character as to evoke from the critics some amusing speculations as to his position and pursuits. While one has conjectured that the writer must have been in the habit, throughout his life, of travelling from one fair to another, associating with clowns and acrobats, another has surmised that he is a veteran revolutionist who has kept himself dark, and that his associates in the past have been the foreign refugees who haunt the cafés around Leicester Square. How near these conflicting ideas are to the truth will appear in the following pages.

CONTENTS.

CHAPTER I.

My birthplace—Topographical changes—Ghastly traditions of the "George Inn"—Mother Hotwater's closet—Gipsy camps at Penge and Anerley—Story told by the late Dr. Gardiner 1

CHAPTER II.

The forwarding branch of the contraband trade—"Smuggler's Hall"—Lawyer Drummond and Farmer Sharpe—Biggin Hill—A well-kept secret—The Beulah Spa Gardens—Charles Cochrane 17

CHAPTER III.

The southern suburbs fifty years ago—A ghastly discovery in an osier-bed—The murder of Hannah Brown—A reminiscence of Sarah Gale—Forgotten localities in Lambeth . . 32

CHAPTER IV.

My apprenticeship in typography and literature—Correspondence with Henry Hetherington—My first appearance in print—*Chapman's Miscellany*—A mysterious disappearance—The lost sheep found—A singular elopement 38

CHAPTER V.

Holywell Street and "Satanic literature"—The notorious Dugdale—My experiences as a publisher—James Blackaby, poet and shoemaker—A literary policeman—The *Penny Punch*—Threatened action for libel—Conspiracy against my life 52

CHAPTER VI.

The Communist propaganda in England—Goodwyn Barmby and the *Communist Chronicle*—The short-lived *Communist Journal*—Successful ventures in a new field—Retirement from business—First attempt at dramatic writing—At a stage-door and a tavern bar—Biddles, of the Bower—William Rogers, the comedian 65

CHAPTER VII.

Transactions with a broken-down publisher—A glimpse of the canvassing trade—A lecture which I did not deliver, and books which I did not write—The turn of the tide—Engagement on "Papers for the People"—David Page and the *Fifeshire Journal*—Successful return to fiction . . . 76

CHAPTER VIII.

The Fraternal Democrats—Julian Harney—Carl Schapper—Colonel Oborski—A strange story—"Where's Eliza?"—Fortune frowns again—A typographical Chamber of Horrors—Writing to plates—Canvassing for a life assurance company—Some peculiar people 85

CHAPTER IX.

Reading for the press—A theatrical journal in embryo—Bookmaking—Parliamentary reporting—G. F. Muntz and the Wolverhampton lock-maker—Ernest Jones's unfinished novel—I take up the broken thread 100

CHAPTER X.

At a loose end again—My first editorship—A reminiscence of Miss Meteyard—James Hain Friswell—George Frederick Pardon—A gigantic scheme that was never realized . . 111

CHAPTER XI.

Introduction to journalism—Leader-writing for the *Birmingham Journal*—Michael Feeney—Liverpool journalism—The

Beans and the *Albion*—The leader-writers of that day—John Wade—John Pope Hennessy—Michael James Whitty and the *Daily Post*—Henry Greenwood—Mr. E. R. Russell, M.P. 117

CHAPTER XII.

Roche, of the *Courier*—James Mahony, the artist—"The Book of the Baltic"—Samuel Lover—Sir Cusack Roney—"A Month in Ireland"—A dishonest publisher—The *Shrewsbury Chronicle* 127

CHAPTER XIII.

A shadow on my path—An electioneering mission—A search for a young lady—A visit to York—Newsome's circus—Vivian, the ring-master—The brothers Francisco—Alfred Burgess—A circus-man's criticism of Dickens 135

CHAPTER XIV.

Kean's revivals at the Princess's—Phelps at Drury Lane—The fire at the Adelphi—Realistic failures—Ramo Samee—The rope trick—Redmond and the butcher—Bunglers with the rope—Lizzie Anderson—Amateur practice 155

CHAPTER XV.

The London Pavilion—Willio, the contortionist—The dead alive—Olmar, the gymnast—Little Corelli—Boy or girl?—Transformation of Lulu—Parelli and Costello—Luke Majilton—Who's who?—Professional names—The Brothers Price—A slice of good fortune—Madame Senyah—Back-slang . 166

CHAPTER XVI.

The return of sunshine—Writing for a periodical—What is a "penny dreadful"?—Writers for the penny periodicals—Lady novelists—"Bob Lumley's Secret"—Another attempt at dramatic writing—Shepherd, of the Surrey—Managerial courtesies—Townsend, the dramatist—Anecdote of Yates . 175

CHAPTER XVII.

The London letters of the *Albion*—Blunders of Mr. Grant—Mr. Kelly—Death of Charles B. Bean—Controversy with Sir Howard Douglas—Article in the *United Service Magazine*—A mysterious individual—Another dishonest publisher—Contributions to *Et Cetera*—Arthur Raggett Cole . . 187

CHAPTER XVIII.

Editorship of the *Gentleman's Journal*—A misunderstanding about a presentation—Experiences of writing for the magazines—The fortunes of a farce—Mr. J. S. Clarke and Mr. Joyce—A Durham journalist's experience—Cessation of my connection with the *Shrewsbury Chronicle*—Mr. B. H. Grindley and the *Albion*—Mr. William Hind—At a loose end again . . 203

CHAPTER XIX.

A batch of literary projects—"Half-hours with the Early Explorers"—The "pot-boiler" that became a great success—A friendly hint—Dr. Manning—On the staff of the Religious Tract Society—George Belmore and the Cookes—Charlie Keith, "the roving English clown"—"The Old Showmen and the Old London Fairs"—"Circus Life and Circus Celebrities"—A reviewer's error—Mistake in a railway-carriage 213

CHAPTER XX.

An old volume of letters—A literary mystery—Researches at the Museum—Study of the letters—Correspondence with Lord Lyttelton and Lord Edmund Fitzmaurice—Help from Hagley—The statement of Combe brought to light—A banshee story—"The Secret Societies of the European Revolution"—Opportune references to the subject by Lord Beaconsfield and Cardinal Manning 225

CHAPTER XXI.

Removal to Croydon, where I find myself forgotten—Mr. Frederick Baldiston and the *Croydon Chronicle*—" Recollections of an old Croydonian "—Another flitting—Rural rambles, and their literary results—An Irish Colenso—An extraordinary project—Correspondence concerning literature for boys 243

CHAPTER XXII.

" In Kent with Charles Dickens "—Letter from a lady—" Forty Years' Recollections "—How publishers' readers sometimes read manuscripts—Letter from Mr. John Morley—Reviews—Dr. Mackay's protest—My reply, and a friendly comment—Mrs. Victoria Woodhall 262

CHAPTER XXIII.

Mr. H. H. Murphy and the *Sheffield Evening Post*—First impressions of Sheffield—Mr. Murphy prosecuted for libel—Mr. J. E. Bloomer—Result of the trial—Sheffield sewage—The children of Thomas Miller, the poet—Letter from Lord Wharncliffe 273

CHAPTER XXIV.

Barnsley journalism—Reporting in the country—Lost in a fog—Zigzagging in a swamp—" Life and Times of John Vallance "—John Hugh Burland—Thomas Lister, the Barnsley poet and naturalist—Yorkshire dialects—Reuben Hallam and Charles Rogers 285

CHAPTER XXV.

A disappointment and another change—First impressions of Liverpool—The *Evening Albion* and the *Telephone*—My Italian host—A priest in search of relatives—Transfer of the papers to a company—Letter from Mr. Moy Thomas—Return to Barnsley 308

CHAPTER XXVI.

The *Barnsley Independent*—Drawbacks to its success—Controversy with a correspondent—The general election—Split in the Liberal camp—Mr. C. S. Kenny—Mr. Pickard—Liberal compact with the miners—National Association of Journalists—Deterioration of journalism—Results of a career considered successful 313

REMINISCENCES

OF A

COUNTRY JOURNALIST.

CHAPTER I.

My birthplace—Topographical changes—Ghastly traditions of the "George Inn"—Mother Hotwater's closet—Gipsy camps at Penge and Anerley—Story told by the late Dr. Gardiner.

Though my memory does not carry me back in time so far as that of a deceased relative, who used to gravely aver that the first thing he remembered was hearing his mother's keys rattle in her pocket three days before he was born, I can remember living, some time about the year 1828, in a wooden house, painted white, a few doors north of the "Bricklayers' Arms" public-house, in the main street of Croydon, then a country town nine miles from London, but now absorbed into the metropolitan suburbs. That old house exists no longer, having been demolished more than forty years ago. Indeed, the changes in that part of the town have been so great that old inhabitants who have been absent for thirty or forty years find themselves lost in the new streets between the Old Town and the southern portion of High

Street, or the villa-lined roads of Addiscombe and the Common, which I remember as green pastures and cottage gardens. Katherine Street was then known as King's Arms Yard, and Park Street as Markby's Yard.

The best shops were then in the narrowest portion of High Street, north of the "Green Dragon." There were very few in North End, and those of little repute, much of the frontage there being occupied with the yards of builders and masons. George Street consisted entirely of private houses, with the exception of the still existing veterinary forge and the draper's shop at the south-western corner, which had the reputation of being haunted, a belief which arose from the fact that it had formerly been an inn, and that, a century or more ago, several travellers and pedlars were known to have been entertained in the house, and were never seen afterwards. They were supposed to have been murdered by the people of the inn, which was thereupon believed to be haunted by their troubled spirits. This house, formerly the "George Inn," which gave its name to the neighbouring George Yard, was many years ago in the occupation of a linendraper named Stapelton, one of whose daughters informed a cousin of my own that there was a closet in the house, the door of which had been nailed up by some former tenant, perhaps a century before, and had never been opened since.

If my memory does not deceive me as to these traditions, this was the house in which lived a singular old woman, who was long remembered by the name of Mother Hotwater, and of whom many strange stories used to be told when I was a boy. One of these was, that she had a closet into which she placed the household gear whenever it needed cleaning; and on opening the door on the following morning found the work done. Some domestic sprite, akin to the brownies of Scotland, washed the dishes, cleaned the knives, and performed any similar office that the old woman required of it. Among the needlewomen and domestic servants of the town it used, forty years ago, to be a common saying when they were busy, "I wish we had Mother Hotwater's closet."

Another tradition attributed to the old witch a prophecy that, when she had been dead a hundred years she would rise from her grave. It is said that the time when this prediction should have been fulfilled is past, but the year of the dame's decease is unknown, and even her name, as it is now pronounced, does not occur in the list given by Ducarel of persons buried in the vaults and precincts of the parish church. The only name resembling it of which any record exists is Atwater, still borne by a family in the parish, which is preserved in a copper token, impressed with the name of Edmund Atwater, without any date. This may have been the name of the old lady who possessed such a very remarkable closet, corruptions of the names of persons and places by the substitution of *o* for *a* being not uncommon. Croydon, for instance, was formerly called Craydon, and the name of another Surrey town has been similarly changed from Darking to Dorking, the older forms being in use among the rural population down to a period within my own recollection. Tolworth, again, in old maps and records is written Talwarth.

Norwood, half a century ago, where not covered with oak-woods, was a furze-clad waste, with a few patches of cultivated land; and the inhabitants, a few farmers and labourers, with almost as large a shifting population of gipsies who pitched their tents about Anerley and Penge. I remember Parchmore Road as a green lane, impassable in winter, while the ground eastward, now intersected by the villa-lined road from Whitehorse Road to Upper Norwood, was a thick wood, in which I have seen rabbits running and heard the nightingale sing. The gipsies who frequented the woods and green lanes were not held in such disrepute as in some other localities, perhaps from the circumstance of the Lees and Coopers being reputed rich. Stories were current in my boyhood of Adam Lee—hanged with his son, Thomas Lee, at Horsemonger Lane Gaol, for an alleged robbery with violence at Hersham, between Esher and Walton, but generally regarded as victims of a mistake as to identity—having his coat-buttons made of guineas, and his vest-buttons of seven-shilling pieces, and giving his daughter a peck measure full of gold coins as her dowry. An old master baker, named Theobald, told me, forty years ago, that he and Adam Lee had played the violin at farm-houses around Norwood and Streatham, when a dance was given on the occasion of a birthday or a wedding; and an old woman, the mother, I believe, of Gipsy Cooper, of pugilistic renown, was for many years allowed to pretend to reveal the fortune of all inquirers who crossed her palm with a piece of silver in the Beulah Spa Gardens, a once famous summer resort which has long ceased to exist.

Fifty years ago there was a considerable breadth of pasture-land between the upper and lower portions of the hamlet, respectively within the parishes of Croydon and Lambeth, and the former was still surrounded on the south and east by thick woods, in which rabbits and hedgehogs burrowed, and the cooing of the ring-dove formed an accompaniment to the melody of innumerable finches and warblers. The houses with which the northward slope of the ridge was beginning to be dotted stood at long intervals, and there were not half a dozen shops in the place. The household of my maternal grandmother, who was one of the oldest inhabitants, was supplied with bread from the neighbouring village of Streatham, and with fish by an old Irishwoman, mother of the famous pugilist, Ned O'Neale. Peggy O'Neale carried her fish in a flat basket, poised on her head, and decked her neck and shoulders with a handkerchief of yellow silk. Pugilism was not considered disreputable in those days, when it was patronized by royalty and the aristocracy, and Peggy had no little pride in the achievements of her bull-necked son, which she would recount to her customers with evident relish, and unfailing fluency of language. I well remember her sitting on the doorstep, with her basket of fish by her side, relating to my grandmother and one of my mother's sisters, in a very graphic manner, the incidents of Ned's great fight with White-headed Bob, in which the former scored a victory. Like most of the prize-fighters of that day, O'Neale retired from the ring when he had won enough money to purchase the goodwill of a public-house, and for many years kept the "Rose and Crown," in the cross-road leading from Norwood to Streatham.

My mother remembered Norwood when the hamlet consisted of about a score of farm-houses and cottages scattered at considerable intervals along the lanes which intersected the woods, and the only means of communication with the metropolis was the carrier's tilted cart. From the parish churches of Lambeth and Camberwell to that of Croydon there was not a single place of worship, so sparse was the population, the former places, now so populous, being then but villages, and the latter, now a suburb of London, a quiet country town. The greater part of the ridge over which the southern portion of the hamlet was scattered was covered with thick woods of oak and hazel, which extended southward to Croydon Common (no longer existing), and eastward to the villages of Sydenham and Beckenham. The lower northern portion, sloping towards the valley of the Thames, was a rushy waste, upon which two or three small farmers grazed their cows and their geese.

Of this Common there was still a remnant forty years ago, upon which I have often, when a boy, caught the nimble lizard and cut sods of turf for my lark's cage. It was a square space of about an acre in extent, opposite the detached houses known as Boat House and Hollingbourne House, and bounded on the farther side by the Tivoli Gardens. From time to time a company of strolling players set up their canvas theatre there, or a mountebanking circus troupe selected the smoothest spot for their uncanopied arena. There I more than once saw Clark's circus pitched, with the old man in a scarlet coat and white cords acting as his own ring-master, his daughter Laura leaping through "balloons" and over banners from the back of a horse, and the Polish Brothers tying themselves into knots and performing serpent-like evolutions among the rungs of a ladder, with other performers whose names my memory has not retained. There, too, I saw "The Charcoal Burner" played in Newman and Allen's portable theatre, and a performing tiger act a prominent part in a sensational drama setting forth the perils of a British traveller in Africa.

The road skirting the western side of Thurlow Park (from which Lord Thurlow's mansion on the hill had then disappeared), and meandering between verdant pastures to the foot of Herne Hill, was still spoken of in those days as "the green lane," though the increased traffic had then deprived it of that character; and, in like manner, that portion of the road to Croydon between the top of Leather Bottle Lane and the church, was referred to by old inhabitants as "between the woods," having originally been a lane between thick oak-woods, though the eastern side was cleared and cultivated at a date to which my memory does not extend. On the other side of the road the wood remained until it became the site of the Beulah Spa Gardens, which were for several years a fashionable resort; and all along the border of Kent there stretched a fringe of woodland, intersected by the lanes leading to Sydenham and Beckenham.

These woods had been from a period far beyond the memory of the oldest inhabitant, and perhaps from the dim and distant epoch of the gipsies' first appearance in England, a favourite camping-ground of that singular remnant of an Asiatic nomade race. Less than a century ago they were in the habit of camping every summer in large numbers upon the patches of waste bordering the lanes that intersected the woods of Anerley and Penge. The men made clothes-pegs and butchers' wooden skewers, which were hawked through the neighbouring villages and hamlets by brown-faced boys and girls; or perambulated the vicinity with the treadle-wheel and fire-basket of the itinerant tinker and knife-grinder. Some who had acquired or inherited a little money, made the round of the country fairs as horse-dealers, not without incurring the suspicion that they sometimes sold horses which they had not bought or bred. The women practised palmistry, in which their repute was so great as to furnish Monmouth Street publishers with the title, "The Norwood Gipsy Fortune-Teller," a little book in great demand among young women of all classes.

A temporary encampment was sometimes formed upon a piece of rushy waste near White Horse Farm, on the northern verge of Croydon Common. Railway extension and building operations have obliterated the site, but no longer ago than 1853 it might have been found opposite Fir-Tree Cottages, in one of which I resided at that time. Gravel was then being dug there, and near the road stood a strange-looking nondescript habitation, partially formed of the body of an old omnibus, in which lived an old man named Batt. A little farther northward a brook which rises at Woodside, and flows into the Wandle, ran beneath the road, then bounded on both sides by hawthorn hedges; and I have often paused on the bridge to watch the water-rats as they swam the stream, or ran in and out among the sedges.

I remember hearing my father relate the story of a fright which he got at that spot from unexpectedly coming upon a gipsy encampment while returning one night from Norwood to Croydon, accompanied by the late John Skelton Chapman, master of Archbishop Whitgift's School, who married one of my mother's sisters. It must have been about 1812, at which time there were not more than two houses between the top of Leather Bottle Lane and White Horse Farm. They had crossed the brook just mentioned, and were close to the waste, when the moon shone out suddenly from the clouds which had obscured it, and showed the rushy strip of common-land covered with tents, little tilted carts, and tinkers' barrows. Chapman took to his heels at the sight, and my father, catching his panic, followed, both leaping the low hedge, and running at their utmost speed across the green pastures bordering the north side of Croydon Common.

The late Dr. Gardiner, who, during the latter part of his life, lived in a white house facing the verdant slopes of Streatham Common, but had formerly practised at Norwood, used to tell a story, illustrative of gipsy life and character under conditions which have long ceased to exist, which, if only for that reason, is worth telling again.

He was called upon one evening by a wiry-looking gipsy, with black elf locks dangling about his bronzed countenance, upon which sat an expression of the keenest solicitude and anxiety. In a hurried manner the man begged him to hasten to the assistance of his wife, who was lying in their tent in Anerley Wood, in the pangs of maternity. For a moment the doctor hesitated. The night would be dark, and Anerley Wood was a place of evil repute. Where the briars and brambles grew the thickest amongst the hazels there was a hollow which bore the ominous name of Thieves' Den. But the doctor was a kind-hearted man, and his irresolution was of brief duration. He looked at the anxious face of the gipsy, and then put on his hat and went out.

It was growing dark when they reached the lane which intersected the wood, the gipsy striding on in advance, and looking over his shoulder from time to time to assure himself that the doctor was following. They descended into the valley through which the railway now runs, and then the gipsy paused, waiting with evident impatience until the doctor came up with him.

"Give me your handkerchief," said he in a tone that sounded imperative, notwithstanding the respectfulness of his manner. "You must not know the way to our tents. There are reasons for it. It will be only for a few minutes," he added, on observing that the doctor hesitated.

Reflecting that blindfolding did not necessarily imply a design against his life or his property, and that if the man had such intentions towards him, resistance would be useless, as the only human beings likely to be within the range of his voice were fellows of his swarthy guide, Dr. Gardiner took his handkerchief from his pocket, and allowed the gipsy to bind it over his eyes.

"I did not bargain for this," he observed.

"No harm will be done to you," returned the gipsy. "Keep close to me, and in a few minutes we shall be there."

Then he plunged into the wood, and Dr. Gardiner, clutching the skirt of his velveteen jacket, followed at his heels, not without stumbling every two or three yards over the interlaced briars and brambles. There evidently was no beaten track, though the gipsy went on without a pause, as if guided by indications of which the doctor was unconscious. In a few minutes he stopped, and, turning to the doctor, desired him, in a subdued tone, to stop. The doctor obeyed, and on advancing a few steps became conscious that he had entered a closer atmosphere. The handkerchief was immediately removed from his eyes, and he found himself in a dome-tent, with his gipsy guide by his side, and a young woman of the same race lying upon some fresh-cut bracken, with her shining black hair straying about her dark face, upon which stood large beads of perspiration. Two women of the tribe were crouched by her side, regarding her with anxiety and compassion, as the doctor saw by the feeble light of a candle which one of them held in a cleft stick.

About an hour afterwards, Dr. Gardiner left the tent, under the guidance of the gipsy husband, having again submitted to have his eyes bandaged. A fine boy had in the meantime been added to the tribe, and the women who ministered to the gipsy mother were in a position to assure all inquirers that she was "as well as could be expected."

Before the lane was reached, Dr. Gardiner became aware that they were not leaving by the way they had entered it, but he prudently abstained from making any remarks. The route was a more circuitous one, and the wood was quitted at a point near the by-road leading to Sydenham. Then his conductor paused, removed the handkerchief from his eyes, and drew forth a small canvas bag, from which he took a guinea.

"No, no," said the doctor, declining the proffered fee. "You are a poor man—I hope an honest one. Give it to your wife, and let her do as she likes with it."

"She won't want for a guinea while I have got one," returned the gipsy, as he dropped the coin back into the bag, which he thrust into his pocket. "But if you won't have it, all I can say is, that I hope I may find an opportunity of paying the debt in another away. Look here, doctor. If you ever come into contact with any of our people in an unpleasant kind of way, you just say you are a friend of mine, or ask if Ned Righteous is in the camp, and you'll find the mention of that name very much to your advantage."

Wishing his guide "good-night," the doctor was hurrying away, when the gipsy volunteered to accompany him a short distance, observing, "There's some rough fellows about that it wouldn't be good for your health or your pocket to meet with." At the nearest houses they parted, the gipsy enjoining the doctor not to forget his name, and then disappearing into the darkness in which the neighbouring fields were by that time steeped.

A year or more after this adventure, Dr. Gardiner was riding homeward one night, after a visit to a patient who resided near Beckenham, when his horse reared suddenly, and the bridle was grasped almost at the same moment by two men, one on each side, who, with menacing tone and manner, demanded his money. There was light enough in the sky for him to discern that both the footpads had the deep brown complexion of the pure gipsy race; and the injunction of Ned Righteous at once recurred to his mind.

"You will not rob a friend of Ned Righteous?" he observed, not, however, without a doubt of the efficacy of the charm there might be in that name.

"The friends of Ned Righteous are our friends," said one of the robbers, in an altered tone, but without loosing his hold of the doctor's bridle. "But how are we to know that you are a friend of his?"

"It's a stall!" exclaimed the other with a forcible adjective before the slang noun.

"If the man I mention is anywhere near here, he will answer for me," said the doctor.

"Come on, then," returned one of the gipsies. "We'll interduce you to Righteous in less time than it would take you to reach the 'Jolly Sailor.'"

Reflecting that they could rob him on the lonely road as easily as in any place to which they might conduct him, Dr. Gardiner allowed them to lead his horse into a narrow path that meandered through Penge Wood. In a few moments they stopped, and one of them uttered a peculiar cry like the "too-wit!

too-woo!" of an owl. The signal was answered almost immediately, and in a short time the cracking of twigs and rustling of foliage announced the approach of another. Presently the hazel-stems parted, and Ned Righteous stepped into the dim light upon the woodland path.

"Here's a broadcloth cove as claims to be a friend of yours, Ned," said one of the gipsies. "You haven't many friends among the house-dwellers, have you?"

Righteous raised his dark eyes to the benevolent countenance of the doctor, whose own were fixed upon the brown face of the gipsy who had conducted him, blindfolded, to the encampment in Anerley Wood. The recognition was mutual.

"You know me, Righteous?" said the doctor.

"Dr. Gardiner!" exclaimed the gipsy, his face brightening with gratification.

"Dr. Gardiner!" echoed one of the footpads, instantly loosing his hold of the doctor's bridle, which example was followed by his companion. "Why, if we had knowed it was you, sir, or you had only jest told us your name, that would have been enough. You saved Righteous his child, and perhaps his wife, taking no gold for it, and your name is remembered for that in all the tents of the Romany."

"I am glad to find that the Romany are not ungrateful," returned the doctor, with a feeling of relief, which probably enhanced the earnestness of his utterance. "You have fulfilled your pledge, Righteous. I hope your wife and child are well?"

"Quite well, sir," replied Righteous. "The boy gets on finely."

"I am glad to hear it," said the doctor. "Now I wish you a good-night."

"Good-night, sir," they all responded, and one of them added, as the doctor turned his horse's head towards the road, "Hope you'll say a good word for the gipsy when you can, sir."

"I shall think better of gipsies from this time," returned Dr. Gardiner, looking over his shoulder, and then he urged his horse to a trot, and was soon ascending the rise towards Norwood.

The gipsies have disappeared with the woods and wastes. I have not seen any considerable company of the swarthy race since 1839, when I had the privilege of being the only house-dweller in a large party of both sexes assembled at the "Greyhound Inn," at Streatham—not the existing house, but the old one, then kept by stout old Michael Keatley. There was about that time, and for some years afterwards, a gipsy named Stevens, who, with his two dark-eyed daughters, used to go the round of the south of England fairs with a refreshment and dancing booth, having for its sign a green bough. Naturally all the gipsies who frequented the fair to buy or sell a horse, or preside over the exercises of the votaries of Aunt Sally, resorted to Stevens's booth; but a far larger number of persons visited it from curiosity, as one of the sights of the fair. I have only a dim recollection of Stevens, but I have heard him spoken of as a quiet, well-conducted man, and that the late Nelson Lee, who had a good opinion of the gipsy race, was in the habit of giving him and his party an occasional free admission to his portable theatre (formerly

Richardson's), a treat which afforded them the greatest delight.

The descent from the higher part of the hamlet to what is now called South Norwood was then known as Beggars' Hill, and was undotted by a single house. Even when the railway was made, the only houses near the line at that part were two or three cottages and the solitary public-house at the corner of Selhurst Lane, before which hung the sign of the "Jolly Sailor," represented by a capering blue-jacket with a pot of beer in his hand. Now there is a railway-station at Penge even, which I remember as a rushy waste, bordered by an oak-wood, with half a dozen cottages scattered along the road, and a little, old-fashioned public-house, called the "Crooked Billet," standing back a little from the lane leading to Beckenham. The pleasant green lanes about Penge and Woodside are now fringed with villas, the wood has been cleared, the common enclosed, and the old hostelry long ago succeeded by a suburban tavern, flanked by a row of shops.

CHAPTER II.

The forwarding branch of the contraband trade—"Smugglers' Hall" —Lawyer Drummond and Farmer Sharpe—Biggin Hill—A well-kept secret—The Beulah Spa Gardens—Charles Cochrane.

I MUST say something here about the old smuggling days. We are apt, misled perhaps by the ballads and romances of which Will Watch is the hero, to associate the smuggling of the last century and the early part of the present exclusively with the creeks and "gaps" of the coast, forgetting that the contraband goods had to be distributed over the whole country. There were members of my mother's family living less than twenty years ago who remembered deceased relatives who had been engaged in the forwarding branch of the contraband trade in Surrey and Kent; and I remember being one day, about thirty years ago, at the house of a spinster aunt at Norwood, when a bottle of hollands was placed on the table with the remark, "This was smuggled by old Will Fox. It is the last bottle!" The said Will, whose bones, with those of many more of the Foxes, Sharpes, and Ayreses, rest in Beckenham Churchyard, was engaged in the inland smuggling trade at the beginning of the present century.

Spirits and tea, silks and laces, upon all of which very heavy customs duties were then levied, were the chief commodities of the "free trade" of those long bygone days. The agents on the coast knew when a sloop or lugger in that trade was expected to arrive, and were on the look-out, provided with well-understood signals wherewith to inform the skipper whether it was safe to land his cargo at the usual place, or more advisable to run with it to some creek or gap where the officer of the preventive service was not on the alert. Landed under cover of darkness, the casks, chests, or bales were removed in carts or by means of pack-horses to the warehouse of the agent to whom they were consigned, and under whose superintendence they were afterwards forwarded to the owners' customers by like modes of conveyance.

Feversham Creek, the marshes between Reculver and Westgate, the gaps between Margate and Kingsgate, and the "guts" of Romney Marsh were the landing-places most in use by the smugglers on the coast of Kent. The numerous green lanes and bridle-paths through the extensive woods stretching from Feversham to Canterbury, and thence to the coast, the marshes bordering the Swale, and the broader tracts extending west and south from Shorncliff to the borders of Sussex, afforded ample facilities for unobserved inland conveyance. A trot of ten miles over the level country between the north-western edge of Romney Marsh and the little town of Cranbook brought the smugglers to the borders of the thickly-wooded Weald, the villages and hamlets of which were inhabited by a rough population of iron-workers and charcoal-burners. Thence the green lanes were continuous at that time to the Thames, below Greenwich, or through the woods between Croydon and Camberwell to Southwark. Along these byways strings of pack-horses, laden with smuggled goods, could pass for miles without attracting observation, or seen only by those whom fear or self-interest rendered silent.

I remember hearing, when a boy, that smuggled goods had, within the recollection of persons then living, passed by night along what was then called Back Lane, now Park Road, on the east side of Croydon, and within five minutes' walk of the main street of that town. These probably came from Kent over Cockham Hill and through Warlingham, and passing Croydon, were conveyed into the metropolis across Croydon Common and along the green lanes of Norwood. The risks of the trade were not always at an end when the goods were started from the coast, however, for the newspapers of the period contain an account of an affray that occurred one night in the early part of the present century, not very far from the spot where the "Elephant and Castle" now stands, when some smuggled goods were seized in transit, the customs officers having received warning and being on the alert. Cutlasses were drawn and blood was shed, but no loss of life resulted from the conflict, which ended with the smugglers abandoning their goods and taking to flight, making their escape under cover of the darkness.

Upon the coast such affrays were not unfrequent, and as the smugglers often lost their goods, and sometimes were killed or wounded in the struggle for their possession, it is not surprising that the evil passions thus excited sometimes led to the commission of fearful crimes. The smugglers could not be convinced that the goods which they had bought and paid for in France or Holland were not as much their own as if they had bought them in England; and they had always with them the sympathies of the people, who were equally hard to be convinced that because a Parliament representing only the wealthy imposed heavy duties on foreign goods, it was their duty to purchase such goods at double the prices at which they could be procured from the " free traders." Hence the seizure of their goods was regarded by the smugglers as nothing less than robbery, and our criminal annals record terrible acts of vengeance arising out of the conflict between the natural rights of the majority and the laws made by the representatives of the minority.

Of the general lawlessness engendered by the temptation to engage in the contraband trade which was offered by the heavy customs duties of that period, and the advantages which the community derived from dealing with the distributors of smuggled commodities, a striking instance was afforded, somewhat before my time, in the escape from Horsemonger Lane Gaol of a noted smuggler named Johnson. I heard my father relate the story when I was a very small boy, and found it as exciting as I some years afterwards found the apocryphal ride to York of Turpin, the highwayman, as related by Mr. Ainsworth for the regalement of the readers, not of " penny dreadfuls," but of three-volume novels. All the arrangements for Johnson's escape from prison and his flight to the Continent appear to have been made beforehand, and a large number of persons must have been in the secret; yet the whole plan was successfully carried through, without a hitch. A post-chaise awaited him near the prison, relays of horses were in readiness at every stage between London and Dover, the turnpike gates were thrown open at his approach, and a fast-sailing lugger was lying off the coast with her sails set and her anchor weighed by the time he reached it. " Guineas flew right and left," as my father expressed it, to secure the smuggler's escape.

There is a mansion in Surrey, within six miles of the metropolitan bridges, standing in beautiful grounds and commanding a charming and extensive view westward, which I remember hearing mentioned in the neighbouring village, about forty years ago, by the name, certainly not conferred by its wealthy owner, of Smugglers' Hall. On inquiring why it was so called, I was informed that it had been built by a silk-mercer who had made a large fortune in the contraband silk trade at the time when customs duties, so heavy as to be almost prohibitive, were levied upon the productions of the looms of Lyons. What stronger testimony could there be to the unwisdom of imposts which, upon the plea of protecting native industry, enabled fortunes to be made by evading the payment of them, and gave ninety-nine per cent. of the population an interest in their evasion?

One of the Sharpes mentioned on a preceding page married the sister of my maternal grandmother. He was a small farmer at Beckenham, and it is of him that the story is still told that, meeting one day the father of the late head of the legal firm of Drummonds and Co., of Croydon, when he was carrying a plant, and being asked, "What plant have you there,

Farmer Sharpe?" he replied, "It is a plant that won't thrive in a lawyer's garden, Lawyer Drummond; it is called *honesty*."

Some of my earliest recollections are connected with Biggin Hill, the only rural spot remaining in Norwood at the present day. From the brow of that, where we have the grounds of White Lodge on the left and the residence of Dr. Epps, whose name is a "household word" in connection with his homœopathic cocoa, on the right, we have a fine view towards the North Downs, the stand on the race-course at Epsom being distinctly visible. Descending lower, we reach the once celebrated mineral well, formerly resorted to by swarms of persons from London, whose belief in the curative properties of the water was so great that, besides drinking a mug or two of it, they carried large quantities of it away in stone bottles. Its character was similar to that of the well at the pump-room at the Beulah Spa Gardens, and did not differ much from that for which the spring on Epsom Common was so famous until the manufacture of the salts which it contained by the chemists caused it to be neglected. The latter is now choked and overgrown with brambles, and the well at Biggin Hill has been closed by order of the local Board of Health.

We have green fields on the right and on the left, with the ground rising in both directions, as well as before and behind us. On one side is a large old house, to which every generation has added a wing or a story, until it has grown utterly unlike any other house that ever was built;—a rambling, old house, with old ivy on the eastern end, which was the original house, constructed of wood, old fruit-trees in the orchard, and older yews partially screening the other end from the road;—a strange, old house, with which are associated strange memories of former occupants, which linger about the old rooms like restless ghosts that no exorcism can lay.

The rambler will not think of the house, however, in his pleasant surprise at finding so pretty a bit of rural scenery within half a dozen miles of the metropolis. Standing with his back to the hill, the old yews and the old fruit-trees are on his left; green pastures, bounded by a remnant of an old wood, are on his right; and before him the road ends at a red mansion, with a lawn before it, which was called the Hall in the old days when the old house on the left was a wooden cottage. Blackbirds and thrushes sing in the garden and the orchard, and the cooing of the ringdove is heard in the wood. A gate crosses the road at the point where the land attached to the Hall commences, and the gleam of water is seen between the slender branches and greyish-green foliage of some pollard osiers. But the rambler's way is not barred by this gate, for beyond it there is a bridle-way through the fields into a pleasant cross-road leading from Streatham to Croydon.

I remember this road when it was a green lane, impassable in the winter; and that portion of it between Leather Bottle Lane and Lower Streatham remained in that condition until within the last few years. It is still bounded by green hedges, beyond which in summer corn may be seen waving, and the delicate fragrance of the bean-flower be inhaled; and all around Biggin Farm retains the same rural character as it did a century ago. But from Leather Bottle Lane, which bounds Biggin Farm on the south, to White Horse Farm (mentioned in the first chapter), there are now houses all the way, with rows of shops, a school-house, and a church.

Forty years ago there were only two farm-houses in that length, the first called Parchmoor, now a beer-house, and the other Collier's Water, situated at the corner of the lane of that name, leading to Thornton Heath, where, it may be observed in passing, there has not been a sprig of heath growing within the memory of any person now living. Parchmoor Farm passed, about twenty years ago, into the possession of the National Land Society, by whom it was sold in building lots, an enterprise which, by raising the value of the adjoining land, caused the frontage of the other side of Parchmoor Lane to be sold or leased for the same purpose. The homestead of Collier's Water Farm remains unchanged, with the tall firs before it, which have stood there as long as I can remember, and may have been planted by John Gilpin, the hero of Cowper's well-known ballad, if it be true that he was a real personage, and once the possessor of this house.

Now for a strange story. From the earliest time I can remember until I came upon my own resources, I used to hear much of a thriving farmer whose holding was divided only by a couple of fields, with a green lane on one side and an occupation-road on the other, from the little freehold of my maternal grandmother, herself a farmer's widow. The farmer in question used to be quoted by the old lady and a spinster daughter who lived with her as a striking example of the well-earned fruits of industry and perseverance. "Look at Mr. T——," they said. "He came into these parts a raw Yorkshire lad, seeking a job at potato-digging; and see what he is now." I saw what Mr. T—— was then; he farmed some two hundred acres, had lately bought a farm of a hundred or two more, and owned a mill, a score of cottages, and a share in a collier. But I was incredulous as to that amount of property having had for its nucleus the savings made by the most frugal of Yorkshiremen out of the wages of potato-digging. My incredulity was not lessened by extended observation and experience; for though I heard of other instances of fortunes made by industry and frugality, they proved fabulous on investigation.

This particular case of the thriving farmer who had begun life as a potato-digger baffled me, however, for many years from the time when his bright example was first commended to my attention and emulation by my octogenarian grandmother and spinster aunt. In fact, it was not until a year or two ago that the mystery was solved. Forty years before that time, however, I got a glimpse of a secret in Mr. T——'s life, —a private view, as it were, of the skeleton in his cupboard.

It was in this way. I had entered the parlour of a roadside public-house in the village near which the farm of the remarkable individual was situated, though in another parish; for the day was hot, the roads dusty, and the old-fashioned house—long ago pulled down—looked quiet and comfortable, and very suggestive of a glass of ale. I was alone with my glass, for few persons ever assembled in the parlour until the evening; and while resting I could not help hearing, through the open window, the conversation of two or three rustics who were seated on a bench outside, smoking short pipes, and at intervals lifting to their lips a pewter measure of Barclay and Perkins's London porter.

"Wasn't it a queer thing that T— didn't prosecute him for stealing that sack of wheat?" one of them said.

"He didn't lose the wheat, did he?" returned another, in a tone that seemed to imply that the wheat-stealer ought not to be prosecuted for the larcenous intention.

"No," said a third speaker. "He copped Joe as he was coming out of the granary, with the sack on his back, and he made him drop it."

"He might have prosecuted him all the same," said the first speaker.

"Ah!" ejaculated No. 3. "But, you see, Joe knew something which he didn't know was knowed by anybody, and which he wouldn't have known for a trifle."

"How so?" one of the others asked, and I began to feel very much interested in the dialogue.

"Something that he wouldn't like talked about," returned No. 3, lowering his voice a little, "and there's a young fellow inside who—"

He lowered his voice until it became almost inaudible to me, and I quietly changed my position, and got nearer to the window.

"You see," I then heard the man say, in a whisper, "Joe had got into the saw-pit out o' the rain, and he hadn't been there long when he sees T— comin' along—leastways he didn't know it was him when he first see him, but he reco'nized him when he stepped into the pit,—with a spade over his shoulder and something under his arm. Joe shrunk into the darkest corner, and the old man—though he wasn't so old, nayther, at that time—he didn't see him, but put down the thing that he carried under his arm, and began digging a hole."

The narration ceased on footsteps approaching, and greetings were exchanged between the loungers on the bench and the new-comer. I sat a short time longer, hoping to hear the sequel of a story that had broken off at the most interesting point, like a week's instalment of a serial fiction; but the new-comer sat down, a pint of the aforesaid Barclay and Perkins's brew was brought him by the hostler, and it became evident that the story of the adventure in the saw-pit had become like Butler's

> ——" story of the cat and fiddle,
> Begun and broke off in the middle."

Forty years had passed away. Farmer T— had long departed this life, and his remains reposed beside those of his first wife in the parish churchyard. All his progeny, except two daughters, who had emigrated to Canada, had also gone over to the majority, and his grandchildren were scattered all over the world. Of those forty years the last twenty-five of my own life had been passed far away from the scenes amid which I had lived in my youth, and the story of Farmer T—'s extraordinary rise in life had long ceased to have any interest for me.

One day, when I and a relative who was visiting at my house were talking of old times, the subject was revived in my mind by some reference to a great-uncle who had accumulated a little property in the days when farmers wore gaberdines, such as the Sussex labourers wear, and have worn for more than a thousand years, and their wives carried butter and eggs to market.

"There was old T—," said I. "I could never make out his wonderful rise."

"Don't you know," said my guest, with an air of surprise, "how he got his first start in life?"

"No," I returned, "but I don't believe he got it out of potato-digging."

"I'll tell you," said he. "I have known it for some time, though for family reasons it has been kept pretty close. It is quite true that old T— began his career as a labourer on the farm, the profits of which afterwards became the nest-egg of his fortune. You have heard, I suppose, that his first wife was a lady? Well, I will tell you how she came to be his wife. She had been seduced by his master, who, finding that he had brought a hornet's nest about his ears, and having perhaps other reasons for taking the step he did, arranged with T— that he should marry the girl, and in return should become his bailiff, as he contemplated going abroad. T. agreed; the girl was induced by her betrayer's desertion and the condition in which she found herself to consent to the arrangement; and they were married. T—'s master went to America, and T— was to send a yearly balance-sheet and remit the balance of profits. Whether he ever did so I can't say, but I think it is very doubtful. His master never returned to England, and T— became tenant of the farm in a few years after he became bailiff."

"The secret is out, then," said I, after a pause, during which my memory ran back to the time when I had heard the commencement of the story of Joe's adventure in the saw-pit.

What was it that the farmer was going to bury there? That can only be conjectured, but there was no doubt in my own mind that he buried there a child of shame, whether still-born or a victim of crime the great searcher of hearts alone knows.

I have, on a preceding page, mentioned the Beulah Spa Gardens, in connection with which there was a curious history. Fifty years ago, these gardens, with their pump-room, rosary, archery-ground, maze, camera obscura, &c., were one of the most fashionable resorts near London, and, on the occasion of the visit of Marshal Soult, they attracted such a large assemblage of the upper classes that the carriages extended from the neighbouring church of All Saints to Crown Lane. Associated with the gay scenes which the gardens presented, until the site was occupied by the villas of Grange Road, was a handsome young man known as the Spanish Minstrel, who sang love-lyrics on the lawn in the intervals of the band programme, accompanying himself on the guitar, and, with his dark complexion, ample cloak, turban hat, and the national instrument of the sunny south, looked his assumed part to the life. "Who is he?" was a question which every visitor to the gardens asked, and which no one could answer. The mystery with which he contrived to surround himself enhanced his attractiveness, and doubled the interest with which he was regarded. The secret was well kept, however, or he had contrived to render it impenetrable; for, on the day when he twanged his guitar for the last time in public, he remained as profound a mystery as on his first appearance.

When, however, the handsome Charles Cochrane appeared in "society" as the husband of a wealthy widow, there were many persons who recognized in him the Spanish Minstrel who had turned the heads of so many younger ladies by his good looks while singing and strumming at the Beulah Spa Gardens. Mystery and romance ended with marriage, and Charles Cochrane became a useful member of society (what a different meaning that word has when it is not "quoted"). He interested himself in the welfare of the London poor, subscribed largely to charitable societies, instituted the corps of street-sweepers, and even entertained the design of associating himself with the movement for the extension of the franchise. In politics he made a mistake at starting, however, and the mistake threw him out of the movement. Without any arrangement with the accepted leaders of the masses, he convened a meeting in Trafalgar Square, just after the French revolution of 1848; and, on receiving an intimation from the authorities that the meeting was illegal, and would be suppressed by the police, he did not venture to present himself before the thousands whom his placards attracted to the Square, notwithstanding the warnings issued from Scotland Yard. The opportunity of achieving demagogic fame which Cochrane cast away was eagerly seized by the late George W. M. Reynolds, the novelist, who, mounting a wall, delivered himself of a flood of fervid declamation which procured him a seat in the Chartist Convention, and prepared the way for the establishment of the democratic journal to which he gave his name and devoted his pen. It must have been a moment of sadness and mortification to Cochrane when he learned how many heads were broken by the staves of the police and the missiles of the mob, with no better result than the elevation to temporary popularity of the author of the "Mysteries of London."

CHAPTER III.

The southern suburbs fifty years ago—A ghastly discovery in an osier-bed—The murder of Hannah Brown—A reminiscence of Sarah Gale—Forgotten localities in Lambeth.

At a period well within my recollection, Camberwell was approached from the south by a devious lane, bordered by hawthorn-hedges, which extended from Norwood to the foot of Herne Hill. Lord Thurlow's house, on the summit of the green hill behind which Dulwich lay, had been demolished before this time, and not a single house then existed on the right-hand side of the road, between an old house, surrounded by venerable elms, from which the name of Elm Grove was derived, near the church at Lower Norwood, and the old-fashioned wayside hostelry on the site of the present tavern at the corner of the road leading to Dulwich, still bearing the old sign of the "Half Moon." There Camberwell Park, surrounded by a belt of ancient trees, stretched away on the left; and beyond Herne Hill, to the right, was Camberwell Grove, with its rows of stately elms, in the shadow of which George Barnwell shoots his uncle in Lillo's lugubrious tragedy, while across the green, on which a fair was held in August, was the main street of the village, with the sign of "Father Red-cap" swinging before the old hostelry at the corner.

There was at that time a little stream called the Effra, which, rising near Dulwich, flowed tranquilly by the side of Cold Harbour Lane, and there turned northward as far as Kennington Common, where it curved westward at the point at which it was crossed by the road, and thence meandered towards the Thames. Where is it now? To the eye it is lost, and its course can be traced only by the aid of old maps and plans. It began to disappear more than a quarter of a century ago, when, having been for years contaminated by the deplorable drainage system of former days, the extension of building operations along Brixton Road caused it to be arched over, its appearance and the odour emanating from it becoming more offensive every year. I remember the white railings which formerly fenced it from the footpath, and the black stream which flowed along its bed in dry weather, but swelled to turbid flood when water poured into it from the hills of Norwood and Sydenham after heavy rain. All that part of the road through North Brixton which it skirted was then called the Wash Way, and persons were living within the last twenty years who remembered seeing the roadway flooded by its overflow on several occasions.

From the site of the old watch-house nearly to Vassall Road there were, at a period within my own recollection, no houses on that side of the road, all the area now covered by Angell Town being then pasture-land and market-gardens. In one part was an osier-bed, and there it was that my brother made the ghastly discovery, the recollection of which haunted his memory long afterwards.

He was walking along a footpath near the osier-bed, when he observed a dog, which had been prowling in quest of a bone or a crust, snuff the earth at the edge of the swampy ground on which the osiers grew, and then disappear amidst the slender stems. Boyish curiosity led him to leave the path and follow the dog's example. His horror and surprise may be imagined when he found the animal intently regarding some object amidst the osiers which at the next moment he saw was a pair of human legs! For a moment he gazed at the ghastly remnants of humanity with widely-dilated eyes and pallid cheeks; then he ran from the spot as fast as he could, and told the first man that he met what he had seen. He would not return to the spot himself, but for weeks afterwards he seemed to see the legs skipping and dancing before him whenever he went near the spot, and memory recalled the spectacle which had given such a shock to his nervous system.

A horrible sensation had been caused a short time before by the discovery of the headless trunk of a woman amongst the rushes of Battersea Fields, and the relatives of missing women were enduring the most dreadful suspense while awaiting the elucidation of the mysterious crime to which the ghastly discovery pointed. Shortly after the finding of the legs in the osier-bed at Brixton, the head of a woman was found in the canal at Paddington; and in the opinion of the surgeons who examined them, these relics of mortality were severally portions of one and the same corpse.

The head was recognized as that of a woman named Hannah Brown, who was engaged to be married to a mechanic named Greenacre, living in Bowyer Lane, now Wyndham Road, Camberwell. Suspicion being directed to Greenacre, whom the woman was known to have visited, the results of the inquiries instituted by the police and a search made in his house convinced them that he was the murderer, and he was apprehended, as was also a woman named Sarah Gale, with whom he had formed an unlawful connection. Link by link, a chain of circumstantial evidence was forged which established the guilt of the man beyond a doubt. His object had been to possess himself of Hannah Brown's property, and then, after murdering her, to marry Sarah Gale, whose complicity in the crime was so clearly proved that she was convicted as an accessory, and sentenced to transportation for life, Greenacre being condemned to death. One of my cousins saw Sarah Gale, a year or two afterwards, serving as assistant in a confectioner's shop at Sydney, a circumstance which affords a striking illustration of the difference between the old system of transportation and the present system of penal servitude at home.

The broad tract of pasture and garden ground upon which Angell Town now stands was a portion of the estates which for so long a period suffered the blight of the Chancery suit which arose out of the extraordinary will of the eccentric John Angell; who, more than a century ago, lived in what was then the neighbouring hamlet of Stockwell. Dying childless, he bequeathed his property in trust for the benefit of the nearest of kin to him who might be found at the expiration of a hundred years, during which time the rents, &c., of the estates were to accumulate. For some time no claimant could be found, but the rightful heir at length turned up in the person of a poor old basket-maker, a widower, with an only child, a daughter, who, by her father's death a few years after he emerged suddenly and unexpectedly from poverty and obscurity to wealth and independence, became the possessor of an estate of which a peer of the realm might be proud. The whole of the ground surrounding the osier-bed in which my brother discovered the dismembered limbs of the murdered woman, and extending from Brixton Road to Camberwell, is now, and has been for some years, covered with new streets and long lines of villas.

Many persons find their imagination unequal to the task of picturing to themselves green fields where the streets and squares of Marylebone and Finsbury now are; yet there were living only a few years ago octogenarians who remembered the time when the space between Blackfriars Road and Westminster Road consisted of market-gardens and marshy wastes, dotted here and there with an isolated building, generally a wretched hovel; and a person standing a little beyond, and to the right of, the spot now occupied by the Surrey Theatre, had an uninterrupted view of the Thames from the rows of squalid buildings forming the Clink Liberty of Southwark, amidst which rose the towers of St. Saviour's Church, to the grey walls of Lambeth Palace and the ancient elms of the archiepiscopal grounds.

One of those octogenarians—the gentleman who was so scared by finding himself close to a gipsy encampment, as related in the first chapter—told me, many years ago, that he remembered this now thickly populated district when St. George's Fields and Lambeth Marsh presented an aspect more consonant with their names than they have done at any time within the recollection of persons still living. He remembered the "Dog and Duck," a solitary house of entertainment in what is now St. George's Road, with a tea-garden and a bowling-green attached, the resort of all the disorderly characters of the scattered and not very reputable neighbourhood, and the rendezvous of the highwaymen and footpads who infested all the wastes of Surrey and Kent within a dozen miles.

He remembered the broad ditch, crossed by a swivel-bridge, in the line of the present Waterloo Road, and the cottage known as the Halfpenny Hatch, where a toll of the amount indicated was taken for the privilege of passing through the market-gardens by a narrow footpath, from which those who availed of it emerged upon another, leading across a marshy waste to St. George's Bun House, near what is now Great Surrey Street. He remembered the time also when the riverside tract, now called Belvedere Road, was still known as the Pedlar's Acre, a tradition concerning it being that a pedlar dreamed on three consecutive nights that he found a treasure buried beneath a tree near the monastery of the Black Friars, and on digging at the spot thus indicated to him, found some money, with which, or a part of it, he bought the strip of low-lying land which afterwards received its name from the circumstance, and bequeathed it at his death to the poor of Lambeth.

CHAPTER IV.

My apprenticeship in typography and literature—Correspondence with Henry Hetherington—My first appearance in print—Chapman's Miscellany—A mysterious disappearance—The lost sheep found—A singular elopement.

Some of my readers are probably, by the time they have read the preceding chapters, beginning to grow impatient of my recollections of the topography of Old Lambeth and Croydon, and to turn over the leaves in search of reminiscences of my early ventures into the realm of authorship and journalism. But, in beginning at the beginning, I came upon so many old memories of the places familiar to me in my boyhood, and now so changed as to be unrecognizable, that I could not resist the temptation to record them, hoping that they may be interesting to present dwellers in the old places.

I have incidentally mentioned that my parents removed from Croydon to Norwood when I was between ten and eleven years old, and my home for the next four years was in the latter place, where I attended a day-school, kept by a gentleman named Westwood, at Hollingbourne House, which has already been mentioned. On leaving school I became an apprentice in the printing-office of my cousin, Cornelius Chapman, situate a few doors from the market-house at Croydon, since pulled down, the offices of the *Croydon Chronicle* now occupying the site.

It was while working at what I then supposed would be my future occupation, and when I was about eighteen years of age that I made my first essay in authorship. I have always had the strongest objection to any obtrusion of my religious views upon other persons; but it is necessary that I should here explain that I had, soon after leaving school, drifted away from the creed I had been taught into deism. I had written a treatise on the Thirty-nine Articles of the Episcopal Church, bristling with arguments, deistical and necessitarian, against every point of the Church's belief. I offered the MS. to Henry Hetherington, a well-known Radical bookseller of that time, and famous in the history of the agitation for the repeal of the stamp duty on newspapers. He was then incarcerated in the Queen's Bench prison, as the result of his prosecution for the publication of Haslam's "Letters to the Clergy." My proposal to him was declined, and I received no encouragement to publish on my own account, Hetherington expressing his belief that "nobody cares anything about the Thirty-nine Articles."

I committed the manuscript to the flames, and pursued the search after truth of which it had expressed the first outcome. Professor Nichol's "Architecture of the Heavens" had just been published, and the views expressed therein as to the origin of the celestial bodies, with some passages from Lamarck which I had read, combined with the results of my own observations on the development of the most simple forms of vegetable and animal life, formed the basis of a paper which I contributed to the *Freethinkers' Information for the People*, one of the numerous printed apostles of unbelief which were then issued, and of which the *Reasoner* was the latest survivor. In the three or four pages which constituted my first appearance in type I anticipated the hypotheses which subsequently produced so much sensation in the anonymously-published "Vestiges of the Natural History of Creation."

My only copy of the number in which the article appeared has long since gone to the butter-shop; but I remember that the coincidence of the hypotheses advanced in it with those of the author of the "Vestiges" struck me forcibly on reading the latter work several years afterwards. There was not much encouragement for such speculations then, however, and I turned my attention from physical cosmogony to the genesis of a new moral world. But it was necessary for me to work as well as think, and out of this necessity grew another change in the direction of my intellectual exercises.

There was not always work enough in Chapman's office for himself and two apprentices, and there is nothing more irksome to me than compulsory attendance for certain hours daily with nothing to do. I had, besides, a strong and growing desire to be occupied with something more interesting than commercial circulars and auctioneers' catalogues. I began to ask myself, why should we not bring out a local periodical? Chapman read French and German, and had, while an apprentice, published a volume of poems, original and translated, entitled "Leisure Hours." I credited myself with some literary ability, as yet untried, and flattered my employer and myself with the belief that, in default of other local contributors, he and I could supply all the literary matter that would be required.

"Why not get up a magazine?" said I one day, towards the close of 1842, when we had not an order in the office, and had all been standing idle for two or three days.

"That is what I have been thinking of," rejoined my employer with a reflective air.

There was a few minutes' silence, during which I was waiting for him to say something further, and he, it seemed, was waiting for me to follow up my opening.

"Have you any ideas upon the subject?" he at length inquired.

"Only," I replied, "that, as the circulation would be exclusively local, it would be essential to give it as much local interest as could possibly be infused into it. To that end, the matter should be furnished entirely by local contributors, and the distinctive features of the publication should be the antiquities, history, and traditions of the town and neighbourhood."

"Yes," he responded thoughtfully; and then another pause ensued, which was terminated by his saying, "Well, put your ideas upon paper, and I will turn over the matter in my mind."

Revelling in a dream of literary fame, of which the magazine, as yet in embryo, was to be the foundation, I was not long in producing a prospectus, which, being approved, was printed at once, without any alteration, and distributed all over the town, announcing that the first number of *Chapman's Miscellany* would appear on the 1st of January, 1843.

The contents of the first number were not so easily provided. The possibility which I had foreseen of our having to supply most of the matter ourselves became an actuality. Blackaby, the Chartist shoemaker-poet, could have provided poetry or politics, but the former department was filled by Chapman, and the latter subject it was thought desirable to exclude. We enlisted, therefore, only one contributor, namely, Dr. Berney, who had recently established himself in the town, and having been to Australia, and returned *viâ* Cape Horn, undertook to furnish a series of articles relating the incidents of the voyage and what he had seen in Tasmania.

The first of these papers, with an archæological article gleaned from an old history of the town, and a story of the fifteenth century, with the attraction of local associations, which I had commenced as soon as the publication was decided upon, constituted the more prominent features of the first number. It was published at sixpence, and, as there were no illustrations, and none of the contributors were remunerated, while the cost of the production was very little more than that of the paper, the "composition," as the setting of the type is technically called, being done in time during which I and my fellow-apprentice would otherwise have been idle, the profits were fairly remunerative.

Four numbers were published, to which I contributed two other and somewhat longer stories, and Chapman some translations from Schiller and Uhland, and the commencement of a serial story of a domestic character, the scene of which was laid in the town and neighbourhood. The sale of the third number showed a decline in the circulation, however, and the greater part of the fourth issue never left the counter. It was therefore discontinued, and Chapman's story remained unfinished.

I must now relate some reminiscences of a different character. One evening, on entering the house at which I lodged, I was informed that a gentleman had called, asking for me, but declined to give his name. From the description which I received of his personal appearance I was, however, led to surmise that he was a cousin whom I had not seen for some time, and as I had never received a visit from him, his unexpected appearance at a time when he could not be engaged in his duties as a commercial traveller, caused me some little perplexity.

Dining at my father's house on the following Sunday, I learned that Charlie had not been seen since Monday, either at his employer's place of business in London, or at his own residence. Nothing was known, or could be discovered, that could suggest a motive for a voluntary disappearance, and his wife and parents were in the greatest trouble and bewilderment. It could not be learned that there was anything wrong in his relations with his employer, or that there had been any quarrel, or even the most trivial disagreement, between himself and his amiable young wife. On the Monday he had been at his desk in his employer's counting-house, but from the hour when he left it he seemed to have dropped out of existence.

His supposed visit to me on that evening increased the mystery in which his disappearance was involved. I say "supposed," because the description which had been given me of the young man who had inquired for me was too vague to warrant more than a surmise on the subject. The hypothesis accepted, the apprehensions of secret crime which were at first entertained by his anxious wife and parents would, if not entirely dispelled, be considerably lessened.

The idea of suicide was scouted by every one who knew him. Though that crime as well as others has frequently been committed by persons who have been considered not at all likely to perpetrate them, and without any apparent motive for their commission, the hypothesis was considered to be disposed of by the declaration that Charlie had no reason for committing suicide, and was not a likely man to do so in any circumstances that could be imagined. The only other conceivable hypothesis being voluntary retirement from the little circle in which he was known, and that being rejected with scorn by relatives and friends, his disappearance was regarded as an inscrutable mystery.

I often wished that I had seen him on the evening of his disappearance, for he had never sought me before, and I could not divest my mind of the thought that he had done so on that occasion with the intention of making some communication which would have enabled me to lift the veil of the mystery. But why had he not awaited my return? That was beyond conjecture.

About six months after his disappearance, which was still an inexplicable mystery, I sojourned for a few days at Gravesend. I had visited Tully's Lounge and tried my luck at the "wheel of fortune," promenaded the Tivoli Gardens,—smoked a Manilla, and quaffed lemonade on Windmill Hill, and was beginning to feel like the Roman emperor, who offered a reward for a new pleasure, when a walk to Northfleet was suggested to me. So I strolled thitherward, looked in at the old church, one of the oldest in Kent, walked round the churchyard, and explored the picturesque chalk-pit, now the site of the Rosherville Gardens, persistently advertised during the summer as "the place to spend a happy day." The day was warm, the chalk-dust of the roads in that part of Kent is provocative of thirst, and, as I left the chalk-pit, the sign of the "Leather Bottle," swinging before a low-roofed, old-fashioned village inn, was suggestive of a cool mug of ale.

As I stepped into the road again, I found myself face to face with the missing man. Jack Robinson, renowned in nautical song, could not have been more surprised when he recognized Polly Gray in the person of the smart hostess of the Portsmouth public-house in which he and the strange man had just disposed of "as much grog as came to half a crown," than I was at that moment. I could scarcely believe what my eyes told me. I opened them wider, and regarded him steadfastly. They had not deceived me. It was Charlie himself, in the garb of an ostler, and looking rosy and well, though surprised and confused by the unexpected meeting.

"Charlie!" I exclaimed, regarding him with wonder. "What is the meaning of this?"

"Who would have thought of seeing you here?" he rejoined, blinking a little under my steadfast gaze. "You didn't come down to look for me, did you?"

"No," I replied. "I had not the least idea that you were here, and I suppose nobody else has."

"Well, come and have a glass of ale," said he, entering the inn. "You don't mind coming into the tap-room, do you? There is nobody there."

I followed him into a room with a smoke-blackened ceiling and a sanded floor, and we sat down upon a settle, at a narrow iron-bound table, scored with lines for playing the game of "shove-halfpenny."

"How are they all at home?" he asked, after a few moments' silence.

"All well, I believe," I replied.

"What do they think has become of me?" he inquired.

"I doubt whether any one in the family has any opinion on the subject," I replied. "Your disappearance has now come to be regarded as an insoluble mystery."

For a few minutes he was silent and thoughtful, sitting with his eyes lowered towards the sanded floor.

"It has been a foolish affair," he at length observed.

"Then the sooner you put an end to it the better for all who are concerned," I replied.

"Can you keep a secret?" he asked.

"As close as the grave, if I think it is one that ought to be kept," I replied.

"Well, look here, Tom," said he. "I can't leave here at an hour's notice, and I don't want anybody to come down here and haul me over the coals. When do you go back?"

"To-morrow, or next day," I replied.

"Well, no one will be much the worse on account of this escapade of mine in that time," said he. "What I want to ask of you is, not to mention having seen me."

"For how long a time do you wish me to keep silent?" I asked, for I hesitated to accede to his request without knowing what his intentions were.

He fidgetted on his seat for a few moments, and then replied, without looking at me,—

"I will get away from here as soon as I can, and then get another situation, I suppose."

"Well, do it as soon as you can," said I. "Of course, you want to get another berth before you show yourself, and I trust you will soon succeed in doing so. If that is your plan, I will say nothing that might interfere with it. But what made you go away?"

Upon that point, however, I could elicit from him no information. Nearly a month elapsed after my visit to Gravesend before he was seen by any of his relatives and friends, having then obtained another situation. What explanation he gave to his wife I am unable to say, but presume that it was acceptable, if not quite satisfactory, as his strange escapade did not appear to have any permanent ill-consequences. But I never discovered the cause of his mysterious disappearance.

There was living in Croydon about this time a middle-aged spinster, who carried on the business of a stationer and librarian, in which she was assisted by a niece. One morning the young lady, who, though beyond her "teens," could scarcely be said to have arrived at the age of discretion, was missing. She had risen earlier than usual and gone out, as her aunt at first thought, for a walk. But the breakfast-time passed, the hours crept on towards noon, and she did not return. The worthy stationer became anxious, and then alarmed. On searching her niece's chamber she found that the best and largest portion of the young lady's wardrobe was also missing; and, having made that discovery, she wrote to her brother, imparting to him the disquieting intelligence that his daughter had eloped.

The distressed spinster could form no idea of her niece's motive for leaving her, or of the direction in which she was likely to have gone. But the young lady's father was soon on the spot, and was not long in finding a clue. It was only a slight one, but it pointed to Dover as his daughter's destination, and for that ancient port he started by the next train. Ten minutes after his arrival he was on the track of a young lady whose person and attire, as described to him at the railway-station, corresponded with those of his daughter, but who was said to be accompanied by an elderly woman of unprepossessing and, in such companionship, suspicious appearance.

The anxious parent hurried from one hotel to another until he found the young lady whom he had been pursuing, and with her the anything but respectable person by whom she was accompanied. In the former he recognized his daughter, greatly to that young lady's confusion; but the old woman was a source of surprise and perplexity to him. What could his daughter be doing in a hotel more than sixty miles from her home, with such a wrinkled, disreputable-looking harridan as he had found her with?

Not all at once was a full explanation forthcoming. The young lady, surprised and confused by her father's unexpected appearance, stammered one or two broken and unintelligible sentences, and then sought refuge in tears. The old woman seemed glad to escape when ordered to leave the room, and the young lady returned to Croydon with her father. There, by degrees, and with many tears and blushes, the story of her folly was told to her aunt.

The old woman was a reputed fortune-teller, named Stacey, whose cottage on what had once been, and was still called, the Common, was much resorted to by foolish young women who wished to penetrate the mists of futurity. The young lady had been there several times, and had been assured that a certain gentleman, who had nearly completed his studies at Addiscombe, was deeply in love with her. "Mother Stacey," as the fortune-teller was called, did not venture to name him, but the description she gave corresponded so well to a young man who had been a customer of the young lady's aunt that the credulous aspirant to knowledge of the future was convinced of the identity. Finding the fair librarian as impressionable as she could wish, the old woman pursued her aim so adroitly that she succeeded in inducing her to elope, with the intention that they should travel together to India, whither the supposed lover had gone, and where he was represented as longing for the young lady's arrival, eager to make her his wife.

Will it be believed that this foolish girl had never received a line from the gentleman whom she had been led to believe was so deeply in love with her, had never heard a word of even ordinary gallantry from his lips, was not even sure that she knew him? It was so; and yet, relying upon the representations of an artful, disreputable old woman, she was ready to leave her home and her friends, and go with that woman to India, to unite herself in marriage with a man of whom she knew nothing, and with whom she had never exchanged a dozen words, except in the way of business. Surely feminine folly and credulity could go no further. Mother Stacey had to answer for her share in the affair to the magistrates, who sent her to the county gaol to meditate upon it, and the fair stationer returned to her duties a sadder (and it is to be hoped) a wiser woman.

The young gentlemen of the college were not in such odour with the townsmen as with romantic school-girls and milliners' apprentices. There had been two or three riots, bearing a close family resemblance to the "town and gown" rows of Oxford. On one occasion, when a collision was provoked by the cadets, as they were called, the offenders retreated up the High Street, stopped a waggon loaded with faggots, drew it across the street, armed themselves with sticks from the faggots, and charging the townsmen, obtained a temporary advantage. Their opponents were reinforced at every moment, however, and they were ultimately driven back the second time, and forced into flight.

On another occasion, during the fair formerly held close to the town, a party of the young collegians visited Richardson's travelling theatre, and stood on the external platform, professionally called the parade, while awaiting the commencement of the next performance. A remark addressed to one of the ladies of the company by one of them proved offensive, and was so promptly resented by one of the comedians that he saw stars that were not shining, and found himself flying off the parade before he knew what had happened to him. A general fight immediately commenced, ending with the cadets being put to flight. The consequences did not end there, however, for the chief offender was expelled, and from that day thenceforward the cadets were not allowed to enter the town during the three days the fair lasted, whilst at other times the liberty was confined to a limited number each evening.

CHAPTER V.

Holywell Street and "Satanic literature"—The notorious Dugdale—My experiences as a publisher—James Blackaby, poet and shoemaker—A literary policeman—The *Penny Punch*—Threatened action for libel—Conspiracy against my life.

My cousin becoming bankrupt, soon after the collapse of the magazine, and before I had completed the term of my apprenticeship, it became necessary for me to seek employment away from the town. I was eligible for employment during the next few months only as what is termed in the trade a "turn-over," that is, an apprentice who, after serving a portion of his term, is transferred to another employer. After applying unsuccessfully to the other printers in the town, I went to London to seek employment, which my fellow-apprentice had there found on the *Watchman*.

One day, while wearily trudging through Holywell Street, I saw in a bookseller's window a notification that "a turn-over at case" was wanted, and applicants were requested to "inquire within." Entering the shop, I found there a stout, middle-aged man, who, after a few questions, desired me to follow him to the printing-office. Turning into Wych Street, we passed through a dark and narrow passage on the north side, and into a dirty little yard, at the rear of which was a dingy and dilapidated building, the ground-floor of which was closed, and the room above approached by wooden steps from the outside. Following my conductor up the steps, I entered a dirty, cobwebby room, in which seven or eight compositors were at work, and was introduced to the overseer, who immediately assigned a frame to me.

When I had filled my cases with type, reprint copy for a song-book was given to me, and upon that I worked a fortnight. As the books displayed in the shop window in Holywell Street were chiefly translations of comparatively unobjectionable French novels as Eugene Sue's "Mysteries of Paris," varied with such works as Voltaire's "Philosophical Dictionary," and Carlile's "Manual of Freemasonry," I was unaware that I was on the premises of the arch-offender of that day in the dissemination of a species of literature which has been termed "Satanic," and which the fitful efforts of the Society for the Suppression of Vice, aided by Lord Campbell's Act, have failed to extinguish. 1 knew that my employer was William Dugdale, but I did not then know that all his publications were not of such good repute as those I have named.

I remember a correspondent of the *Times* stating, during the political excitement of 1848, that, judging from the contents of Dugdale's window, the literature of the working-classes was a *mélange* of sedition, blasphemy, and obscenity. The grounds upon which the conclusion was arrived at that the works there displayed constituted the special literature of the working-classes were not stated; but it is obvious that working-men do not buy guinea books of erotic engravings, imported from Paris, such as were more than once seized on Dugdale's premises. That these were purchased by wealthy sinners may be inferred both from the price and from the influences brought to bear upon the Home Office when Dugdale, after being repeatedly prosecuted and convicted, was at length sentenced to two years' imprisonment. Some months after his conviction, I was induced to enter his shop, by observing in the window an old and rather scarce volume, entitled, " God's Revenge against Adultery," which I thought might be useful to me in the compilation of a collection of *causes célèbres* upon which I was then engaged, and which was subsequently published, with steel engravings, by MacGowan and Co., of Great Windmill Street, Haymarket. To my surprise, the book was handed to me by the hoary sinner whom the public believed to be expiating his iniquities in prison.

The mystery was explained by a paragraph which afterwards appeared in the newspapers, and from which I learned that the man had been liberated by order of the Home Secretary, on the surgeon of the gaol certifying that his longer incarceration would endanger his life. It may be that he was an adept at malingering. I only know that when I saw him, immediately after his liberation, his sodden and sensual countenance presented its ordinary appearance. No indication of ill-health was visible, and he seemed to be in a condition of semi-intoxication. It would be an instructive lesson in the science of promoting public morality to learn at whose instance the certificate was given, and by whom it was supported when laid before the Home Office.

I left Dugdale's employment at the end of the fortnight, and, in the course of my perambulation of the metropolis in quest of work, I met the tradesman, a wholesale stationer in Watling Street, who had been my cousin's principal creditor. He intimated to me that an arrangement might be made, on easy terms, whereby my fellow-apprentice and myself, or myself alone, might carry on Chapman's business. Believing that bad management had been the chief cause of my cousin's failure, I had a conference on the subject with my father, who had recently retired from business, and attained what to him seemed the summit of felicity in the possession of an orchard and a garden, a couple of pigs, and a score of poultry. But no arrangement could be effected. As my father remarked, my mother "held the purse," and she pronounced an emphatic judgment that I was too young— I was then in my twenty-second year—for either business or marriage, which latter state she supposed would be the next thing I should be thinking of. My father emitted a peculiar low and prolonged whistle, as he was wont to do when he was perplexed, and said nothing.

"Then let me have my own money," said I, referring to a sum of about 25*l*., the accumulated gifts and bequests of earlier years, "and let me do the best I can for myself."

"And run headlong into trouble!" rejoined my mother, the noun with which she concluded her vaticination being her ordinary synonym for marriage.

My resolution had, however, the desired effect. The money was not immediately procurable, and the interval enabled a calmer and sounder judgment to be formed. The opportunity offered me by the stationer was lost by the delay; but, as the plant and stock of my bankrupt cousin had been sold by auction, and the premises closed, there was still a fair opening in the town. The refusal of the parents of my fellow-apprentice to allow him to join me in the enterprise, on the ground of his being a minor, caused a further delay; but my mother at length consented to advance me the smallest amount that would suffice for the purchase of an Albion press, a small assortment of type, and a few reams of paper, and I went down to my native town to look for suitable premises.

In this matter I had no choice. The premises lately occupied by my cousin were already let, and there were only two unoccupied houses in the town that were eligible for the purpose. These were both on the east side of Surrey Street, which is parallel with High Street, and in the centre of the town, in the rear of the markets. As the owner of one of them declined to let it for the purpose for which I wanted it, on the ground of there being, in his opinion, as many printers in the town already as could get a living in it, I was reduced to Hobson's choice.

So the premises were taken, my press, type, and paper came down from London, and I first married one of the best wives a man ever had, and then took down my shutters. I soon found that I had to compete with London printers by steam, at prices which would not have paid wages, or content myself with such casual work as lower prices might cause to be brought to me in preference to my local competitors. I found it expedient, therefore, to employ my too abundant leisure in printing the productions of my own brains and pen, which I could do, in the circumstances, at cost of the paper. My first experiment in publishing was made with an amplification of my cosmogonical article in *The Freethinkers' Information for the People;* and, as the sale of a hundred copies resulted in a profit of 15s.—not taking into account my own labour, either as author or printer—I was satisfied with my very limited success.

About the same time I made my first appearance as a newspaper correspondent in the columns of *Lloyd's London Newspaper*, and my next publishing venture was a reprint, in pamphlet form, of four letters on such a modification of Owen's social system as would render it more readily practicable by that generation. Of this pamphlet I sold as many copies as of the other, but they did not go off so quickly. The men who were glad to have their doubts of the creed of Christendom confirmed, or their arguments against it strengthened, seemed to be more numerous at that time than those who were disposed to study societary science.

Mention has been made in a previous work[1] of James Blackaby, a shoemaker, who devoted his leisure to politics and poetry, and with whom I had become acquainted during my apprenticeship. He was at this time living in the hamlet of Wallington, about a mile from the town, and had just completed a poem, in

[1] "Forty Years' Recollections." London: Sampson Low and Co.

blank verse, entitled "A Vision of Judgment," informing the reader, by two words in parentheses, after the title, that it was "not Byron's." The subject was the then recent death of Lord Abinger, and his appearance at the bar of the celestial court before which Byron arraigned George III. He submitted the manuscript to a friend for his opinion of its merits, and his friend's judgment was favourable enough to induce him to guarantee the cost of printing fifty copies, which he calculated could all be sold by himself. Most of them were, in fact, so disposed of, the remainder being sold by me. Blackaby was continually scribbling verses, but the only other production of his pen that attained the honours of print was a poem on the night-flowering cereus, and that owed its appearance in type to being enclosed by myself in a letter to Mr. G. W. M. Reynolds, then conducting his *Miscellany*.

About the time when I renewed my acquaintance with Blackaby, another bard of humble position in the social scale introduced himself to my notice on the common ground of friendship with the shoemaker-poet, whom he had known while in the town. Reflecting upon the failure of *Chapman's Miscellany*, I had conceived the idea that the sort of publication most likely to obtain a remunerative sale in a community that had suffered an excellent literary institute to be closed through the spirit of class-exclusiveness, and in which there was no political organization (for the local branch of the Charter Association had been dissolved), would be something humorous and satirical, well spiced with local allusions and personalities;

and some clever parodies and droll stories in rhyme, *à la Ingoldsby*, which had been shown me by the newly-discovered bard, who was a constable in the metropolitan police, told me that his talent in that line might be turned to capital account in the pages of such a publication. As soon as I broached the idea to him, he took it up *con amore*, and not only placed all his effusions, past and future, at my service, but undertook to gather up for my use all the *on dits* and *facetiæ* of the town and neighbourhood.

With such an ally, it was not difficult to produce a good first number, the chief items of which, both contributed by the policeman, were the first of a series of curtain lectures, the couple introduced in which were readily recognizable, and a parody on Hood's "Song of the Shirt," supposed to be chanted by the ill-paid women employed in a large laundry in the town. A great commotion was created in the town by its appearance, as may be supposed, everybody being apprehensive of being morally gibbeted in its pages. If the reader will imagine a *Little Pedlington Punch*, he will understand the situation. Mr. Overton, the brewer, who was my landlord, warned me, in a significant manner, not to venture upon liberties with his family; and an irascible neighbour, whom I was unconscious of having done anything to offend, bounced into my shop an hour after the publication of the first number of the *Penny Punch* had commenced, and demanded to know what I meant by insulting him in that manner.

"I am not aware that I have insulted you in any manner," said I, probably exhibiting some surprise at the frantic appearance of the man.

"What do you call this?" he exclaimed, slapping one hand violently upon a copy of my first number which he held in the other. "You have coupled me with a sweep—me, a respectable tradesman—with a chummy!"

I could not suppress a smile as the cause of the man's ire was revealed to me by his complaint. He had recently introduced what he had advertised as a "polka clog," and a brief paragraph in the offending publication had announced that Oliver, the chimney-sweeper, an old inhabitant of the town, and a character in his way, had invented a polka sweeping-machine.

"I am sorry such a trifle should have annoyed you so," I said, beginning an endeavour to mollify my irate neighbour.

"Trifle!" he exclaimed, interrupting me. "It is no trifle, and that you shall find to your cost. I will sue you in the Court of Common Pleas, and I should like to pull your nose."

I leaned over the counter, but he did not avail himself of the opportunity. He bounced out of the shop, and never entered it again; and as I received a letter from a solicitor, enclosing two postage-stamps, and desiring the publication to be sent to him, I presume that he really contemplated an action for libel, for which, however, there was no ground whatever.

Many more of the shopkeepers were as thin-skinned as the inventor of the polka clog, and even those who laughed at the humours of Constable T—, or the satirical reflections that emanated from myself, when the follies or eccentricities of their neighbours were the theme, were disposed to resent them when it became their own turn to provide a provocative of risibility. The result was that, while the sale of the publication increased very rapidly during the first two or three months of its issue, the number of those whom it offended increased also, until something very like a conspiracy was formed for its suppression.

One evening, when the publication had been in existence two or three months, I received a message by a boy, informing me that a butcher, who was one of the aggrieved parties, but with whom I had never exchanged two words in my life, had an order to give me, and requesting me to wait upon him at a public-house opposite his shop. The statement was incredible, the rendezvous suspicious; but I went. The parlour was crowded, but the red face of the butcher shone through the haze of tobacco-smoke like the sun through a fog, and I threaded my way through the chairs until only the length of a table was between that glowing visage and my own.

"Glass of ale, Polly," said I, as the dark eyes and cherry-coloured ribbons of the waitress beamed upon me through the haze; and then I turned to the butcher, and accosted him with a calm and courteous "good evening."

He returned my greeting with a portentous gravity of demeanour that confirmed my suspicion, and the singular silence that prevailed in the room, filled as it was with an unusual number of customers, indicated that something was expected in which those assembled were deeply interested.

"You sent me a message just now?" I observed, half-interrogatively, after a pause, during which the eyes of all present were turned towards the butcher and myself.

"I have just a few words to say," returned the butcher, after clearing his voice, and knocking the ashes out of his pipe. "A few words upon a subject that we all feel strongly about, and which we want to talk to you about seriously, in hopes that what we have to say will be taken as a warning."

"Your messenger informed me that you had an order for me," said I, availing myself of his first pause. "Am I to understand that I have been brought here by a false pretence?"

"It is for your own good," he replied, with undiminished gravity. "You have gone on with that pestilent publication of yours, without sparing even the most respectable people of the neighbourhood, until it has become a nuisance which must be put down. A joke is very well, but I don't see the joke in 'I doubt it won't weigh so much as I expect, as the butcher said of his pig,' and to bring in such a nice-hearted lady as Miss H— in the way you did, was, I must say, shameful."

"It didn't ought to be allowed," said one of his supporters, and the remark elicited a response of "hear, hear."

"Suppose," continued the butcher, "she did ask for some book which wasn't read by servants, what is there ridiculous in that?"

"Excuse me, Mr. B—," said I, rising, "I did not come here to discuss with you the manner in which I conduct my property, which will continue to be conducted in the manner which I conceive to be most conducive to my interests."

As I left the room chairs were pushed in my way and legs stretched out to throw me down, but not a word was spoken, and, carefully avoiding the obstacles to my egress, I reached the door in safety, and without molestation.

A week or two afterwards I received a note, purporting to come from a gentleman named Russell, whose residence was at the corner of Addiscombe and Wellesley Roads, and requesting me to call upon him at a late hour in the evening, to receive an order for printing. The caligraphy and orthography of the note were so evidently those of an illiterate person that I at once pronounced it a forgery, and on Constable T— coming into the shop, I asked him what he thought of it.

"It is a forgery safe enough," he replied, after perusing it, "and it may be only a hoax; but I will tell you more about it between now and night."

Just as I was lighting the gas he came in again, so completely disguised that I did not recognize him until he spoke.

"This is more than a hoax," said he. "It is a plot to decoy you to the place, and throw you into the pond."

He then proceeded to tell me in detail what he had discovered, and how he had discovered it. The house to which the note was intended to lure me stood at some distance from the road, between which and the grounds there was a large and deep pond, overshadowed by weeping willows. The night would be moonless, and at the hour named for my visit it would be quite dark. There was no lamp near, and, had I gone to the spot, it would have been easy for fellows lurking in the shadow of the fence which divided the road from the water, to have suddenly pounced upon me, and thrown me, before I could utter a cry for help, into the deep black pool.

Of course I did not wait upon Mr. Russell, and the base attempt was not repeated. But, after the third or fourth month of its existence, the public interest in the *Penny Punch* began to diminish, and by the end of the sixth month its circulation had fallen below paying-point. It ceased to appear, therefore, and I had again to deliberate upon the question of the ways and means of keeping the pot boiling.

CHAPTER VI.

The Communist propaganda in England—Goodwyn Barmby and the *Communist Chronicle*—The short-lived *Communist Journal*—Successful ventures in a new field—Retirement from business—First attempt at dramatic writing—At a stage-door and a tavern bar—Biddles, of the Bower—William Rogers, the comedian.

IT was in the circumstances stated at the close of the last chapter that I revived, in 1846, a publication devoted to the dissemination of Communism, which had been started and carried on for some time as a monthly by the late John Goodwyn Barmby, but had been discontinued for financial reasons. It was agreed between its founder and myself that I should produce the paper at my sole cost and receive all the profits, he retaining the copyright and the editorship, while the business arrangements should be under my control. These matters being satisfactorily arranged, I converted the publication into a weekly, reduced it in size from eight quarto pages of three columns each to four of the same size, and in price from threepence to a penny. The history of that publication, and of the Communist Church, of which it was the organ, has been so fully told in my "Recollections" that it cannot be repeated here, nor would it, perhaps, interest a large proportion of those who will read the present work. The *Chronicle* came to an end through a difference of aims between Barmby and myself, and its successor, the *Communist Journal*, which was my own property, and entirely under my own control, had, owing to the schism, a very brief existence.

When, in May, 1847, a conference of social reformers was proposed by Barmby, he laid much stress on the desirability of the establishment of "a general chronicle of all the associated efforts, not only in this country, but also in the world." I brought this proposal before the Croydon branch of the National Land Company, in which unfortunate enterprise I was a shareholder and office-bearer, and thus was again brought, for a time, into correspondence with Barmby. The proposition was taken up by several co-operative organizations, but difficulties intervened which, for some time, prevented it from being carried out. The discussion of the matter suggested to me the idea of a Communist League, of which I made Barmby a present. He did not use it, however, his ever-changing mind being occupied with a Communist Covenant, which had at that time succeeded the Communist Church.

The insufficiency of my gains as a printer to meet the cost of maintaining a family impelled me into the flowery path of fiction, there being at that time a demand for serial stories of a popular character, which found a large sale in penny numbers. I took Eugene Sue for my model, and was tolerably successful. The stories were published anonymously, and I was somewhat surprised, and not very well pleased, when I, many years afterwards, found the titles in the catalogue of the British Museum library, with my name affixed as that of the author. I was able to understand how the authorship had been traced to me, but the discovery that rewarded the compiler's search was certainly not worth the trouble he must have taken.

The first attacks of the *cacoethes scribendi* take the form, in most cases, of an irrepressible inclination to write verses, which the unfortunate victims of the malady regard as poetry, because their effusions conform, in some degree, to the requirements of rhyme and metre. Generally, as every editor knows, the themes are threadbare, the rhymes of the "room" and "spoon" sort, and the metre so defective as to suggest that the matter has been written as prose and then cut into irregular lengths. But, being written in verses, the writer calls it poetry, though there may not be a scintillation of the poetic fire in it; and if he can induce an editor whose ear for harmony is as defective as his own to give it a place in a magazine or newspaper, he is a happy man, and feels proud when he is spoken of as "one of our local poets."

My own case was an exception to the general rule. I had gone into the ranks of the literary profession with the conviction that it could be made to pay, and with the determination to make it pay. So of course I did not attempt to write poetry. Publishers shake their heads at much better stuff than the average, and magazine editors will pay for it only when they have half a page to fill up, and a contribution above the average quality is offered them. Fiction and the drama afford the best routes to fame and fortune, and sometimes a short cut, though success at one bound is exceptional. So I tried my hand at fiction, and as ten thousand copies of my first tale were sold, on its first issue, and it was twice reprinted, I was very well satisfied with the result.

After a second successful trial of my powers in the construction of a plot, I conceived the idea that the story was well adapted for dramatization. There was a mysterious murder at the beginning, and there were two characters that seemed likely to "fetch" the pit and gallery, an erratic baronet who indulges in piracy, abduction, and murder, and a dashing highwayman of the Tom King school. There were some effective situations on which to bring down the act-drop, and plenty of scope for picturesque scenery, the scene being laid on the rocky coast and wild moorlands of Cornwall. The Pavilion, then under the management of Mrs. Edwin Yarnold, was suggested to me as a probable house for the production of the drama, and when it was completed and a fair copy made, I waited upon that lady, with the MS. in my hand, at her residence, adjoining the theatre.

"She is not up yet," said the servant who responded to my tintinnabulary summons. (This was at noon.) "You had better see Mr. Gerrish," she added, glancing at the roll of manuscript in my hand.

"Where shall I find Mr. Gerrish?" I asked, pleased rather than otherwise with the intimation, for, like most of my masculine fellow-humans, I disliked doing any kind of business with a lady.

"Ask for him at the stage-door, up the court," was the reply. "If he isn't there, you'll perhaps find him at the bar of the public-house, up the court."

The court referred to was Baker's Alley, a passage between the theatre and a public-house called, if I recollect aright, the Pavilion Tavern. Arrived at the stage-door, I looked into a dark passage at the end of which a tiny jet of gas twinkled like a distant star. For a moment that was all I could see, but as I gazed into the darkness I saw a door dimly outlined just within the passage, and on stepping forward and tapping on it with my knuckles, an old, shabbily-dressed man made his appearance, something after the manner of a house-dog disturbed by a strange footstep.

"Well, what's your business?" demanded Cerberus, with a look and a snarl that completed the resemblance.

"Is Mr. Gerrish here?" I asked.

"No, he isn't," was the snarling response, and the surly janitor turned into his den.

Bearing in mind what Mrs. Yarnold's servant had said as to the next most likely place to find Mr. Gerrish, I strolled up the court, and entered a public-house, at the bar of which seven or eight men were lounging, all engaged in the consumption of tobacco and intoxicating beverages, and all presenting the unmistakable external characteristics of the "pro."

"Is Mr. Gerrish here?" I asked the barman, when I had been supplied with a glass of ale.

"That's him," replied the dispenser of alcoholic fluids, glancing towards the other end of the bar, "him with the squinny eye."

In a few words I made Mr. Gerrish acquainted with my business, and gave him the manuscript, which he promised to take an early opportunity of reading. A month afterwards, being again in London, I called at the theatre, and after some detention at the stage-door, was guided by a preternaturally knowing-looking boy along the dark passage, and up some dimly-lighted steps, to a small room. There I found the manager seated at a desk, engaged in writing.

"Sit down," said he, without changing his position. "You have called about your manuscript? Ah, I haven't read it. Unfortunately, we are not doing good business here, and Mrs. Yarnold has decided to close the theatre on Saturday week. So I don't see— Do you know Biddles, of the Bower?"

I intimated my ignorance of that gentleman.

"I think he wants something. Suppose you see him. There can be no harm in trying, you know."

I thought so too, and on receiving back my manuscript, in doing which I should have thought myself lucky if I had known as much of such matters as I learned twenty years afterwards, I made my way back to London Bridge, and then to the transpontine region of Lambeth Walk, in the vicinity of which Mr. Biddles resided. Admitted to that gentleman's presence on sending in my name, I was pleased to find him looking much more like a gentleman than the manager of the Pavilion, and most courteous and affable in his manners. I suppose it was true that he did want "something," for he glanced over my manuscript; but he shook his head as he handed it back to me.

"My dear sir," said he, "I could get a better play translated from the French for a guinea. You have written stories, you say; and I daresay you have written them very well, for I should say you had a well-constructed plot in this case; but something more is required for dramatic authorship than the ability to weave the incidents of a story into a dramatic form. Some knowledge of stage business is required, and of that I see that you know nothing."

These observations destroyed for the time—for a very long time indeed—my hope of shining as a dramatic author, and that unlucky manuscript was consigned to the flames. That it contained some of the elements of a good play may be inferred, however, from the fact that William Rogers, of the City of London Theatre, afterwards took the same story in hand. I met him one day at the house of the publisher, and had some conversation with him on the subject. It was agreed that the management should have casts of two or three of the illustrations of the story for use in the bills; but nothing came of it. From some cause or other, unknown to me, the play was never produced.

At this time I had a serial story running with the attractive title of "The Mysteries of Old Father Thames." One day, when this story was drawing to a close, I was passing the Victoria Theatre, on my way to the Strand, when this title caught my attention, prominently displayed in large red type on a bill. I paused in surprise, and found that a drama, founded on my story, was to be produced at that theatre on the following Monday night. Now, this story was not so well adapted for dramatization as its predecessor, and had not been so successful in its original form. Yet there was the title in all the glory of large type; and neither the publisher nor myself had had any communication concerning it with either the dramatist or the manager of the theatre. The copyright belonged to the publisher, however, and as he thought the play would be a good advertisement for the story, the representation was not interfered with.

I had so fair a prospect at this time of being able to keep the pot boiling by my literary labours, that I resolved to disengage myself from the cares and anxieties of business, and devote all my time and energies to literature as a profession. If I had been thriving in business, this would have been a decision that would not have afforded a brilliant illustration of my judgment; but, as an old and decayed tradesman once remarked to me of himself, just before he retired into the workhouse, " I had enough to leave off with, but not enough to go on with."

The truth was, that when I did not provide employment for my printing plant myself, the press stood still, and dust gathered on the type. The receipts of the bookselling and stationery departments of my business were very small, while the working expenses were the same as they would have been for a much larger concern. So, after considering the value of the time occupied in the business, and the difference between the rent of the premises and that of a cottage a mile from the town, I sold the plant to a printer's broker, and the stock of stationery to my successor in the tenancy, and removed to a little white cottage on what is still called the Common, though there has not been an acre of waste within the recollection of any person now living.

This change, which was effected in the midst of the political excitement of 1848, afforded me leisure to double my production of copy, and also to write some letters to the *South-Eastern Gazette*, of which I had been a correspondent during the general election of 1847. Letters on Parliamentary reform were, however, appreciated no longer by the Maidstone editor, and further communications from me were declined, with an intimation that he had come to the conclusion that I was " a dangerous character." That was the greatest compliment ever paid me in type. When a man is able to express his views on politics, and on political and social economy, in a manner which obtains him thousands of admiring readers,—as I had done in fiction,—the confession of his political opponents that they consider him dangerous is the highest compliment they can pay him.

I never could understand why the story which, when dramatized, was a success, should have been less successful in its original form than its predecessors. "The Mysteries of Old Father Thames" was a kind of title which had been made attractive by the sensational fictions of Eugene Sue and G. W. M. Reynolds, and I did my best to carry out the promise of interest which it held out to the reader. I shifted the scenes from the wharves and docks to the marshes, and from the river pirate's boat to the convict-hulk; I visited Ratcliffe Highway and Shadwell, and dropped into the "White Hart" and the "Brown Bear," to obtain the necessary local colouring; and I introduced into the story some well-known waterside characters, such as the crippled mariner who, with a coarsely-executed picture of an ice-girt vessel before him, and a smartly-dressed little sailor-boy by his side, was wont at that time to gather the halfpence of the charitable in the Highway. But the sale was not so large as the publisher had anticipated; indeed, it fell short of the numbers sold of my two former stories.

The comparative failure of this story deterred the publisher from giving me the same amount for my next production, "Edith Gray," a romance of the seventeenth century, with characters drawn from both the Court and Commonwealth parties, and incidents succeeding each other with melodramatic rapidity, now in Whitehall, now in the sanctuary of Alsatia, and anon amid the pleasant scenery of Kent. When this story had reached its twentieth number, with a circulation below even that of its immediate predecessor (though it was, in my own opinion, the best I had yet produced), the publisher declared himself insolvent, a state of things which caused it to be curtailed, and was a source of considerable embarrassment to me.

While I yet had some money to receive from the publisher, I set to work upon another historical romance, going back this time to the fifteenth century, to the story of Perkin Warbeck, and adopting the theory that my hero was really the younger son of Edward IV. This was accepted by Peirce, a bookseller in the Strand, on the understanding that it was to be completed in twelve numbers, unless the sale should encourage him to run it at greater length. Unfortunately, it proved a failure, and the publisher declined to make another venture. This was a state of things which I had had no reason to anticipate when I cast from me the cares and anxieties of business, picturing to myself the pleasantness of smoking my pipe in a flower-perfumed bower, after the literary labours of the day, and listening to the melody of the blackbird and the thrush.

The look-out was not so pleasant when I had been less than a year in my cottage. There were only three or four publishers of serial fictions in the penny number trade, and these were issuing very few works, and not desirous of multiplying them. This class of literature was being superseded by the *London Journal* and *Reynolds's Miscellany*.

CHAPTER VII.

Transactions with a broken-down publisher—A glimpse of the canvassing trade—A lecture which I did not deliver, and books which I did not write—The turn of the tide—Engagement on "Papers for the People"—David Page and the *Fifeshire Journal*—Successful return to fiction.

WHAT was I to do? That question had become one of increased gravity with the advent of another baby, and, as one publisher after another was tried unsuccessfully, the aspect of the situation darkened every day. Whatever I did—to that it came at last—had to be done quickly, or the world would be afforded a striking exemplification of the adage about the growing grass and the starving steed.

I was acquainted at this time with a gentleman named Emans, who had formerly been in business in "the Row," as a publisher, but, having been pecuniarily unfortunate in his ventures, was living in a back street at Kennington, engaged as a commission agent in the sale, through the medium of canvassers, of illustrated works issued serially. Knowing that my circumstances were at this time depressed, and my prospects none of the brightest, he suggested that I should temporarily employ myself as a canvasser. It happened that one of the young men whom he employed, and who were paid by commission on the orders they obtained, came in while we were talking about the matter, and was referred to on the question of earnings.

"It all depends upon the circumstances," said he. "One fellow will make his thirty shillings or two pounds a week, while another can't get an order in the time."

"It requires a little brass," observed Emans.

"That is just it," said the other, who was exceedingly well "got up," and struck me as being just the man for the business, according to the mode of doing it which he proceeded to describe. "I carry my numbers in a portfolio, and go into the best streets, give a strong pull at the bell and a double rat-tat, and ask for Mrs. So-and-so. The slavey shows me into the front parlour, and presently the lady comes. I bow, and ask to be allowed the pleasure of showing her some first-class engravings. She scarcely knows what to take me for, and is surprised into looking at the plates. I expatiate upon their beauties, she admires them, and when I mention the extraordinary cheapness of the work, she does not like to refuse me an order. The plan seldom fails."

I thought no more of the old bookseller's proposition after this conversation, but it led to a more congenial one. Emans suggested that I should compile a work on the plan of Hone's "Every Day Book," and I undertook the task very willingly. When I had collected a portion of the materials, and written a few pages as a specimen, he altered his mind, however, and proposed that I should write a novel, to be published in shilling numbers, with steel engravings.

The rate of remuneration which he offered me was so small that, had my circumstances been different, I should have declined the commission; but my position enabled me to appreciate the adage that "half a loaf is better than no bread," and I accepted it. An agreement was drawn up and signed, by which I was to furnish a certain amount of "copy" every fortnight; and this aggravated the wretchedness of the terms by precluding me from receiving as much as I could earn.

At the end of six weeks, however, Emans informed me that he found himself unable to pay for the stipulated supply of "copy" oftener than monthly. It was now my turn to put the screw on. As he had broken the agreement, I demanded double the rate per sheet which he had agreed to pay me, making that the condition of completing the work. To this he reluctantly acceded, but the next instalment was the last I received. He had not the means, he told me, to go on with the work, and had sold the MS. and copyright to the printer. On calling at the latter's office in Great Windmill Street, I found, however, that Emans had borrowed money of him on the security of the MS., which he had no intention of proceeding with on his own account.

While I was engaged on this abortive undertaking I endeavoured to eke out my resources by lecturing, and chose for my subject "California and its Gold Fields," which everybody was then talking about. Not being able to engage the lecture-hall of the Literary Institution, I hired a large room at a public-house in the populous manufacturing village of

Mitcham, had bills printed, and engaged the services of a respectable mechanic as money-taker.

"I am afraid you will not have a very good audience," observed the landlord, when I presented myself on the night for which the lecture was announced.

"How is that?" I asked.

"Why, you see," he replied, "most of the people here work in the factories, and they are a peculiar class of people—always pull together, and whatever they get into their heads can't be got out again. They have got it into their heads—the Lord only knows how—that you are an agent of the Government, sent down here to tempt them to emigrate; and there will not be a man of them here."

The emptiness of the room confirmed his statement.

Just before the time at which the lecture was to have commenced a solitary individual walked in quietly, and took a front seat. I heard afterwards that he was a schoolmaster. But no one else came, and my money-taker returned the old gentleman his shilling.

I was now at my wits' end. I wrote a prospectus of a work on the revolutions of Italy, and showed it to a publisher of illustrated serials as something likely to be a success while the world was ringing with the name of Garibaldi. But the publisher shook his head, and declined the proposal. I sketched the outlines of a work on the origin of man and the migrations of the race in prehistoric times, in which I proposed to reconcile the existence of several distinct varieties of the genus *homo* with the hypothesis of a common origin by means of the theory of development. This I submitted to Mr. Churchill; but he, too, shook his head, and even the hint that the work, published anonymously, and as a sequel to the "Vestiges," would obtain a large sale on the supposition that it was the work of the same hand, was lost upon him.

I was fast drifting into the slough of poverty when a little glimmer irradiated the darkness. During these weary weeks of suspense and anxiety, I had written a short story, illustrative of the wretched lives of the poorest among the poor of Bethnal Green, and sent it to the editor of a new sixpenny magazine of strong Radical tendencies, called the *Commonwealth*, owned by Macgowan, the printer of the *Northern Star*, and the identical printer of whom Emans had borrowed the money on the security of my unfinished novel. The story was accepted, and, though the magazine was a failure, it procured me an introduction to the editor, Mr. Fleming, who had formerly edited the *New Moral World*, and was now on the literary staff of the *Northern Star*. It led to an engagement to write a serial story of similar character for a new weekly publication, called the *National Instructor*, which was issued, under Fleming's direction, immediately after the discontinuance of the monthly. It was nominally the property of Feargus O'Connor, but I believe it was really the property of Macgowan.

This engagement proved the turn of the tide, and though the flood did not "lead on to fortune," the clouds that had been gathering around me began to break from that time, and the welcome sunshine of competency soon gilded my path. At the commencement of 1850 I was enrolled on the staff of contributors to "Chambers's Papers for the People," and found myself earning fifteen guineas per Paper, and wondering how long the golden shower would last. The history of my connection with that publication has been so fully told in my "Forty Years' Recollections" that I will say here only that my contributions to the series were—"Social Utopias," "The Secret Societies of Modern Europe," "The Secret Societies of the Middle Ages," "Ancient Philosophic Sects," and "Ancient Rites and Mysteries," the last being then and still the only work on the pagan mysteries in the English language.

About the time when the "Papers" ceased to appear I received a letter from David Page, the editor, informing me that he had removed from Edinburgh to Cupar, there to edit and superintend the *Fifeshire Journal*, his own property, and which he described as "a quiet Conservative affair, with a good spicing of literary and scientific information." A copy of the journal accompanied the letter, which concluded as follows:—

"I had thought of asking you for an essay, to run over several numbers, and, if so disposed, I may yet trouble you, though I could hardly promise you the *honorarium* which you received for the Papers. I shall be in your neighbourhood next week, and may give you a Scotch call in the passing.

"P.S.—If you have any matter beside you prepared, or could do so with little trouble, you might let me know, and, if suitable for a newspaper, we might negotiate."

I had nothing suitable by me at the time, and do not remember whether I made any suggestion; but I never heard from the writer again, or received his promised visit. My reply, and a subsequent communication, remaining unanswered, I applied for information respecting my correspondent either to Robert Chambers or Leitch Ritchie, who then edited *Chambers's Journal*; but, strangely enough, my efforts to elicit the desiderated information were unsuccessful. On reference to Mitchell's "Press Directory," a few years afterwards, I found that the *Fifeshire Journal* had changed hands in the interval; but that was all I was ever able to discover. The manner in which David Page dropped out of ken remains to this day an inscrutable mystery to me.

My engagement on the *National Instructor* remained, and, though not one that added much to my income, I could not afford to terminate it. I was writing all the fiction for it, and the favour with which my stories were received prompted me to cast about for a commission in that department. With a dozen chapters of a romance in my hand, I waited upon one of the only two publishers then issuing serial fictions in penny numbers, and offered them for his consideration, with a reference to my former productions in that branch of literature, the success of which constituted their best recommendation. The story was accepted, and as its interest centred about a mystery which, almost to the end, baffled the penetration of most of my readers, it had a considerable sale. Its success induced the publisher to ask me for another, and the success of the second exceeded even that of the first.

I got another story accepted by Mr. Edward Lloyd, and, when it was near its conclusion, received from him an offer to take three or four more, on the condition that I would let him have all my productions in that department of literature. With this condition I declined to comply, and my connection with Salisbury Square was limited in consequence to the story then drawing to a close. While it lasted, however, it was attended with the advantage that, as Mr. Lloyd paid for "copy" on delivery, I could, to a certain extent, regulate my income by sending in the manuscript as rapidly as I could produce it, and supplying Purkess and Macgowan, who deferred payment until publication, at a rate which just sufficed to meet the demands of the printers.

The selection of a title was always a matter of much thought with me, as a good title is one of the chief elements of success, equally with publishers and readers. I was very fortunate with my titles, which were always suggestive of some strong source of interest, without affording any indication of the *dénouement*. As a rule, I submitted the manuscript to a publisher when I had completed a dozen chapters. Of some thirty or forty stories which I have written for publication in numbers or in the pages of periodicals, not more than two or three were completed before the copyright was sold.

That was a happy time! I was "running"—as our American cousins say—four stories at the same time, three in numbers, and one in a periodical, and writing those "Papers" the preparation and composition of which constituted one of the most congenial tasks that could have been assigned to me. Yet, by methodical and steady working, I found leisure to cultivate my little garden, to indulge my love of long rambles in the woods and fields, green lanes and gorsy commons, and to devote my evenings to reading to my wife the sublime poetry of Shelley and Byron, or the glorious fictions of Bulwer and Dickens, occasionally varying the entertainment with an after-tea discussion with a friend on the theory of evolution and development or the doctrine of necessity.

It was too bright to last. There are few persons, I am afraid, who have not felt the truth of the mournful lines of Moore,—

> "All that is bright must fade,
> The brightest still the fleetest,
> All earth's delights were made
> But to be lost when sweetest."

Twelve months of unalloyed felicity came to a sudden and unexpected end in the early days of 1851 with the death of my wife. Then I bade adieu to my cottage and the neighbourhood in which I had lived so long, and made my abode for a time at the pleasant rural retreat of my parents.

CHAPTER VIII.

The Fraternal Democrats—Julian Harney—Carl Schapper—Colonel Oborski—A strange story—" Where's Eliza ?"—Fortune frowns again—A typographical Chamber of Horrors—Writing to plates—Canvassing for a life assurance company—Some peculiar people.

NOTWITHSTANDING my love of the country, born of my sympathy with the beautiful in nature, my father's house did not afford me a congenial home. My tastes and ideas found nothing in accord with them in the narrow and antiquated notions of my father and the cold, hard, practical materialism of my mother. Repelled on one side by this complete uncongeniality, and attracted on the other by old associations and the hope of restoring the domestic paradise which death had blighted, I returned to the neighbourhood which love had blessed.

I did not return alone. It has always been an article of my moral and social code that marriage is the only state compatible with the welfare of the community and the individual; and I testified to my faith in my belief by again entering that state, which, however, my experience would justify me in treating in the strain of alternate laudation and malediction in which Charles Lamb apostrophized tobacco.

The experiences that constituted the shady side of the picture were, however, all hidden in the future.

There was not a cloud on the moral horizon; everything was bright and sunny.

The political world was quiet. A deep calm had succeeded to the storms of 1848. Men who had then been members of the Executive Council of the Charter Association were now directors of a life assurance company. The brethren of the Fraternal Democrats, with whom I had been associated in 1847-8, were now scattered, some of them dead. Julian Harney, who had been the secretary of the English section of that cosmopolitan association, was in Jersey, whence he subsequently emigrated to New York. I heard nothing of him until 1885, when a letter from him in the *Athenæum*, referring to the expulsion from Jersey of Victor Hugo, informed me that he had returned to England and was then residing temporarily at Macclesfield. I wrote to him and received a somewhat lengthy reply, a portion of which I gave to the readers of the *Barnsley Independent*, to the old Chartists among whom he was known.

Ernest Jones, who had suffered two years' imprisonment for saying that "the green flag would soon be waving over Downing Street," had abandoned the press for the bar. Michelot, the secretary of the French section, who had been a member of the secret society founded by Barbes and Blanqui, and participated with them in the conspiracy and insurrection of 1839, returned to Paris after the February revolution, and probably fell in the fight or the massacre of June. Carl Schapper, the secretary of the German section, and an artist, returned to Germany, where he was soon afterwards arrested at Cologne on charges of treason and sedition. Of the former charge he was acquitted, but he was convicted of the minor offence, and sentenced to two years' imprisonment. To that circumstance he not improbably owed his life, as he was safe in prison when his compatriots were being hunted down by Prussian troops and decimated by the Crown Prince after the surrender of Rastadt. He returned to London on the expiration of his sentence, the prospect of German unity having been crushed for the time by the men who have since profited by its realization. Colonel Oborski, the secretary of the Polish section, went, as I understood at the time, to Poland, with the intention of taking part in another rising against the autocratic rule of the Czar; but when I next heard of him he was commanding a regiment of the Baden insurgents, under the leadership of his compatriot, Mieroslawski.

I think it was in 1852 that I became acquainted with the incidents of a strange story, which I can relate only with reservations as to names and localities. The heroine, whom I will call Eliza, was only fourteen years of age at the time when the strange incidents occurred, and, unlike some girls of that age whom I have known, did not look older than her actual age, and had never displayed any symptoms of coquetry or impressionability to the tender passion.

Eliza was living with her father's parents, when the series of strange incidents to which I have referred had their origin, as was supposed, in an intimacy which she formed while walking with a younger sister in the neighbourhood. On the outer border of the metropolitan suburb in which her guardians resided was a line of newly-built villas, and one of those villas—so Eliza informed her grandmother—was hired for the season by Lord D—, with whose amiable and accomplished daughter, Lady Laura, she had the happiness and good fortune to become acquainted.

A morning call upon Lady Laura was followed by an invitation to dinner, the first of a series of such invitations, which delighted Eliza's grandparents as much as they were surprised by them, though it is probable that their surprise would have been much greater if they had been better acquainted with Debrett, and more conversant with aristocratic manners. Every time she returned from the villa, they listened, pleased and wondering, to her rapturous eulogies of the amiability and accomplishments of Lady Laura and the manly beauty and agreeable manners of Lord Henry, and her glowing descriptions of the elegant furniture and the riches and delicacies of the table. If they ever expressed surprise that Lady Laura never visited their granddaughter, Eliza hastened to say that she should not like her aristocratic friends to know how humble her home really was, though they were aware, of course, that she did not move in the same sphere as themselves.

Lord Henry came more and more to the front in the stories with which Eliza regaled the old couple after her visits to the villa, and they, hearing so much of the attention which he paid their granddaughter, began to indulge the hope of one day seeing her fair brow encircled by a coronet. A shawl, a dress, some ornaments, were exhibited to their admiring gaze as presents which she had received from

Lady Laura and her brother. Then a ball was given on the occasion of Lady Laura's birthday, and a note was written, asking permission to keep Eliza at the villa until the next day. The consent of her grandparents was given, and the girl, radiant with delight, went to the ball, returning on the following day with her head brimful of the details of the entertainment, the elegance of the dresses, the gentlemen she had danced with, and the marked attentions of Lord Henry.

The grandmother's pride would not permit her any longer to withhold from the family the knowledge of the aristocratic friends the girl had made, and the presumed matrimonial intentions of her patrician admirer. The family received it with more surprise than gratification. Sisters of the old lady thought that she had done wrong in allowing the intimacy to go on without seeing Lord D——, or any of his family, or even making any inquiries concerning them. An uncle of Eliza's shook his head, and ventured to hint that her story was too improbable for belief. One of her cousins made the discovery that there was no such title or name in the peerage as those which had been assigned by her to her new and charming friends.

The girl's mother became alarmed. Doubts and fears stole into the minds of her grandparents. Inquiries were made. Then it was found that no such family as Eliza described lived in the road in which she had located her aristocratic friends, or anywhere in the neighbourhood. Eliza, accused by her anxious guardians of falsehood and duplicity, exhibited some confusion, but, quickly recovering her self-possession, asserted boldly that her grandfather's informants were mistaken, and reminded her grandmother that she had one day called her attention to Lord D——'s carriage as it passed the house.

It was true that Eliza had one day indicated a passing carriage as that of her friends; but there was no evidence that its occupants were Lord Henry and Lady Laura, or that she knew them. The manner in which she met the charge of falsehood and duplicity staggered her accusers, but it was not to be abandoned without proof of her innocence, and her grandfather insisted that she should accompany him next day to the locality indicated, and verify her representations. Eliza declared her readiness to do so and then retired to her room, where, for the remainder of that day, she as much as possible secluded herself.

Next morning she was missing. All her clothes having disappeared, she was supposed to have eloped. But with whom? Who was the Lothario to whom she had given the fictitious title of Lord Henry? The inquiries that were immediately instituted failed to elicit any answer to this query, or any clue to the direction of the girl's flight.

More than a year passed before she was seen or heard of by those who were interested in her. Then, by one of those strange incidents which, remarkable as they often are, the unthinking ascribe to chance, she was discovered at a distant village, where she was living with a family of good repute in the capacity of nursery-maid. She did not return home until some time afterwards, it being deemed desirable that she should not do so until the gossip to which the news of her discovery gave rise had abated. The lady in whose service she was living knew nothing that threw any light upon the mystery in which her movements before and after her disappearance were shrouded. Being in want of a nursemaid, and being pleased with the girl's appearance and manners, she had engaged her without a reference, believing her statement that she was an orphan, and that her last mistress had gone abroad. False as she now found those representations to have been, she had never any reason for suspecting the girl of untruthfulness, or of any impropriety of conduct, during the time she had been in her service.

From the precedent mystery the veil was never withdrawn. That the time which Eliza represented as having been passed beneath the roof of the Lord D— of her fertile imagination had been passed somewhere near the villa of her story was almost certain, and suspicion pointed in some degree to a small house near the Brighton Railway; but beyond that the mystery proved impenetrable. If Eliza made any disclosure to her mother or grandmother, it was revealed to no one else. Her manner after her return was observed to be subdued and reserved, and whenever any of the circumstances connected with her disappearance were alluded to, she exhibited the utmost reticence concerning them. About four years after her return, she became the wife of a respectable working-man, whom she had not known at the time of the romance of which she made herself the heroine; and she maintained throughout her subsequent life the twofold character of wife and mother in a creditable and exemplary manner.

I must now return to myself. There came a time, while I was taking part in the agitation for Parliamentary reform led by Sir Joshua Walmsley and Joseph Hume, when the *National Instructor* had gone to the limbo of defunct periodicals, and serial stories were asked for no more, the publishers finding that re-issues were more profitable than new ventures. I had to cast about for new engagements, and one day I called upon Macgowan and fished for a commission.

"Does anything suggest itself to you?" he asked. "Any brilliant ideas that would make our fortunes? Any forgotten novel that you could dig up, and clothe the dry bones with new flesh?"

"I would rather provide skeleton and all," I rejoined, with a smile at the suggestion.

"I am afraid the days of novels in shilling or even sixpenny numbers are over," he observed, looking more serious. "I have a notion that all serial literature will come before long to the penny form, and ultimately to a lower form; and I sometimes feel disposed to anticipate the era of halfpenny literature by a bold venture in that direction. If I do, you shall be the editor. What do you say to a *Halfpenny Herald?*"

"It would be practicable," I replied. "Half the size of the penny periodicals, at half the cost of production; and, assuming a circulation of 100,000 to be necessary to the success of such a publication as the *London Journal,* a similar one at a halfpenny, half the size, would pay with the same circulation, but would require a sale of 200,000 to yield the same amount of profit."

"There's the rub," said he, reflectively. "The extreme cheapness of the thing renders necessary to its success such an enormous circulation that the chances in its favour, in the face of so much competition, are proportionately diminished. The risk would be too great!"

He concluded with a sigh, and, after a pause, resumed the expression of the thoughts that were passing through his mind.

"There might still, I think, be something done in the sixpenny number trade, if one could get hold of something sensational,—a Chamber of Horrors in type, like the 'Newgate Calendar,' for instance."

"That would be easy enough," said I, "if you think that is the sort of thing that would sell among that portion of the reading public supplied by canvassers. I could find materials for a series of narratives of crime, gleaned chiefly from foreign sources, and little known in this country."

"Well, write a prospectus, and I will think about it," he returned, after a few moments' reflection.

He did think about it, and gave me a commission for the work, under the title of the "Black Register," the first number of which, embellished with a steel engraving of the murder of the Duchess of Praslin, was issued as soon as it could be produced. Commencing with the story of the Marchioness of Brinvilliers, I gave a series of narratives of remarkable crimes, including those of Marie Laffarge, Marguerite

Gottfried, the Duke of Praslin, &c., selected rather on account of the mystery in which they were for a long time shrouded, or some remarkable circumstances connected with them, than for their surpassing atrocity.

While this work was in progress, Macgowan gave me an introduction to a firm in the neighbourhood of Fleet Street, engaged chiefly in the production of illustrated works. They had purchased some engraved plates from the widow of a deceased engraver, and wished to use them in the production of a gift-book. Proofs of the engravings were given to me, with a commission for the literary matter, which was to consist of short stories, so written as to be appropriately illustrated by the engravings. Some of these, such as a landscape or a feminine figure, were easily fitted; others, in which a story was suggested, required some consideration as to the intention of the artist. The manner in which I fitted the stories to them proved so satisfactory to the publishers that they gave me two or three commissions of the same kind.

The work was very poorly remunerated, however, and it was on that account that, in 1853, I accepted the local agency of the British Industry Life Assurance Company, offered me by Mr. Macgrath, whom I had known as a director of the National Land Company, and a member of the Executive Council of the Charter Association, prior to the stormy period of 1848. The company had been formed for the purpose of bringing life assurance within the reach of the working-classes by adopting the system of weekly premiums, and employing agents all over the kingdom. As I was well known to the working-men of the locality through my former connection with the Chartist movement, and had neither occupation nor income, I accepted the appointment, and entered upon its duties with zeal and energy.

If my principals had been directors of an old and substantial company, looking for proposals from persons who would pay yearly premiums of five or ten pounds, I might have placed a large brass or zinc plate on my door, announcing my agency, and advertised in the local newspapers; but that plan would not have succeeded, in that day at least, with the working-classes. So I spared myself all expense, and, with a parcel of prospectuses in my hand—neat little books, in yellow covers—set out to make a perambulation of the district.

Those who have never undertaken a similar task can have no conception of the amount of ignorance and prejudice which had to be encountered by the assurance canvasser of thirty years ago, or of the patience required for explaining such a subject to illiterate persons, to whom the idea was novel and strange. That was then the state of mind with regard to life assurance of all but the cream of the working-classes, the skilled artisans and mechanics. With these I had to encounter only the indifference and selfishness which many of them felt, and which were, and are, shared by quite as large a proportion of the middle-classes. It was in the slums where the labourers dwelt, in the midst of the squalor and wretchedness which are such fertile sources of callousness and selfishness, that I found my work the hardest.

In the oldest part of the town, within a stone's cast of the parish church, there was a narrow lane of wooden houses, occupied by men whose average earnings ranged from fifteen to twenty shillings per week. It was a fine summer evening when I canvassed that locality, and many of the inhabitants were lounging at their doors, the men in their shirt-sleeves, smoking short clay pipes, and the women nursing their babies and indulging their love of gossip.

"May I ask you to read this little book?" said I, as I paused at the first door in the lane, at which a little, middle-aged man, who looked like a bricklayer's labourer, was standing.

"What's it about?" he asked, regarding the prospectus I offered him rather suspiciously, without taking it.

"It explains the principles of life assurance on a new system, which is being introduced for the benefit of the working-classes," said I.

"I don't believe in it," he replied. "We must all die when our time comes, and I look upon them as pays to insure their lives as fools and them as takes their money as swindlers."

"You don't appear to understand the matter," said I. "We can't, as you say, prolong our lives by the payment of money; but by paying a trifle weekly you assure the payment of a certain sum of money at your death to your widow, or any one you may name to receive it."

"But I have neither wife nor child," he rejoined.

"Still you would like to leave enough to bury you, would you not?"

"The parish must bury me," he replied. "They daren't let me rot above ground."

I went on to the next house, where a younger man, apparently a "navvy," was sitting just inside the door, nursing a child, and sending up a curl of blue smoke from lips closed upon a dirty pipe.

"Look here, master," said this man when I had explained my business to him, "I does my best for the missus and the kids, and when I am gone they must do *their* best for themselves."

"But the children are too young to do anything for some years, and you may be taken from them to-morrow," I said. "It is a hard trial for a woman to be left with three or four children to keep out of the little she can earn; and for the price of a quart of beer per week you might leave your wife enough to set her up in some little business in the event of her being left like that."

"She must do the best she can," he returned. "If a man does his best for his family while he lives, he can't be expected to do more."

"I hope you will think better of it, my friend, for the sake of your wife and little ones," I said, and I passed on to the next cottage.

The occupier, who was knocking some hob-nails into the thick sole of a very dirty boot, was a middle-aged man, less stolid-looking than the bachelor, though his superior sharpness was of the kind often found in company with ignorance and narrow-mindedness. His wife was ironing, and two or three children were playing upon the bare floor.

"I haven't any opinion of them companies," this

man said, when I had offered him a prospectus and explained the proposed investment. "All the money I has to spare I can take care on myself, I can tell you."

"Aye, and more, too!" added his wife, resuming her ironing, which she had suspended while I was speaking.

"I am glad to hear that you know how to take care of your money, my friend," I said. "But, supposing you save sixpence a week, that will amount to only twenty-six shillings a year, with eightpence or ninepence added for interest, if you put it into the savings' bank. Now, if you pay sixpence a week to this company, they would pay fifty pounds to your widow at your death. You might die before the year is out, and then what a handsome sum fifty pounds would be to your widow."

"That's all very fine," returned the man, twisting upon his chair, "but I can take care of my money myself, and I don't mean to let anybody else have the handling of it."

"I hope you will change your mind," I observed, and I left the prospectus on the table, fancying that I saw a glimmering perception of the value of life assurance expressed on the countenance of the woman.

At the door of the next cottage a young woman, with long gold pendants in her ears, and dark hair smoothly parted upon a sun-browned and freckled forehead, was sitting upon a stool, occupied with some needlework.

"May I leave you one of these little books?" I asked, offering her a prospectus.

"It is not my religion," she replied, without looking up from her work.

I told her that it was not a religious tract I offered her, and proceeded to explain the principle of life assurance to her; but to all that I said she had only one response—"It is not my religion." Finding that she was a Catholic, too much in awe of the priest to risk reading a book that might contain what her spiritual guide would regard as heresy, I passed on, with a smile and a shrug.

In other quarters, and with men and women better instructed or more intelligent, I was more successful, and for some weeks proposals came in very well; so that, as I received a half-crown for each accepted proposal, the business was, for the time, satisfactory. When, however, the district had been thoroughly worked, and my income from the agency was reduced to little more than the commission on the premiums I collected, I resigned my appointment, and sought other employment.

CHAPTER IX.

Reading for the press—A theatrical journal in embryo—Book-making —Parliamentary reporting—G. F. Muntz and the Wolverhampton lock-maker—Ernest Jones's unfinished novel—I take up the broken thread.

LEAVING, not without some regrets, my cottage-home in the pleasant road between Croydon and Norwood, I took apartments temporarily in one of the back streets between Mile End Road and Arbour Square. My income being reduced at this time to the ten shillings per week I received for converting popular dramas into short stories for Purkess's "Library of Romance," the practicability of obtaining employment as a printer's reader occurred to me. Reference to the advertising columns of the *Times* resulted in the discovery that two persons were just then required in that capacity, one in a private office near the Houses of Parliament, the other in a large jobbing-office in Whitechapel. I made an appointment with the gentleman from whom the first announcement emanated, and, on a snowy and slushy evening in the last days of 1853, presented myself at his residence.

Ascending to the second floor, under the conduct of a servant, I was shown into a front room, in the centre of which stood a large office-table, covered with books, magazines, and Parliamentary papers.

The curtains were drawn, a bright fire burned in the grate, and at a desk near one of the windows a stout, middle-aged gentleman was rapidly driving pen over (and sometimes through) paper.

"One moment," said he, scarcely looking up. "Take a seat."

I drew a chair towards the fire, and awaited the leisure of my correspondent, whose pen flew on for a few minutes longer, when he touched a bell, hastily folded and enveloped his epistle or manuscript, and threw it upon the floor, to be picked up and posted by the boy who responded promptly to the tintinnabulary summons. Then he approached the fire, and seated himself opposite to me.

"You have not held a readership before, I think you said," he observed, after stirring the fire vigorously.

"No," I replied.

"Then what, may I ask, leads you to suppose that you are qualified for such a situation?" he asked.

"Because I am a practical printer, and have also had some experience in literary pursuits," I replied.

"They are good reasons, though the implied qualifications don't necessarily follow," he rejoined. "Supposing I engaged you, what wages would you expect?"

"Two pounds," I replied.

"I am afraid I should not have reading enough to occupy you fully," he observed after a pause. "Mine is only a private office, employing two or three men; but I require a man competent to read the proofs of an important work which they are now setting up, and if you could come two or three days a week we might arrange."

"I am afraid that would not suit me," I returned. "By accepting your offer I might lose the chance of obtaining full and permanent occupation."

"Very well," said he, rising. "If I can see my way to fully employing you I will write."

I left him, and on the following morning waited upon the Whitechapel printer, who, having succeeded on the death of a brother, to a business of which he had no practical knowledge, had been so hard to convince that a reader was necessary that the proof-reading had hitherto been performed by the overseer. On presenting myself at his office, I was conducted by a grimy-faced boy along a dirty and dimly-lighted passage, and shown into a dingy office, the walls and ceiling of which were blackened by smoke, while cobwebs festooned the corners, and the windows were almost opaque with dust.

A moment afterwards a stout man came into the room with long strides, the skirts of a dressing-gown of shawl-border pattern flowing in the draught, and flopped himself down upon an ancient stool.

"Sit down," said he, indicating a similar and rather rickety seat. "You have not been employed before as a reader, your letter informs me, but you are a practical printer, and have been engaged for some years in literary pursuits."

"Those are my qualifications," I observed, on his pausing.

"Well, I have hardly got reading enough to require a reader, or I should have had one before," he resumed. "But I print the bills of several theatres, and I have been thinking of a theatrical publication, combining displayed advertisements with critiques and all sorts of theatrical odds and ends."

"Such a publication might be made interesting to play-goers and useful to professionals," I observed, finding that he seemed to expect some response from me.

"You think so?" he returned. "Well, if you would edit the publication in the leisure that the reading would leave you, I think we might come to terms."

I saw that his aim was to obtain the services of both an editor and a reader for the wages of the latter, but I thought something better might come out of the arrangement, and I accepted his proposition, though it was coupled with the condition that I was to go for a fortnight "on trial," and I was to receive only thirty shillings per week—less than the wages of a compositor. I was at once installed in the reading-closet, where the proof of a play-bill was immediately brought to me by another grimy-faced boy.

The publishing project was not realized, however, and at the end of my probation I was informed that there was not reading enough to occupy the ten hours and a half daily that I was expected to be at my desk, and that, therefore, my services were no longer required. It happened most opportunely that I had that morning received a letter from the gentleman who had the private office near the Houses of Parliament, asking me to call upon him again. He, too, had come to the conclusion that, if I could and would assist him in certain literary undertakings, it might be to his and my advantage to come to some arrangement.

His immediate purpose, however, was to arrange with me to read his proofs at home, at a stipulated price per sheet, and to write two articles which, he informed me, he had not time to write himself. One of these was a memoir of Hincks, the Canadian minister, for which he supplied the material; the other was a paper on the advantages of western Canada as an emigration-field. I performed both tasks to his entire satisfaction, and, after reading the articles in manuscript, he engaged me in the double capacity of reader and general literary assistant at the usual reader's salary of two pounds per week.

It was with a feeling of curious interest that I read my article on emigration in an evening journal, in which it appeared as a "leader," and discovered some time afterwards that the memoir of Hincks had appeared (anonymously) in a magazine. I could only console myself for getting no credit for them by the reflection that I should not have had the opportunity of earning anything by their production if I had written them under other circumstances.

The book which I was engaged to read for press, and which was published by Messrs. Longman, was one of the most extraordinary examples of bookmaking which has ever come under my notice. It bore on the title-page the name of a gentleman who had, for commercial purposes, made a voyage to Buenos Ayres, calling at Pernambuco, Bahia, Rio Janeiro, and Monte Video; and, with a view to the interests of the enterprise with which he was connected, it was deemed desirable that a book should be produced which should direct attention to Brazil and the Platine republics as promising fields for European emigration and commercial undertakings of every description. As the gentleman who had gathered the materials for the book was unpractised in literary work, his journal and memoranda had been handed to my new employer, who, having his hands full of commissions from other persons who desired literary aid in various enterprises, sought my assistance in moulding the raw material into a book.

Portions of the work were already in type, though the whole was not yet written, and, as fresh information was supplied every week, odd pages and half-pages, with blank folios, crowded all the galleys in the office, and the two compositors employed on the work had not the faintest idea as to their ultimate places. I can compare the "making-up" of that book only to the putting together of one of the geographical puzzles designed for the amusement of children.

Other interests had to be served, besides those of the firm of Liverpool steamship owners with whom the ostensible author of the book was connected. There was a Manchester merchant interested in the development of the natural resources of Brazil, especially of the province of Amazonas; and there was a Liverpool gentleman interested in turning to a good account the supposed natural advantages of the Falkland Islands. But the gentleman who was to be announced as the author of the book had not explored the valley of the Amazon, or visited the dreary Falklands; and the information concerning those strongly-contrasted parts of the world had to be drawn from other sources. My employer undertook to impress the public mind with the idea that the Falklands, besides being a most eligible emigration-field, afforded the best sites in the world for a naval station, a harbour of refuge, and a convict settlement; and to me he entrusted the task of showing that the region watered by the Amazon would make the fortunes of those who would undertake the development of its vast natural resources. Mr. Wallace's interesting volume on that region, and the then recently-published narrative of the American explorer, Lieut. Herndon, furnished ample and excellent material for my share of the work, and I had the satisfaction of seeing the chapter on Amazonas described by the reviewer of the *Economist* as " the best in the book."

Parliament met soon after I entered the service of the gentleman in whose office this book was manufactured, and that event brought an unexpected, though not unwelcome, addition to the variety of my tasks. I was asked to report, for the *Birmingham Daily Post*, the Select Committee to which the House of Commons had delegated the consideration of the comparative advantages of the contract system of supplying the army with weapons and those which might be expected to accrue from the establishment of a State factory. Reporting was quite new to me when I first gazed at the frescoes which adorn the walls of the palace of the Legislature, and trod the long corridors into which the committee-rooms open; and, as I had not the slightest knowledge of shorthand, it may seem to have been an act of temerity in me to have undertaken such duties. But, being a rapid writer, and accustomed, in making literary memoranda, to use a system of abbreviations, which I now found very useful to me in the place of shorthand, I felt myself competent to perform the duties I had undertaken.

Every newspaper reader who has ever been in any court during a trial knows that the evidence is not given in the form of a continuous narrative, as it is reported, but in a series of answers to questions addressed to the witnesses by counsel or from the bench. To give the evidence in any other form would be impossible, as a rule, though it is sometimes done in cases which attract an extraordinary amount of public interest, such, for instance, as the Tichborne trial, which was reported *in extenso* in the *Daily Telegraph*. Parliamentary committees and royal commissions, the evidence before which abounds in repetitions and irrelevancies, are reported in the same manner. On the second or third day of the Small Arms Committee, the late George Frederick Muntz, then one of the members for Birmingham, was examining a lock-maker from Wolverhampton as to the rejection of locks by the Government viewer.

"If the viewer happens to be drunk, I suppose the rejections are more numerous?" said the honourable member.

The witness responded affirmatively, and of course I reported him as having said, "If the viewer happens to be drunk the rejections are more numerous." At the next meeting of the committee Muntz came up to the reporters' table when he entered the room, and asked if I was reporting for the *Daily Post*. Being answered in the affirmative, he complained that the report of the preceding sitting was incorrect; and the lock-maker, whose name, I think, was Jackson, leaned over the table, and said, with a grave countenance, and a tone of utmost distress, "You made me say that the viewers were drunk."

"I did nothing of the kind," said I. "What I reported was precisely the sense of what was said by Mr. Muntz, and assented to by you."

I then repeated the question and the answer, on which both gentlemen subsided silently into their places.

In connection with this subject I may observe, as the result of my own experience, and observations of the work of the reporters I have been brought into contact with, that for ordinary reporting the man who recommends himself on the score of the number of words he can take in shorthand per minute is, as a rule, inferior in the quality of his work to men who have not learnt shorthand. The *verbatim* reporter is usually deficient in the art of condensation, and the best reporter for all ordinary work is the man who can preserve all that is important or interesting, and omit all that is trivial or irrelevant, without obscuring the sense. There is an old story of a Parliamentary reporter who, being a rapid note-taker and transcriber, took in so long a report that the editor told him there was space only for half what he had written, on which he divided his copy, and asked the editor which half he would have. I can match that with the case, which came under my own observation, of a reporter who took such copious notes of a lecture that, when he had transcribed as much as would fill the space I had assigned him, he found that he had written out only two-thirds of his notes, and thereupon closed his report.

One qualification of no little importance in reporting which I possessed at this early period of my journalistic career was the great amount of miscellaneous knowledge which I had gathered in the course of my varied reading and occupations, and which an excellent memory had enabled me to retain. I soon found that, whatever might be the subject before any Parliamentary committee which I had to report, I knew enough about it to discriminate readily between what was important in the evidence and that which was trivial or irrelevant. After I had gained some experience, I found myself able to write my report at the table, taking notes only when I could not write rapidly enough to dispense with them, and transcribing in the intervals afforded by explanations and irrelevancies.

I had been employed five months in the various occupations I have indicated when the South American book was sent to press, and the need for my services which its preparation had created ceased to exist. It was a fortunate circumstance, upon which I now congratulated myself, that I had only the week before my engagement terminated undertaken, at the request of Macgowan, to take up the broken threads of a novel entitled, "The Lass and the Lady," which had been commenced by Ernest Jones, who, however, for some reason unknown to me, had declined to complete it. Plates had been engraved, and half the work printed, so that its abandonment would have involved a considerable loss to the publisher. Having read the printed sheets and the unprinted portion of the manuscript, to acquaint myself with the characters and the plot, as far as it had been developed, I set to work upon it; and though there was no suggestion of the intended *dénouement* in what Jones had written, and I had in consequence to shape my course by such light as was afforded by the characters of the persons who figured in the story, and the relations in which they stood to each other, I succeeded in carrying on the story to a natural and satisfactory conclusion.

CHAPTER X.

At a loose end again—My first editorship—A reminiscence of Miss Meteyard—James Hain Friswell—George Frederick Pardon—A gigantic scheme that was never realized.

THE prospect which I had before me in the middle of 1854 was not a brilliant one. What I had done during the last five months was useless to me as a stepping-stone in my career. If I advertised for a press engagement, to whom could I refer applicants for my services? Mr. Jaffray knew nothing of me, might not even be aware of my existence. My late employer, who alone could give the requisite recommendation, might have reasons for declining to forward my views. Something had to be done, however, and done quickly; so, after glancing over the columns of the *Times*, without finding any announcement of a want which I considered myself qualified to supply, I put on my hat, and walked to Ludgate Hill, with the intention of calling upon John Cassell, to whom I had introduced myself soon after my removal to London. I had then left with him copies of my "Papers for the People" on the pagan mysteries and the ancient schools of philosophy, in the hope that, as his publications ran in the lines of those of William and Robert Chambers, he might be induced by their perusal to give me employment. That he was then unable to do, but he promised to bear my application in mind whenever a vacancy occurred in his staff; and it was to freshen his memory with regard to that promise that I now sought him.

On inquiring at his office, on the old, tumble-down premises forming a portion of the site of the present great pile of buildings, I was informed that he was then in New York, and would not be in London for two or three weeks. Disappointed in that quarter, my thoughts turned again to journalism. That profession had a great attraction for me, and my recent experiences had increased its fascinations in my eyes. Believing that I could exercise it, the opportunity being given to me, with credit to myself and advantage to the cause of social progress, I determined to invest four or five of my limited number of shillings in an advertisement of my desire and my qualifications. The venture made, I walked home, and sat down to continue Ernest Jones's novel, and await the result.

The investment did not pay. The only response I received was from the proprietor of the *Buckinghamshire Advertiser*, who required an assistant in the threefold capacity of sub-editor, reporter, and reader, but declined to pay for the service I was prepared to render the wages I could have earned in London as a compositor. I did not feel inclined to risk any further investments in the same speculation. I worked hard at the novel, and perused every morning the advertising columns of what used to be called "the leading journal." It was all in vain. Though I answered several advertisements for editors, sub-editors, and reporters, including one from Bombay and another from Georgetown, Demerara, I had not the good fortune to be the selected candidate for one of the vacant posts.

Day after day passed, and the days grew into weeks, the moral horizon daily becoming more gloomy and contracted, and my means as scanty as my credit was limited. Here I am tempted to remark that, though the advantage of cash over credit is great for both tradesmen and their customers, the latter find it very difficult to get credit, when reduced by misfortune to ask for it, if they have always paid ready-money previously. The tradesman knows that the application means poverty, and is not inclined to open a ledger account with one whose impecuniosity is thus evident and confessed.

Just as I had finished the concluding chapter of "The Lass and the Lady," I received a letter from John Cassell, who had just returned from New York, requesting me to call at his office. Precisely at the hour named by him I turned under the arch of the old inn yard, and ascended to the publisher's private office.

"Still doing nothing?" he said, in a pleasant tone of interrogation.

"Doing very little, unfortunately," I rejoined.

"There is just now a vacancy here that may suit you," said he. "Professor Wallis is leaving me, and Mr. Millard succeeds him, vacating the editorship of the *Magazine of Art*. Do you think that will suit you?"

Of course it suited me. I must have made anything suit me just then, so the terms were soon arranged between us, and I commenced my editorial duties on the following Monday.

My pleasant little friend, John Tillotson, was editor of *Cassell's Family Paper*, and the staff of contributors to that widely-circulated publication and the *Magazine of Art* comprised the Howitts, Miss Meteyard, Mrs. Burbury, James Hain Friswell, J. E. Ritchie (now editor of the *Literary World*), Percy St. John, Dallas, and my friend, E. B. Neill, then London correspondent of the *Liverpool Albion*. "Silverpen," Friswell, and the latter two were the only members of that staff with whom I ever came into personal contact. Of Friswell I remember only his curly hair and rather dandified manners. A reminiscence of "Silverpen," which I have elsewhere related, produced a contradiction from one of the reviewers of my description of the lady as being "fair-haired." As my critic contented himself with denying the correctness of my statement, the question between us may be limited to the point, whether the lady was what those of her sex who amuse each other by telling fortunes with cards would call "hearts" or "diamonds." I venture to assert, however, that the difference between my description and the reality was very much less than that between the pen-portraits which two well-known writers have left of Thackeray.

About the time when Cassell's bankruptcy occurred, and again caused me to be cast adrift, Friswell conducted a serial which combined some of the features of a newspaper with those of a literary periodical somewhat after the manner of the magazines of the last century. Having, when I began my career as a journalist, opportunities of occasionally gleaning political information of an important and exclusive character, which I thought would be useful to him, I offered my services to him. To my surprise, and equally to my amusement, he informed me that "exclusive intelligence would be acceptable, and would be remunerated at a moderate rate;" but that my information on any subject must be condensed into a line and a half. I did not inquire what would be the moderate rate of remuneration for that quantity of matter.

Among other literary men who occasionally came up to my room at Cassell's was George Frederick Pardon, who had the singular reputation of having written the best book on billiards and playing the worst game of any man out. He was or had been connected, as founder, editor, or contributor, with more publications than any other man living, according to an announcement which appeared as the printed heading of the paper on which he wrote his correspondence. His claim to the sole right to produce a Welsh edition of the works of Dickens, on the ground that he had suggested such an edition to Messrs. Chapman and Hall, will be in the recollection of many of my readers. As a contributor to the periodical press, and the originator of much of it, the world does not know, and probably never will know, the extent of its indebtedness to Pardon in respect of the popular literature of thirty years ago. I had no conception of the matter myself until I read, thirteen or fourteen years ago, the announcement I have mentioned at the head of a letter I received from him.

I was walking westward one day, after a call upon Tillotson at Cassell's office, shortly after I left that establishment, when I was overtaken by Pardon, whose mind was then gestating a work of the most original character. The idea, as he unfolded it to me as we walked along Fleet Street, comprised a metropolitan directory and a topography of London, interleaved with advertisement pages and sections of a street panorama. Every shop, warehouse, and office in the modern Babylon was to be pictorially delineated, and to have its place in the directory and its advertisement—if the occupier availed of that medium of publicity—on the opposite page. The very vastness of the project invested it, however,—in my own mind, I mean,—with the littleness which the most stupendous objects assume to the eye when they are far distant, for the means of its realization were not very obvious. He was very desirous of my assistance in carrying out the enterprise; but it never advanced beyond the embryonic form which had been conceived in the fertile brain of its projector.

CHAPTER XI.

Introduction to journalism—Leader-writing for the Birmingham Journal—Michael Feeney—Liverpool journalism—The Beans and the Albion—The leader-writers of that day—John Wade—John Pope Hennessy—Michael James Whitty and the Daily Post—Henry Greenwood—Mr. E. R. Russell, M.P.

RETURNING to my lodging in Westminster from the dingy old house in the City, after the incident with which my last chapter closes, I found a letter awaiting me from Mr. E. B. Neill, who combined the duties of consul-general of the republic of Uruguay with those of London correspondent of the *Birmingham Journal*, the *Liverpool Albion*, and the *Bengal Hurkaru*, and had been an occasional contributor to the *Magazine of Art*. It contained an invitation to me to give him a call, and I immediately proceeded to his residence in New Palace Yard, hoping that something might come of the interview that would at least enable me to float over the breadth of broken water that seemed to separate me from fortune.

I found him at his desk, up to his eyes in newspapers, magazines, pamphlets, proof-sheets, and Parliamentary papers, and wound up by the constantly-growing demands upon his brain and pen to a high pitch of mental excitement.

"Don't speak to me," he said, looking up for a

moment as I entered. "I am in the agony of catching the post."

In ten minutes the pen flew over the paper, and slip after slip was rapidly turned off. Then he hastily folded them, thrust them into an envelope, and rang the bell.

"Run with this to Charing Cross," said he, as a sharp-looking boy answered the summons. "If you are too late, jump into the 'bus and take it to Euston."

The boy ran off, and the journalist rose wearily, with a sigh of relief, and, crossing over to the fire, dropped heavily upon an arm-chair.

"I was at that desk at four o'clock this morning," he observed. "And this has been my life for a dozen years."

Not knowing what remark would be the most suitable to the circumstances, I remained silent.

"You understand the emigration question?" he observed, after a pause. "You reported John O'Connell's committee?"

"Yes," I returned. "It was while that committee was sitting that the Mayor of Waterford, conversing with me in the corridor, made an amusing comment on the evidence of one of the witnesses: 'He is an Irishman; he'll say anything.'"

"I want you to write me an article on emigration," he said. "It is to serve the interests of the Grand Trunk people, and you must say as much as you can in favour of Canada as an emigration-field for all classes of emigrants. There is a blue-book on the table there that will give you all the data. To-morrow will do. What are you doing?—anything?"

"Nothing," I replied.

"You are well up, aren't you, in such matters as co-operation, trade unions, sanitary reform, workmen's dwellings, and the like?"

"I have studied them for years," I rejoined.

"Industrial and social questions are coming to the front more and more, and there is a demand for thoughtful writing on them. I supply the *Albion* and the *Birmingham Journal* with leaders, but I don't write them myself, and you might come on the staff. But we'll go into that another time."

We did, and the result was my engagement to write the leaders of the *Birmingham Journal*, and to report Select Committees and Royal Commissions, and furnish *résumés* of Parliamentary papers, both for the *Birmingham Daily Post* and the *Liverpool Daily Post*, the latter being the property of Mr. Neill's brother-in-law, the late Michael James Whitty.

The *Birmingham Journal* was at that time one of the best and most lucrative of the provincial newspapers, yielding its proprietors, Messrs. Jaffray and Feeney, an annual net income of nearly 5000*l*. I never met either gentlemen, but I have one pleasant recollection in connection with Mr. Feeney, and that is that he one Christmas sent me a goose. His brother had died about six months previously, and I had looked after the erection in Kensal Green cemetery of a marble monument which had been executed in Birmingham. For that trifling service the goose was the acknowledgment. "I think," wrote Feeney to Neill, "you told me Mr. Frost is a married man; and he shall have the best goose in Warwickshire."

My connection with the journal ceased about 1859. I then began to write leaders for the *Albion*, but on that paper there were other writers, and I had, in consequence, to confine myself for some time to social questions. The staff of leader-writers at this time was equal, numerically at least, to that of any daily paper, either metropolitan or provincial, the London correspondent being entrusted with the responsible duty of engaging for the supply of "leaders" writers specially acquainted with the matters to be commented upon, and to call upon them as occasion required. Only articles on local topics were written in Liverpool, all others being produced by London pressmen, and sent down as parcels by an earlier train than the mail on Sunday evening, with an arrangement for delivery the same night. The leader-writing staff comprised John Pope Hennessy, who wrote only on the proceedings of the Education Department; Matthew Daly, an officer of the Customs Department, to whom budgets, commercial treaties, and foreign tariffs were assigned; John Wade, the author of the "Black Book" and the "Chronological History of England," who occasionally contributed an article on some passing whim or folly of the day; and the present writer, whose field of labour comprised foreign politics and social questions. Of these one only, John Wade, who then lived at Chelsea, has passed away; he died some years ago, an inmate of the Charterhouse.

John Pope Hennessy was not, however, Sir John, nor a colonial governor, at that time, but a clerk in the Education department of the Privy Council. On leaving Downing Street he studied for the bar, and was called, but never held a brief. In 1858 he obtained a seat in Parliament as member for King's County, in which capacity he harassed the Government with questions and motions to such an extent that he had no difficulty in inducing them to appoint him to the governorship of the Gold Coast. He did not remain in that torrid and notoriously unhealthy locality, being shifted to the more agreeable surroundings of the island of Barbadoes, and subsequently to West Australia.

The *Albion* was founded in 1825, by William Bean, an enterprising printer and stationer in that town, and, as may be supposed, a man of superior education to most tradesmen, as printers were in those days. At that time the journals of the large towns were beginning to take a more prominent part in the discussion of political questions than they had hitherto, and Bean was not behind the times; but, in order to attract readers of all parties, he adopted an independent and impartial course, untrammelled by allegiance to either Whig or Tory.

Bean was one of the best stenographers of the day, but Canning, whose speeches he reported during the greater part of the time that eminent statesman and orator represented Liverpool in the House of Commons, was so extremely fastidious about the rounding of his periods, notwithstanding his eloquence, that he was always anxious to have the reporter's notes submitted to him for revision. His alterations were so numerous as to be equally annoying to the reporter and the printer; but Bean had a greater annoyance than the minister's corrections in the insulting behaviour of the wife of Colonel Bolton, whose guest Canning was whenever he visited Liverpool. Mrs. Bolton had a great contempt for "newspaper men," and evinced it when Bean called upon Canning, at her house in Duke Street, by invariably desiring the servant to bring a chair from the kitchen for his use while he was engaged with the statesman. Bean is said to have felt the insult very deeply, and to have occasionally referred to it in after years in terms not very complimentary to the lady; but it does not appear that he ever resented it, and the story illustrates very forcibly the distance which separates the present time from fifty years ago as regards the influence of the press, and the independence of the persons connected with it.

On the death of William Bean, the newspaper and the printing and stationery business with which it was connected passed into the hands of his sons, Charles Birch Bean and Thomas Bean, the former of whom conducted the *Albion* for many years with great success on the lines laid down by its founder. Being published at that time on Monday morning, its readers were presented with all the news of the two preceding days at the same time as they were given in the morning papers of the metropolis. The distinctive features of the paper were, however, its London correspondence and the copious extracts that were given in its columns from the best of the new books, these selections not unfrequently being given before the book from which they were culled was published, a copy being in such cases obtained from the publisher in sheets. The *Albion* was then and for many years afterwards the best newspaper in Liverpool, whether as regards its literary matter or its reports. I remember hearing Charles Turner, then M.P. for Liverpool and chairman of the Dock Board, observing to a friend, in a committee-room of the House of Commons, during the inquiry which preceded the amalgamation of the Liverpool and Birkenhead docks under one board, "We shall see the best report in the *Albion*."

Fourth in order of time among the existing journals of Liverpool is the *Journal*, which was commenced in 1830, by the late Michael James Whitty. Distinctly Liberal, and conducted by a man of ability and enterprise, it took from the first a front place in Liverpool journalism. It was well edited, and its "Talk on 'Change," written by Whitty himself, was a feature of the paper to which every business-man turned on unfolding it. Whitty had the knack of making personal matters in connection with commerce and finance readable by converting into pleasing gossip what a writer of the Dryasdust order would have simply succeeded in making repellent.

Whitty had several sons, only one of whom has made any mark in the world. This is Mr. Edward Whitty, the author of "Friends of Bohemia," who, after the publication of that amusing novel, emigrated to Australia in quest of "fresh fields and pastures new." It was time, for the journalistic profession was even then becoming crowded. Miss Whitty evinced so much musical talent that at an early age she was sent to Milan to complete her studies, with a view to her appearance on the operatic stage. She made a most successful *début* at a London concert, and after singing at a series of entertainments at the Crystal Palace and other places, in conjunction with Mr. and Mrs. Tennant and Herr Formes, she made a provincial tour with the Carl Rosa Opera Company.

The late Henry Greenwood, the founder and first proprietor of the *Liverpool Journal of Commerce*, was a relative of Whitty, and, like him, originally migrated to Liverpool from Ireland, where his father, a Yorkshireman, held a Government appointment. He was employed by Whitty as a journeyman printer, and afterwards promoted to the position of manager of the *Liverpool Journal*. He subsequently started business as a printer and an advertising agent, and purchased the business of Mr. Smith. He removed from Canning Place to the present extensive premises in Harrington Street and Castle Street, where he built up a considerable printing business. He was also the proprietor of the *British Journal of Photography*, a paper which had an insignificant beginning, but has become the leading photographic journal of the world, and in that publication, together with the Photographic Almanack, he has left a monument of his energy and perseverance, which form the chief features of his character. He long since ceased to have any connection with the *Journal of Commerce*, which he sold to the late proprietor, from whom it came into the possession of the present owner, who was associated with him in its foundation. He died in December, 1884, in his sixty-fourth year, much respected by a large circle of friends.

In 1855, encouraged by the removal of the last penny of the stamp duty on newspapers, Whitty brought out a morning paper, the *Liverpool Daily Post*, which, unlike many similar ventures, was a great success from its first appearance. He was very fortunate in his editor, Mr. E. R. Russell, to whose ability and experience the success of the paper was, in a great measure, due. The *Daily Post* became so great a success that the services of Mr. Russell, to whose ability that success was so largely due, were recognized by the proprietor as indispensable to its existence. After having his salary raised on several occasions, Mr. Russell was taken into partnership by Whitty, and on the latter's death he, in conjunction with Mr. A. J. Jeans, became proprietor of both the *Post* and the *Journal*. That partnership has continued to the present time, the offices of the two papers having, meanwhile, been removed to more commodious premises in a more commanding situation. In 1878, various considerations of a commercial character induced Messrs. Russell and Jeans to bring out another weekly journal, the *Weekly Post*, and in the following year the publication of the *Liverpool Echo*, a halfpenny evening paper, was commenced. Competition between the Liverpool dailies, both morning and evening, has been keen, but the *Echo* has held its ground, and is undoubtedly the best of the evening journals issued in the city of that mythic bird, the liver.

I am anticipating, however, and must hark back. There were two other writers whom I have not mentioned who occasionally contributed a leader on questions of foreign politics to the *Albion*, namely, Major Rolland and Mr. Collet, the editor of the *Diplomatic*

Review, the organ of the Foreign Affairs Committees organized by the late David Urquhart. Both gentlemen being disciples of that one-idea'd politician, I invariably had their contributions consigned to me to be made suitable for nineteenth-century readers, a process which the antagonism of Urquhart's sixteenth-century constitutionalism to my democratic views rendered somewhat difficult. This antagonism once brought me into collision with Urquhart himself, who did me the honour of transferring one of my *Albion* leaders to the columns of the *Review*, and assailing me in his usual violent and unfair manner as " either an imbecile or a traitor."

CHAPTER XII.

Roche, of the *Courier*—James Mahony, the artist—"The Book of the Baltic"—Samuel Lover—Sir Cusack Roney—"A Month in Ireland"—A dishonest publisher—The *Shrewsbury Chronicle*.

THOUGH, as the years wore on, I wrote a much larger number of the *Albion* leaders, my journalistic duties did not absorb all my time, especially when Parliament was not sitting, and, as I had a family growing up around me, I welcomed every opportunity that presented itself of adding to my income by the performance of any literary task that came in my way.

The London reporter of the *Liverpool Courier* at this time was an Irishman named Roche, whom I sometimes met in the lobby and committee-rooms of the House of Commons.

"What do you do when Parliament is not sitting?" I one day asked him.

"I write pamphlets," he replied.

"Do you find that pay?" I asked him, with an air of doubt, well knowing that pamphlets, as a rule, do not pay the cost of paper and printing.

"Very well," he rejoined, with a smile in which self-satisfaction mingled with amusement at my surprise.

"What topics do you find this generation willing to read pamphlets upon?" I asked.

"Well," he replied, "there is nothing that pays so well as a strong-flavoured polemic. As soon as Parliament is prorogued, I take up the most exciting religious question of the day; and the more difficult it is to understand, the more eager I find people to read all that can be said on either side of it. There was Colenso's attack on the Pentateuch, for instance. I went into the controversy that arose out of it with a pamphlet entitled "Moses Right and Colenso Wrong," and it went immensely. What do you do when Parliament is not sitting?" he asked in his turn.

I can answer that question at greater length now than I did then. As I have shown in an earlier chapter, there are gentlemen who aspire to the honours of authorship without possessing the literary ability or enjoying the leisure to achieve them by their own unaided efforts. Well, just after the conclusion of peace with Russia, James Mahony, a very clever artist, whose views of Spanish and Moorish scenery in the *Illustrated London News* may be remembered by middle-aged readers of that journal, crossed Schleswig and Zealand by rail, steamed up the Baltic to St. Petersburg, and travelled through Russia to Moscow and Nijni-Novgorod. On his return to England, with his portfolio full of sketches of Danish and Russian scenery and illustrations of Scandinavian and Muscovite manners and customs, it was suggested by a friend that his journal and his sketches should be utilized in the production of an illustrated volume that should serve as a handbook for tourists and others availing of the newly-opened communications of the North of Europe Steam Navigation Company.

The result was "The Book of the Baltic," in which Mahony's rough notes were elaborated and amplified by his friend and myself, and supplemented by descriptions of the land route from Christiansand to Christiania and the inland navigation between Gothenburg and Stockholm. These sections were committed to me, but those descriptive of Denmark and Russia were a curious piece of literary mosaic, in which I can, thirty years afterwards, pick out each man's contributions, paragraph by paragraph. What did it matter that neither " Our Mutual Friend " nor myself had ever crossed the North Sea? Does not Moore tell us that " authors of all work "

> ——" can take a day's rule for a trip to the tropics,
> And sail round the world, at their ease, in the fleet " ?

Like the gentleman who had never been in Germany, but had a cousin who played the German flute, if I had never been up the Baltic, I had once been on board one of the North of Europe Steam Navigation Company's vessels. That was the *Hesperus*, the steamer which was chartered to convey to the Crimea the navvies who constructed the Balaklava railway. I went down to Blackwall on that occasion as a reporter, and stood on the bridge with Lord Robert Clinton, who represented the Government and made a speech to the men, Captain Andrews, the Company's secretary, and Captain Cruikshank, the commander. I do not remember a word of Lord Robert Clinton's address, except his exhortation to concord, clenched by the reminder that "union is strength," to which one of the rough fellows demurred. "Except," was his comment, "when they put too much water in the grog."

To return to the book, it came out in green and gold, with Mahony's name on the title-page, though there was not a sentence of his writing in it which had not been revised by another hand, and at least two-thirds of the contents were written independently of even his notes.

It might have been supposed that at least so versatile a genius as Samuel Lover, who wrote novels and was a later Moore in the field of Irish song and ballad,—who composed music for his lyrical productions, and illustrated his stories of Irish life and manners with designs drawn and engraved by himself,—would have been independent of such aid as was invoked by his compatriot Mahony. It is, however, one of the things not generally known, and one which was unknown even to his biographer, Mr. Bayle Bernard, until I acquainted him with it, that the manuscript of the handbook which he wrote for Mr. T. H. Friend's panorama of Canada and the States was revised by me, the need of such revision being shown by such awkward phrases as "a quantity of churches," which I recollect as occurring in his description of New York.

Another gentleman, also an Irishman, to whom I gave literary assistance, and to a much greater extent, was the late Sir Cusack Roney, a gentleman for many years connected with railway enterprise in both hemispheres, especially as the organizer of the Irish tourist traffic, which set in strongly about thirty years ago, and of the Canadian Grand Trunk system. In the year preceding the Dublin exhibition it was suggested to or by this gentleman that the expected influx of English tourists into Ireland called for the issue of a new guide-book to the Emerald Isle, which, by the exclusion of everything that would not interest the ordinary tourist, such as historical and anecdotal matter, should be more portable and popular than the well-known volume with the pea-green cover and profusion of illustrations. Sir Cusack had not the leisure, and perhaps equally lacked the inclination, to write the book himself, and, though his name appeared on the title-page as the author of " A Month in Ireland," the matter which he contributed was limited to the preface, the explanation of the through-ticket system of railway arrangements, and the brief eulogy of his friend Dargan, interpolated in the description of Bray. The whole of the book, with those exceptions, was mine. There was, at the outset, an intention that I should go over to Ireland, and run through the districts most frequented by tourists; but it was abandoned, and I had to draw upon the most recent works of Irish travel for my materials, in default of being able to present the results of my own observations.

One of my literary undertakings of this period resulted unfortunately, owing to the dishonesty of the intending publisher. A bookseller in the Strand, with whom I had been acquainted many years, recommended me to the proprietor of a periodical, who wanted a serial story to succeed one then approaching its conclusion. I obtained the commission, worked hard during the still hours of night, and sent in the copy promptly and punctually; but, to my surprise, there appeared in the pages my story should have filled the opening chapters of a story which had previously appeared in an American magazine. I called upon the proprietor for an explanation, but was denied access to him. I wrote to him, but received no answer. I wrote again, asking for the return of the manuscript, or a cheque for the sum agreed to be paid for it, but still no answer came.

At length the man's name appeared in the *Gazette* as a bankrupt, and I scarcely need add that I never received a penny of the hard-earned money that was due to me. Some time afterwards, however, his clerk returned to me the manuscript through the post, stating that he had found it in the waste-paper basket; and adding something very much like Frederick Yates's insulting query to Townsend, the dramatist, when returning the manuscript of a play, "Is this your rubbish?"

My connection with the *Birmingham Journal* ceased about this time, but I wrote more frequently for the *Albion* thenceforward, and also began writing the leaders and leaderettes for the *Shrewsbury Chronicle*, the oldest of the Salopian newspapers, having been established in 1772. It was, and is, the property of Mr. John Watton, whose tact and experience have retained for it, in spite of the journalistic competition of the last five-and-twenty years, the reputation of being the best newspaper in the district in which it circulates, and the most impartial in its treatment of political questions, especially those into which the religious element enters. This course is required from it, indeed, by the extent of its circulation in the neighbouring Welsh counties, the Methodistic tendencies of whose population modifies and softens the support which it gives to the Established Church.

I may here remark that my experiences have not made me acquainted with those extreme strains upon the consciences of leader-writers, some rather ludicrous instances of which have been recorded by Mr. James Grant, in his interesting, but very imperfect, history of the newspaper press of the United Kingdom. As a rule, I have been very little interfered with by the proprietors or chief editors of the papers with which I have been connected, with regard to my manner of dealing with the political and social questions of the day. Both the *Albion* and the *Birmingham Journal* were then Liberal, but Liberalism is a very elastic term, admitting of many interpretations, as too-confiding electors have sometimes been taught by the difference between the professions made on the hustings and the course taken in Parliament; and there was a marked difference between the Liberalism of the *Journal* and that of the *Albion*. Hence, while I had full swing for my Radicalism in the former journal, I was occasionally admonished to write more guardedly and vaguely for the latter, especially on the question of franchise extension, which I was told the merchants and shipowners of Liverpool cared nothing about. The *Liberalism* of the *Chronicle*, though more earnest and decided than that of the *Albion*, which was tempered very much by local influences and commercial considerations, was less advanced than that of the

Journal, clinging rather more than I liked to the traditional creed of the Whigs.

It was easy, however, at that time, to put my Radicalism aside, as its assertion would have been a mere waste of power. The electoral body was content to give a majority to Lord Palmerston, and that majority had become so abject in their submission to the Minister that a deputation of the Commons actually waited upon him with a humble prayer that he would reduce the public expenditure and give the nation some relief from taxation, thus abdicating into the hands of the Minister their functions as guardians of the public purse. Even the more Radical of them were content with the reflection of the French Liberals before 1848, in reference to Louis Philippe,—" Wait till the old fox dies, and then—"

CHAPTER XIII.

A shadow on my path—An electioneering mission—A search for a young lady—A visit to York—Newsome's circus—Vivian, the ring-master—The brothers Francisco—Alfred Burgess—A circus-man's criticism of Dickens.

IF, in the last three chapters, I have subordinated my life to my work, it is because the years of which they treat were untroubled by the vicissitudes of literary Bohemianism, while in other respects they were like a voyage upon a Dead Sea. A dark shadow had been cast upon the pathway of my life, and I could not escape from it. It clung to me as relentlessly as the Old Man of the Sea to the shoulders of Sinbad, and I had no power to shake it off. It paralyzed all my efforts for material advancement, and reduced me to the position of a horse in a mill. In some respects the horse had the advantage.

Seven years passed, with the grip of my devilish burden constantly tightening. Desperation at length gave me strength to cast it from me, but the shadow still pursued me, and came at unexpected turns across my path, poisoning my life with the consciousness that we were still breathing the same air.

But this is a riddle, the interpretation of which would not greatly interest my readers, even if I were disposed to open the closet in which my domestic skeleton of those years was concealed.

As old Mucklebackit, the fisherman, in Scott's "Antiquary," says, "The like o' us maun to our wark again, if our hearts were beating as hard as my hammer." Children must be fed, and rent must be paid; and well it is for the individual and for society that the necessities of life oblige most of us to go on working whatever griefs may cast their shadows across our path.

Several years had elapsed since I had taken any active part in politics, when an incident occurred which enabled me to make myself practically acquainted with the opinions and feelings of the lower grades of the middle class, which since 1832 had formed the majority of the electoral body. It was my custom at that time to indulge myself with an annual holiday of a week or ten days, after the prorogation of Parliament, and that brief period of relaxation I had always passed at some town on the coast of Kent; or, to speak more correctly, I had made Ramsgate, Deal, or Dover my headquarters, sallying forth therefrom every morning for long walks along the beach or the cliffs, or over breezy slopes inland, dining wherever I found myself when my stomach reminded me of the time that had passed since breakfast, and returning at sunset to a meal that was tea and supper in one.

"Is there any place to which you have made your mind up to go?" I was asked in 1864, when the period of my annual excursion drew near, by a gentleman who need not be more particularly mentioned.

"No," I replied. "I have been thinking of Hastings; but I have not decided yet."

"Must it be Kent? Are you particular as to where you go?" my querist inquired.

"I prefer the Kentish coast, because the air is so bracing," I replied.

"If your expenses were provided for, would you mind going in a different direction?"

"No," I said. "There are few places on the coast that would not be new to me."

"Then I think I can arrange that for you," he rejoined. "If you don't mind combining business with pleasure I can give you a commission that will interfere very little, if at all, with your enjoyment of your holiday."

My instructions were not given me until the day before I started, when I was informed that a wealthy gentleman, engaged in trade in the City, aspired to a seat in Parliament, and proposed to offer himself, at the next general election, as a candidate for the representation of a little borough on the south-west coast, to which he was personally a stranger. It was desirable, therefore, that he should employ an agent in the collection of information concerning the constituency, and for this confidential mission I had been recommended. I was to go down to the place, and, without disclosing the purpose of my visit, gather the views and feelings of the electors, ascertain the public wants, and glean all the facts I could that would enable my principal to see his way in the matter.

The name of the candidate was not unfamiliar to me, as I had been concerned on his account in carrying through one of the most extraordinary transactions with which my journalistic experiences have made me acquainted. I had been asked to write an article on the excessive use of chicory in the mixture with coffee authorized by the Treasury, showing how it operated with respect to the coffee-dealer, the consumer, and the revenue. Having reported the Select Committee on the adulteration of food and drugs which sat in 1859, under the chairmanship of Mr. Scholefield, I was conversant with this subject, and at once wrote the required article, which duly appeared in the *Albion*, and was immediately quoted in the London dailies, which were supplied with printed slips for the purpose. Then another article was written, suggesting the desirability of doubling the duty on chicory, and urging the advantage of the proposed augmentation of duty to the trade and revenue of the country, as the importation of coffee would increase in the same ratio as that of chicory would diminish. This also went the round of the press.

When the question had been ventilated in the newspapers for some time, a deputation of wholesale dealers in coffee waited upon Mr. Gladstone, who was then Chancellor of the Exchequer, and represented to him the advantages that would accrue to the revenue, the trade, and the consumers from the augmentation of the duty on chicory to the extent of 100 per cent. An agitation for an increase of taxation is, I believe, unique; and Mr. Gladstone might have been excused if he had suspected that a keen regard for other interests than those of the revenue and the public was at the bottom of the movement. He was ignorant, it is to be presumed, of the real facts of the case, which were known only to a few persons, and were not allowed to transpire. He acceded, therefore, to the request of the deputation, and the duty on chicory was doubled.

Now, the gentleman who aspired to the honour of representing the little seaport town at which it was proposed I should spend my holiday was the largest importer of chicory in this country, and had at that time a very large stock of the commodity, having conceived the idea of making a fortune at one stroke by obtaining possession of all that was procurable, and then forcing up the price. The first step to that end was the creation, through the agency of the press, of a certain amount of public opinion in favour of the augmentation of the duty; the second was the bringing a gentle pressure to bear on the Chancellor of the Exchequer through the medium of some of the principal importers of coffee, whose commercial interests made them, consciously or unconsciously, the ready instruments of the speculator.

The Budget resolutions having been adopted by the House of Commons, the merchant who had been the chief wire-puller in the business paid the old rate of duty on his immense stock of chicory, which he afterwards sold at the enhanced price to which the commodity was raised by the doubling of the duty, the profits of the transaction amounting, according to a statement that was made to me by a gentleman likely to be well informed, to no less than 70,000*l.*

I found the town which the principal in the fiscal incident I have related aspired to represent one of those old-world places which in 1832 had been saved from inclusion in the schedule of rotten boroughs by the device of including a neighbouring village within its boundary. It was partly urban, therefore, and partly rural—one of those composite boroughs which seemed to have been designed for the purpose of furnishing an additional argument for the assimilation of the county and borough franchises and the division of the country into electoral districts of equal population. It did not seem a very lively place, for on going out about nine o'clock on the evening of my arrival to post a letter, I found the streets in darkness, and the solitary constable, who was lame, informed me that the gas was not lighted during the summer.

I devoted the following morning to a walk about the town and the harbour, and in the afternoon made a little circular tour of the vicinity, passing through the village included within the boundary of the borough, and returning to the town by the beach. My attention had been directed to the harbour, the breakwater of which was being extended by the Corporation, who were prevented by want of funds from adding more than a few yards to the work yearly; and it was thought that the prospect of obtaining a grant from the Consolidated Fund would induce the electors to withdraw the support hitherto given to the venerable Conservative who had represented the place for several years, and give it to a Liberal.

In the evening I strolled into a public-house near my lodging, and, sitting down in a quiet corner of the parlour, rolled a cigarette, and prepared to glean all the information concerning local interests and predilections that might fall from the lips of the assembled neighbours. I had not long to wait.

"So we are to have a contest at the next election," observed a stout, red-faced man, on a pause occurring in the conversation that was going on when I entered.

He spoke very deliberately, and his respectability, in the conventional sense of the term, was vouched for by the black broadcloth he wore and a heavy gold chain.

"It seems so," said another of the company, in what seemed a very cautious manner.

"Well, the old colonel has represented us for some years, and I don't say that we have any reason to complain of the manner in which he has represented us," said the red-faced man. "But he has had a good innings, and a new broom, they say, sweeps clean."

"Are we likely to do better?" said a third member of the company, removing a long clay pipe from his mouth. "That's the way to look at it. He lives among us, and deals with us, and subscribes to our charities; and, if he don't say much in the House, he goes up and votes when there is anything important on, and I don't think any one can say that he don't always give his vote on the right side."

"I don't know so much about that," observed a fourth, speaking with rather more energy than the others had done. "And, as for his charities, he has never given so much as five shillings to the British School since he has been our member."

A pause followed this expression of dissent, and the

speaker subsided into quiescence. Presently the red-faced man, who I afterwards learned was a coal-merchant, spoke again.

"I am not sure," he observed, "that we might not do better, though of course I don't mean to say that any change would be for the better. I should want to see my way very clearly before I gave my vote to a stranger. But this gentleman from London that the *Advertiser* speaks of as a probable candidate may be all that we want."

"What do we know of him?" asked the man of few words.

"That's it," said another.

"Vote for the man you know, I say," said the partisan of the sitting member.

Here I saw an opportunity of supporting the candidature of the gentleman by whom the cost of my holiday was to be borne.

"I am a stranger here, and know nothing of your local politics and local interests," I observed, "but I happen to know something which seems to be unknown here, and that is, that the gentleman who has been mentioned as a probable candidate is a merchant of good standing and repute in the City of London, a man of energy and ability, and said to have plenty of money."

"Oh, if he has got that he will do," observed a man who had not spoken before. "We want a gentleman who will spend money in the place, and represent our interests—our local interests, I mean—in Parliament. Now, is he the man to do that, or is he a man of what they call large views, who will go in for Parliamentary reform and secular education, and overlook altogether the wants of the place that elected him?"

"On those points he must speak for himself," I rejoined. "I know him only by repute, and I spoke only because he seemed to be quite unknown to this company."

"Well, there are Liberals and Liberals, it is true," said the coal-merchant, reflectively. "What occurred to me, when I read about his coming here, was, that we are living in a time of change, that trade is not very lively, and that a younger and more active and energetic man than our present member might fall in better with the new lines of thought, and infuse a little more life into us."

"And vote for a Reform Bill that would knock us out of representation," added the Conservative.

I need not repeat more of the conversation, the tenor of which was, the sitting member would have continued to suit the constituency very well if he had been born twenty years later. I made a report which I was informed was "very valuable for the purpose," and received instructions to look at a row of cottages in the town, and a piece of land near it, which were for sale, and report upon their eligibility for the manufacture of votes. A London surveyor who happened to be at Wells on business was instructed to join me, and did so, with the result of a pleasant dinner at one of the principal inns; and at the end of my stay a friend of the would-be candidate came down, with whom I went over the ground for the third time.

The conclusion arrived at was, that the chances of any other candidate than the sitting member were few, the latter being a respected resident in the vicinity; and the appearance of a second Liberal candidate settled the question. The gentleman for whom I was concerned retired, and made an attempt to gain the confidence of another marine constituency; but he succeeded no better on the south-east coast than on the south-west, and, after that second failure, abandoned the pursuit of social distinction through the doors of Parliament, convinced, however unpleasant the reflection may have been, that he was

> ——" born to blush unseen,
> And waste his sweetness on the desert air."

It was about this time that a curious and somewhat inexplicable adventure befell one. One evening, as I was passing along one of the main arteries of traffic south of the Thames, I was accosted by a woman in whom I recognized one who had moved in a respectable sphere, but had abandoned her husband and children, and fallen into the lowest depths of moral and social degradation. She had been looking for me, she said; there was no one else of whom she could ask the favour which she believed she should not ask in vain of me. She desired to enlist my aid in finding her sister, a girl of eighteen years of age, who had been in domestic service, but had lately left her situation, and now mysteriously disappeared. She had been lodging in that neighbourhood, had gone out one afternoon, ostensibly to apply for a situation, and had not been seen since. Would I try to find her, and endeavour, if successful, to keep her from going wrong?

The task which she wished to impose on me was a difficult one, but I did not like to refuse to undertake it. For her sister's sake, I told her I would do my best, though I warned her that to seek any individual in that great modern Babylon was almost as hopeless a task as searching for one particular pebble among the shingle of the beach at Brighton. Could she give me any clue? In response she shook her head despondently, but after a moment's pause remembered having heard her sister mention a house at Brompton at which a girl lived with whom she was acquainted. I may say at once that this clue, such as it was, failed. There was no one at the house in question who knew her sister.

The family with whom the girl had lodged for two or three weeks had removed from Lambeth to Knightsbridge, where I found them living in a back street near Trevor Square. So far as I was able to ascertain, the head of that family was a decent workingman, and the only point which I thought worthy of note on the tablets of memory was that his wife answered my questions in a guarded manner, and mostly in monosyllables. But I was a stranger, and she might feel suspicious as to the object of my inquiries. She could, or would, tell me nothing that was not already known to me.

One night, several weeks after my meeting with the sister of the missing girl, I was leaving the music-hall in Tichborne Street when I was again accosted by the lost woman. Speaking rapidly, and with eagerness of manner, she informed me that she had that evening recognized her sister, who was accompanied by another girl, in Waterloo Road. One of them spoke to a cabman, whose vehicle was standing at the hotel at the corner of York Road, and then crossed over to Tenison Street, the cab following. Ensconced in a doorway near the house at which the cab stopped, she saw her sister issue from it, and step into the vehicle, which was then driven back into Waterloo Road, where it turned towards the bridge.

"Why didn't you speak to your sister?" I asked.

"I didn't like," she replied. "I thought it best not to do so, but to ask you to find her and save her, for I am sure now she is going wrong."

It seemed probable, at the least, Tenison Street being tenanted almost entirely by the frail sisterhood, though as quiet and reputable-looking as any second-rate street in London.

"I can tell you," she added, "the number of the house she came out of, and also the number of the cab."

I made a memorandum of both numbers, that of the cab being the only clue worth anything. Nothing more could be learned at the house than the fact that Miss Wilson had lodged there about a month. The locality to which she had removed was unknown. Now, Wilson was not the name of the young lady for whom I had undertaken to search, but there was nothing more probable in such a case than a change of name. Knowing the number of the cab, it was easy to ascertain by inquiry at the inland revenue office (hackney carriage department), Somerset House, the name and address of the owner of the vehicle; and the following evening found me in the stable-yard of that individual, situate in a street leading from Gower Street to Gordon Square.

There was the cab, and there was the driver. He remembered taking up a girl in Tenison Street on the previous evening, but either could not remember where he had driven her, or was unwilling to give the information. It was somewhere up Pentonville way; but beyond that his memory did not seem to carry him. I suggested that a drink might freshen his memory. He accepted the suggestion, and invited me to take a seat in the cab, as he was just going on the stand. I stepped in, and was driven across Gower Street and into a back street, where the cab stopped before a public-house. In another moment we were at the bar, where, on his expressing a preference for "summat short," he was supplied with a half-quartern of gin, while I refreshed myself with a glass of ale.

"It was Warren Street," he said, when he had drank half of the fiery liquid, and wiped his mouth with the sleeve of his coat. "That's where it was; but blarm me if I know what number it was. However, it was a hodd'un, though I can't say whether it was 3, 5, or 7."

That was near enough to start with, I thought; and I proceeded at once to Warren Street, a quiet, secluded locality in the rear of Pentonville Road. The odd numbers were all on the north side, and the preliminary inquiries were made in a few moments. On asking for Miss Wilson at No. 3, I was informed that the young lady did not live there, but that she might be the one who had arrived in a cab at No. 5 the previous evening. On ringing the bell at No. 5 a stout, middle-aged lady, respectably attired, opened the door, and replied to my inquiries that Miss Wilson was not at home. As my name was not known to the fair object of my search, I left my card, requesting the portly recipient to ask her to write to me.

"A lady has been asking for you," said my landlady, when I returned to my lodgings on the following evening.

"Did she leave her name, or any message?" I asked.

She had left neither; but the description of her personal appearance which I received satisfied me that the caller had been "Miss Wilson," and I felt sorry that I had not been at home. I sat down and wrote to her, begging her to communicate with me at once, and assuring her of my desire to serve in the best manner I could.

Several days passed, but I received no answer to my letter. Sunday came, and I walked up to Warren Street once more, this time at mid-day. The servant who opened the door in response to my tintinnabulary summons informed me that Miss Wilson was at home, and invited me to a comfortably furnished sitting-room on the first-floor.

"Miss Wilson is dressing," said the girl, "but she will be here in a few minutes, if you will take a seat."

I had not long to wait. In a few minutes a door opened, and a young lady entered who, as I saw at a glance, was not the fair one of whom I was in search, though sufficiently like her to be mistaken for her by any person not intimately acquainted with her. The height, figure, complexion, colour of the hair, were the same, and the features similar; but the difference was discernible, though not easy to be expressed. I rose at once, apologizing for the mistake; but she was curious as to its origin, and I resumed my seat while giving the desired explanation. She had seen from my letter that there was some mistake, which was the reason why she had not written or repeated her visit.

I did not succeed in my quest after all. A second visit to the neighbourhood of Trevor Square resulted in my eliciting from the woman I had seen there that she knew where the missing girl was, but she had promised not to divulge, and would assist me no further than in conveying a letter to her. The reply to that letter threw no light upon the mystery. The girl had no desire to see her sister, and saw no good purpose that would be served by seeing me. There was clearly an end of my mission. I made one more effort, however, by going again to Knightsbridge, where I learned, from the same source as before, that the girl had left London for Paris, accompanied by a gentleman, on the preceding day.

This seems the place in which I should say something about the manner in which I acquired some portion of that knowledge of circus life which caused one of the reviewers of a work written by me several years afterwards to remark that I seemed to have passed my life in wandering from fair to fair, conversing with acrobats and circus-riders.

It has been stated that when Dickens was contemplating the writing of "Hard Times," he obtained the *entrée* of the arena at Astley's at the hour when the riders, acrobats, &c., practise feats to be performed in the evening, that is, from eleven to twelve, in order to glean some knowledge of the manners, language, &c., of circus-men, a circus company figuring prominently in the story. This may or may not be true; the fact that the great novelist wrote to a friend, asking where such glimpses of a little-known world could be obtained, renders it probable, on one hand, while, on the other, there is so unreal a picture of circus life and manners depicted in the story that it seems very doubtful.

About ten years after the publication of the novel in question, I one day received a telegram summoning me to York, where a private affair of urgent character required my immediate presence. As it was summer, and only two or three weeks earlier than the time when I usually took my annual holiday at the sea-side, I determined to make the best of the unforeseen occasion, and spend a week at York, taking my yearly dose of ozone while steaming from Hull to London on my return, instead of inhaling it as usual on the cliffs and beaches of Kent. So I left King's Cross by a fast train on the morning after I received the telegram, heard the inevitable story of the Hitchin hermit, disposed of a sandwich and a glass of beer at Peterborough, took a walk at Knottingley while the train was kept waiting for one from Leeds, and reached York late in the afternoon.

It was too late to do anything towards furthering

the object of my journey; and, when I had taken some much-needed refreshment, I descended the steps leading from Ousegate to the King's Walk, with a view to a stroll along the banks of the river. On reaching St. George's Field, as the green between the castle and the river is called, I saw, however, a large wooden building, from the interior of which came the discordant sounds produced by the simultaneous tuning of numerous musical instruments. Walking to the front, I found that the unpretentious edifice was Newsome's circus, and a glance at my watch told me that the overture would commence in a few minutes. I paid my shilling, therefore, and entered a tastefully decorated and well-lighted amphitheatre, all parts of which were filled with spectators eagerly awaiting the commencement of the performance.

I was very agreeably entertained that evening, and, as ten years of journalistic drudgery had not weaned me from the love of studying the varieties of human life and character, I was not displeased when I discovered next morning that all the other guests at the hotel in Micklegate at which I was sojourning were members of the company performing at the circus. I was sitting *solus* in a room over the bar which was appropriated to guests, thinking of the affair which had brought me to York, when a gentlemanly young fellow, with a pleasant, intelligent countenance, joined me at table. I recognized him at once as the ringmaster, and, while we were exchanging the ordinary civilities of the occasion, three other young men entered, two of whom were known to me already as the Brothers Francisco, and one of whom now introduced the third as Mr. Alfred Burgess, the head vaulter and globe performer, whose feats I had witnessed in the arena the preceding evening, and whose name is not unfamiliar to the frequenters of the London and continental circuses.

During my stay in York I was much in the company of these people, and found agreeable companions in Mr. Vivian, the ring-master, who had been successively a lawyer's clerk, a photographer, and a comedian, and the Brothers Francisco, whose antecedents and professional career are related in the volume entitled "Circus Life and Circus Celebrities." The gymnasts, who were intelligent and fairly-educated young men, one having been a clerk, the other a compositor, before they resolved to seek fame and higher "screws" on the double trapeze and the flying rings, conducted me through the circus stables, telling me wonderful stories of their equine fellow-performers; accompanied me to the baths, where I saw Fred Francisco throw a forward somersault into deep water, over a handkerchief held by his cousin and a York acquaintance; and amused me one wet afternoon with juggling and balancing tricks, and the relation of stories of circus life and adventure, some of which may be found in the book just mentioned, and others in tales written several years afterwards for popular periodicals and provincial newspapers.

"You have read 'Hard Times,' Willie," I said, one day to the younger Francisco. "What do you think of it?"

"Rot!" was his more forcible than elegant reply. "Look here," he continued, dropping upon a chair so as to look over the back of it while he spoke, "Dickens puts the whole of Sleary's company—a tolerably strong one—into one little pub. in the outskirts of the town. Why, they must have been as thick as herrings in a barrel! There are more of us here than at any other house in the city. The governor and his family lodge at the confectioner's a few doors down the street, Jem Ridley and his wife at the "Alma," Joe and Sam Sault at the "Sand Hill," and others elsewhere. Then what rot that is about all the men's wives riding bare-backed horses and dancing on the tight-rope."

"Sleary's company must have been exceptionally clever," I observed.

"I should think so," returned the gymnast. "Why, for a dozen women who ride a pad-horse, and fly through balloons and over banners and garters, there isn't one who would attempt an act on a bareback. And as for all the wives riding, and so on, it is rather the exception than the rule. At our show Madame is the only married woman who ever goes into the ring, though both the Ridleys, old Zamezou, and the three clowns, and Sam Sault, and Mr. Vivian are all married. Mrs. Vivian is an actress, and is now fulfilling an engagement in London. Jem Ridley, Zamezou, Franks, Hogini, and the old property-master, who clowns, have their wives with them. Joe Ridley has left his wife in London, and Sam Sault's is in Manchester."

"Then Dickens was not well up in circus life," I observed.

"Can know very little about it," was the rejoinder. "As for the circus slang he has put into the mouth of Sleary's people, it is all new to me."

It was not only on this occasion that I gleaned some knowledge of the peculiarities of circus performers. I conversed with Joe Hogini, the musical clown, at the ring-doors; passed a Sunday evening at the "Alma" with the Ridleys; and strolled along the banks of the Ouse one morning, as far as Bishopthorpe, with Willie Francisco. A new chapter of social philosophy was thus opened to me, and, though circumstances prevented my acquisitions in that hitherto unexplored field from being immediately utilized for literary purposes, I was not the less assiduous on that account in storing them up in the cells of memory.

CHAPTER XIV.

Kean's revivals at the Princess's—Phelps at Drury Lane—The fire at the Adelphi—Realistic failures—Ramo Samee—The rope trick—Redmond and the butcher—Bunglers with the rope—Lizzie Anderson—Amateur practice.

DURING my long residence in London and the southern suburbs of that great city I was a frequent visitor to the theatres and music-halls, and there are few, except those which have been built during the last seven or eight years, which I have not visited. I witnessed several of Charles Kean's revivals at the Princess's—"The Tempest," with Miss Poole as *Ariel;* "A Midsummer Night's Dream," in which the lime-light was introduced with great effect in the fairy scene; "A Winter's Tale," and "Pizarro," with John Ryder as the Spanish conqueror. Never before had the temple scene in the last-named piece been put on the stage as it was by Kean. The Peruvian warriors, white-robed priests, and "virgins of the sun," with their long black hair floating over their shoulders, were grouped opposite a gilded representative of the luminary of day; and as the sunbeams fell upon it, lighting it into splendour, the hymn to the sun was sung.

It was not my fortune, however, to see either Kean or Phelps at their best. The former had lost his front teeth, which affected his voice detrimentally, and was far too old, even with all the aid stage resources could afford him, to give a successful impersonation of *Rolla*. Phelps did not essay youthful parts in his latter years, and was seen to better advantage. I saw him at Drury Lane as *Marino Faliero* in "The Doge of Venice," in which character he was very impressive, and afterwards in "The King o' Scots," in which he doubled the parts of the miser and the king. Both pieces were admirably put on the stage. I have a special recollection of the scene in Alsatia and old London Bridge and the river, seen from Bankside, with the moonlight falling on the face of Dalgarno's corpse—a mask—as it floated up with the tide.

I cannot pretend to give these recollections in strict chronological order. I must follow the example of the Old Bohemian. It was two or three years before I saw Phelps at the Lane that I gained a new experience in being in the pit of the Adelphi while the theatre was burning. The act-drop was down, and I was looking about me, when I became aware that the number of persons who had gone out was much larger than usual, and almost immediately afterwards observed a policeman moving quietly from one row of seats to another, and apparently making some communication to the occupants. Following him with my eyes, I observed that the persons to whom he spoke rose immediately and left the theatre.

"What's up?" I asked him, standing up in my place as he approached me.

"The theatre is on fire," he replied, in a subdued tone. "We want to get the people out without a rush."

Some women near us heard the word "fire," and immediately flew towards the doors. Others caught the alarm, and a general stampede was commencing when the policeman and I made an effort to calm them, and thus perhaps avert a terrible catastrophe.

"There's no danger," I said, ranging myself beside the constable, and stemming the rush as well as I could. "There is plenty of time for every one to get out if you don't go tumbling over one another."

Our calmness helped to calm those who had been scared, and in a few minutes more the theatre was cleared, myself and that cool-headed policeman being the last to leave the auditorium. There were no signs of fire in front even then. It had broken out in the top story of an adjoining house, and thence communicated to the roof of the theatre, the back part of which was destroyed.

About this time the rage for realism set in, and managers expended much money in producing local scenery, which, however, was very seldom a truthful delineation of the places they were supposed to represent. It was rarely that such a scenic triumph was witnessed as was attained at the Holborn Theatre, in the closing picture of "Behind the Scenes." If we take our stand below the second flight of steps in the Temple Gardens, with our back to the river, the fidelity of the scene is recognized immediately by those who saw the play. The steps upon which John Bolton falls, the houses on either side, the fountain, the greenery of the over-arching trees, were reproduced in the scene with rare and commendable fidelity.

There were some good bits of local scenery in the version which was produced at the Victoria, under the title of "Life in Lambeth," of the story which has been made famous by the "Streets of London." The great scenic bit of the piece—the Elephant and Castle by night, with cabs and omnibuses passing between Walworth and Newington Causeway, a train crossing the viaduct in the New Kent Road, and snow falling, and gradually whitening the road and the roofs— would have lost nothing by comparison with the corresponding scene of Charing Cross in the Princess's version, and deserved the applause with which it was greeted. But the scene of the conflagration was more artistic than truthful. It was supposed to represent Fox Alley, better known as Boneboilers' Alley, and so called in the play and on the bills. The house in which Ferret and the orphans lodged occupied about two-thirds of the width of the stage, and there was an open space by the side of it, which afforded a view of the illuminated clock of the Albert Tower. Fox Alley ran—for it has been swept away to make room for the Albert Embankment—at right angles to the river, and a spectator placed as the audience were would have had his back towards Westminster. The clock-tower could not have been seen through the opening towards the river, and a spectator looking in that direction would have had his back towards Fox Alley. The object of the deviation from topographical accuracy was obviously to bring in the clock-tower; and it must be admitted that a more picturesque scene was produced by this device than would otherwise have been possible.

The same excuse could be pleaded for the concluding scene of "Land Rats and Water Rats," which represented the Thames at Westminster Bridge, with the Houses of Parliament and the works then in progress for the Victoria Embankment. These works were elaborately built up in the foreground, and the bridge was seen crossing the river on the left, with the Houses of Parliament seen through the arches. The lighted windows of that long pile of buildings, the moon breaking at intervals through a stormy sky, and the lights and shadows on the river made a most effective picture. But to present it the artist had taken the liberty of transferring the embankment works from the northern side to the Surrey shore; for only from the latter could such a scene be witnessed. The artist had not the excuse which might have been pleaded for the painter of Boneboilers' Alley; for the barges and timber on the Surrey side would have made as good a foreground as the embankment works.

It must not be supposed that these deviations of the realistic from the real are confined to transpontine theatres. In "Lost at Sea," at the Adelphi, there was a scene representing the viaduct and pier at Charing Cross, with a bridge resembling that of Waterloo in the distance. The sketch for this scene had evidently been taken from the Surrey side of the river, and the hypothesis that this is the locality which the heroine has in her mind when she meditates suicide from the pier is supported by the fact that the scene was preceded by a pair of flats representing the land arch of Waterloo Bridge, where she inquires the way to the pier. The pier is on the Middlesex side of the river; and as the view given in the scene could not be obtained from that side, it was evident that the artist transferred the pier to the Surrey side to meet the difficulty of the heroine's position, she having no money, and selecting an imaginary pier at the Belvedere Road end of the viaduct for her "leap in the dark," because she is unable to meet the demand of the tax-collector at Waterloo Bridge.

Play-goers condoned these departures from topographical truth in their admiration of the artistic skill of the scene-painter; but feeling for the picturesque could not be pleaded for managers who presented interiors like anything rather than what they were supposed to represent, or furnished them in a manner which provoked as much derision as their elaborate "sets" elicited admiration. Why did they require us to believe that London garrets are, as a rule, unceiled, and display the bare rafters, like the interior of Kelmar's cottage in "The Miller and his Men"? Why was the feeling for the realistic so mercilessly outraged as it often was by a carpet which covered only the middle of the floor of what we were asked to accept as a Belgravian drawing-room? Why did Mr. Vining, while engaging a comic singer to give an air of realism to one of the scenes in "After Dark," give his supposed music-hall the appearance of a tap-room, with barely a dozen topers at the tables? Such contradictions of policy are beyond comprehension. But theatrical managers were, only fifteen years ago, of all the people in the world, the most difficult to understand. I can only say of their shortcomings in this respect what Townsend said of their refusal to read dramas emanating from authors beyond the circle of their personal acquaintances,—"It is their way." If it is not so now, it was then; and such things as I have mentioned were not so well done in some London theatres at that time as they are now at the little theatre in Barnsley.

I wonder how many play-goers there are now living who remember the looking-glass curtain at the Victoria Theatre, and the performances in front of it of Ramo Samee, the Indian juggler? There was a long interval between Ramo and the Brothers Davenport, and the clever juggler had become a dim memory for most people when the elder of the Brothers Nemo made it known that what was being called the American rope-trick was really an Indian trick, the secret of which had been communicated to him by Ramo Samee when the latter was in England. Nemo thought little of it, but when it was made, about twenty years ago, one of the wonders of the so-called spiritualistic manifestations of the Brothers Davonport, which thousands were flocking to see, he introduced it in the clever juggling performances which he and his brother were then giving at the South London Music-hall.

I never attended the *séances* of the Brothers Davenport, which I regarded as an experiment on the credulity of the public. In the height of their popularity, however, the leading feature of their performance was exhibited, without the pretence of supernatural aid, at Astley's Theatre, and afterwards at the London Pavilion Music-hall, by a young man named Redmond. I was a frequent visitor at that time to the latter place of amusement, where I on more than one occasion witnessed Redmond's performance, or as much of it as was done under the eyes of the spectators. His arms were securely bound with a cord, and he then sat down in a cabinet placed on the platform, and was bound to the seat. The door was then closed, and in less than three minutes an accordion was played and a tambourine banged in the cabinet. In a few seconds more the performer's hand, holding the tambourine, was shown from a square aperture in the side of the cabinet, and in another moment the door was opened, and Redmond stepped out, free!

A speciality in Redmond's performance which was not copied by any of his imitators was, that while he could release himself in three minutes when bound by any other person, he could tie himself up in such a manner that no one else could find either end of the rope. One evening, at the London Pavilion, some surprise and excitement were created at the commencement of his performance, by the appearance on the platform of several gentlemen, one of whom I recognized as M. Loibl, one of the proprietors of the place, the others being unknown to me. It soon transpired that a wager was to be decided between Redmond and a West End butcher, the latter having made a bet that he could untie Redmond in a certain time,—I forget how many minutes. Redmond withdrew into the cabinet, and in a few minutes emerged from it, securely bound, the cord encircling his body and limbs a great many times. The butcher commenced his task at once, and his hands moved with celerity in his endeavours to find one end of the rope. He turned up Redmond's trousers, felt in his boots, and looked up his coat-sleeves; but the end could not be found. The specified time expired, and the butcher lost his wager. Redmond then re-entered the cabinet, and in three minutes came out again, with the rope in his hands.

It was while Redmond's performances were one of the chief attractions of the London Pavilion that Nemo introduced the rope-trick at the South London. He was the best exhibitor of the trick, next to Redmond, that I ever saw; and the only English performer of the sensational feat known as the impalement, first exhibited at one of the London theatres—I think the Adelphi—by a Chinese juggler. Those who have not seen this feat may perhaps have seen in *Punch* the cartoon in which an appalled butler stands with his back against a door, while a lad with a carving-knife in his hand stands prepared to throw it, and cries, " Stand still, Bottles! I am going to do the impalement." As performed at the South London music-hall, one of the brothers stood against some boards in the form of a door, with his arms extended, while the other threw in rapid succession about a score of pointed knives, every one of which stuck in the boards, and some of them within an inch of the motionless figure.

With the exception of Redmond and Nemo, the performers of the rope-trick were, most of them, wretched bunglers. One whom I saw at the Canterbury Music-hall protested against the manner in which the gentlemen who volunteered from the audience to bind him, at his invitation, as "ungentlemanly," because he was unable to release himself. Lizzie Anderson, one of the daughters of the famous conjuror of that name, introduced the trick in her performance, and actually objected to being bound tightly! Being a young lady, the gentlemen who secured her dealt very tenderly with her, reducing the performance to a farce.

Without having seen the *modus operandi*, or received any hint that would have elucidated the mystery, I had an idea of my own as to the manner in which the trick was performed, and this I determined to test by experiment. I bought a dozen yards of new cord, a little thicker than an ordinary clothes-line; and having some business at a printing-office in Westminster, I called there on my way home, with a coil of rope on my arm. The printer asking me, jocularly, if I was going to hang myself, I acquainted him with the object of the purchase, and was asked to make an experiment on the spot. I allowed myself to be tied up, one end of the cord being secured about my right wrist, and then tied round the left, both arms being afterwards bound to my sides. As the operator began to pass the cord round my chest, I quietly inflated my lungs as much as possible, believing that precaution to be essential to the successful performance of the feat. The cord having been tightly drawn round my body several times, was passed over my shoulders and brought down to my legs, which were securely bound together. Then I was shut up alone in the reading-closet, and immediately began my efforts to release myself. In studying the rationale of the business before buying the rope, I had not been unmindful of what I had somewhere read as to the manner in which the notorious burglar and prison-breaker, Jack Sheppard, was able to slip his hands out of the handcuffs. I had found that by depressing the knuckles of the index-finger and the little finger, and turning the thumb inward, the circumference of the hand became very little more than that of the wrist. I now turned this discovery to account, and in a few seconds had slipped my right hand out of the hempen bracelet. With my right hand at liberty, a very few seconds sufficed to free the left and my legs; and as the cord was already slack about my body, owing to the inflation of my lungs while it was being drawn round me, I was free within the three minutes that Redmond required for his liberation.

CHAPTER XV.

The London Pavilion—Willio, the contortionist—The dead alive—Olmar, the gymnast—Little Corelli—Boy or girl?—Transformation of Lulu—Parelli and Costello—Luke Majilton—Who's who?—Professional names—The Brothers Price—A slice of good fortune—Madame Senyah—Back-slang.

I HAVE mentioned the London Pavilion Music-hall in my last chapter as a place of amusement which I very frequently visited twenty years ago. Though one of the leading music-halls of the metropolis, ranking at that time after the Alhambra and the Oxford, there were no stalls, the whole of the floor seats being one charge; and this was one reason for the place which it held in my favour. The proprietors, MM. Loibl and Sonnhammer, are Germans, from Vienna, and all the waiters are, or were, of the same nationality, as uniformly as those at Gatti's are Italians. At the time of which I am now writing, every member of the orchestra, with one exception, were, if not all Germans, all foreigners. The conductor, M. Valckenaere, was a Belgian; the pianist and the flutist were Frenchmen, the cornet a Hungarian, the clarionet a Scotchman, and the two violins and the bass, Germans.

Always reaching the hall in time for the overture,—Rossini's, for "William Tell" was finely given, and more often than any other—I always sat close to the orchestra, and through that proximity and my frequent visits I became acquainted with the Hungarian cornet-player, whose name was Besznak. He had served in the Austrian army, and afterwards came to London in the Hungarian Band. After playing at concerts for some time, he entered the band of the Grenadier Guards. When that regiment was on duty at Windsor, he had to provide a substitute, in order to fulfil his engagement at the London Pavilion.

"You know Willio, the bender?" he said to me one evening. Receiving an affirmative reply, he continued, "Well, he is dead! Went into the country to perform at a gala, caught cold, and died."

I was not surprised to hear, a short time afterwards, this announcement was premature,—very premature indeed; for Willio, a fine young fellow, and of remarkable agility, recovered, and for anything that I know to the contrary may be living still. That the discovery that he was not dead did not surprise me was owing to the many instances in which I had known reports of the death of persons following vocations esteemed by the public to be highly dangerous to be falsified by the facts. "Manchester Jack," the original lion-performer of Wombwell's menagerie, whom I remember seeing in the cage of the lion Nero when I was a boy, had, according to rumour, his head bitten off by the lion many years before he died in his bed, years after he had retired from the profession, and kept an inn at Taunton.

Here is another instance. One of the Brothers Ridgway fell from the trapeze while practising one morning at the Canterbury, and was reported killed. A month or two afterwards, a relative of mine, in the ballet and chorus at Covent Garden, was returning home one evening when he heard his name pronounced, and turning about found himself face to face with the Ridgway who had been reported dead! The gymnast was pale, but well enough to be reckoned worth a dozen dead ones.

"Gymnasts know how to fall," said one of the Brothers Francisco to me, when I met them in London nearly twenty years ago.

He fell from the trapeze one night while performing in Newsome's circus, having missed the catch with his feet in doing "the drop," a startling feat in which the performer appears about to fall headlong, but saves himself by quickly extending his legs, and catching his toes in the angles formed by the bar with the ropes by which it is suspended. He was picked up senseless, and carried into the dressing-room, where it was found that his neck was dislocated. A gymnast named Sault, who had seen such accidents before, with similar results, got hold of his head, reinstated it in its proper position, leaving Fred Francisco little the worse for his misadventure, and the next day none at all.

Olmar was not so fortunate. I was returning home from the London Pavilion one night, and turned into Barnard's—a tavern opposite Astley's, much frequented by theatrical and music-hall professionals—for a glass of my usual beverage, bitter beer. Amongst the men before the bar whom I recognized were the gymnasts, Parelli and Costello.

"Have you heard of Olmar's accident?" the former asked, after the customary salutations.

"No," I replied.

"He fell to-night at the Alhambra, and they say he has broken his thigh," said Parelli.

It was true; and he never performed afterwards. His performance was as unique as it was sensational. He had a ladder suspended horizontally, at a height of forty feet from the floor of the hall, and a triangular framework of spars, also horizontal, and with the point towards the spectators. The two sides meeting at this point were each formed of two parallel spars, to the undersides of which a series of loops were attached, large enough to admit the foot. The performer ascended to the ladder by the climbing-rope, hand over hand, and suspended himself, head downward, by fixing his feet in the ladder in the way in which the "drop" from the trapeze is performed. In this manner he moved beneath the ladder from one end to the other, and then along the sides of the triangle by inserting his toes in the loops.

A similar performance was given at the London Pavilion by a child named Corelli, apparently not more than eight years of age. In this case the height was considerably less; but that, it may be pointed out, is only a matter of importance in the event of an accident, and not of much then, perhaps, for I knew a man who slipped off a doorstep and broke his collar-bone, and another who fell off a house and was so little injured that he walked home with whole bones. Corelli's apparatus was smaller than Olmar's, and the spars formed a square. I witnessed this performance on several occasions, and never observed the slightest trepidation on the part of the child. No net was used, but the child's brother, Charles Corelli, was always on the platform during the performance, and never took his eyes off the performer from the moment he (or she) reached the apparatus until the feat was performed.

The implied doubt as to the sex of the child arose from the fact that he or she was always announced as "Little Corelli," and though I was acquainted with persons who knew Charles Corelli, I was never able to ascertain whether the little gymnast was a boy or a girl. Such a case is not unique. The performer who appeared at Drury Lane some years ago, when the theatre was opened one season as a circus, as Mademoiselle Ella, and was believed by the public to be a young woman, is now a husband and a father. Then there was the famous Lulu. I first saw that lady at the Alhambra in a gymnastic performance, when she appeared as "Young Farini," and at the conclusion sang a song entitled "Wait till I'm a man." By the public she was universally supposed to be a boy, but among the professionals engaged at that time at the Alhambra there was always a doubt as to her sex. The doubt had its origin in the circumstance that she was not only always accompanied by her mother, but used the ladies' dressing-room, which would not have been allowed in the case of a lad of thirteen or fourteen years of age, as Young Farini then appeared to be. It was only when the development of her figure rendered it impossible for her to appear longer as a boy that she began to attract and fascinate the town as Lulu.

I have mentioned, a page or two back, a gymnast named Parelli. This, however, was only his professional name. There was living at that time in Westminster a family named Berrington, consisting, besides the parents, of two sons, named respectively Luke and Francis, and a daughter named Mary. Luke was an artist, and produced, among other things, drawings of different portions of Westminster Abbey, which were much admired by those who had opportunities of seeing them, and were said to be the originals of the illustrations in Dean Stanley's book on the grand old pile. He was better known, however, as a clever and graceful performer of the hat-spinning feat, introduced by the French clowns, Arthur and Bertrand, and afterwards practised with great success by the acrobats Persivani and Duronde. The latter I saw on several occasions at the Alhambra, the London Pavilion, and elsewhere; but the only occasion on which I ever saw Majilton—which was Luke's professional name—was one morning, about twenty years ago, as I was walking towards Westminster Bridge from the Surrey side, accompanied by the younger Francisco. At the corner of York Road we met a rather tall young man, with a pale, intelligent-looking face, brilliant dark eyes, and dark curly hair.

"That is Luke Berrington," observed Francisco.

Frank practised gymnastics until able, in the parlance of the circus, to "do a tidy slang" on the flying rings, when he began performing at music-halls, in the name of Parelli, with a partner named Costello, who had been originally employed by a greengrocer in Westminster to deliver goods to customers, and afterwards an acrobat, "pitching" in quiet back streets and following up his performance with a "nob," otherwise passing the hat round. Frank and "Cos," as his partner was familiarly called by their associates, were together at Barnard's bar when the former told me of Olmar's accident at the Alhambra.

I lost sight of the gymnasts for a time, and was told they were in Paris, engaged at the Hippodrome. When I next heard of them, they were away on a provincial tour, with Frank's brother and sister, giving an entertainment largely made up of hat-spinning, tumbling, knockabout business, and dancing *à la Vokes*.

From that time I heard nothing about the Majiltons until a few years ago, when I saw in a Leeds journal a notice of Charles Majilton's theatrical company. The Berringtons at once recurred to my mind, but Charles was a name I had never heard as that of a member of the family.

"Who is Charles Majilton?" I asked one of my nephews, who, having concluded a professional tour with Madame Soldene's opera company at Huddersfield, had, on his way to London, broken his journey at Barnsley to see me.

"Don't you know?" was the reply. "You know Frank Berrington? Well, it is him."

My nephew was slightly mistaken. Frank, I have since been informed, is now in America, and it is his brother who, under the professional name of Charles Majilton, plays the part of *Hyacinthe*, the sprightly *gendarme*, in "The Gay City."

"Professional names"—*noms de théâtre*—are often

puzzling, and it is not easy to discover the motives which prompt a man to change his name from Powell to Power, or from Berrington to Majilton. The men who have ranked A 1 in the annals of the theatre and the circus—the Keans and the Kembles, the Ducrows and the Cookes—did not change their names, for it was only while Edmund Kean was a lad, performing in Richardson's portable theatre with his supposed parents, that he was known as Master Carey. But the present generation of actors and other entertainers have different ideas on the subject. That ladies of this class should, when they marry, prefer to retain before the public the name by which they have become famous is intelligible; but that a man, on adopting the stage or the arena as a profession, should change his name, is not so. Why, for instance, should the late George Belmore have preferred that name to his real one of Gaston? Why, again, should a foreign name be preferred to an English one? Shakespeare says "a rose by any other name would smell as sweet." Why, then, should Jemmy Lee have called himself Sextillian? Why should a brace of young Englishmen adopt the *nom d'arena* of the Brothers Francisco? There is really, in most cases, no accounting for these caprices.

There is in some cases. There was Joe Welsh, who twenty years ago was an attendant at the Alhambra gymnasium, where he was known to the professional trainers, the Ricardos, and their pupils as Alhambra Joe. He practised the flying trapeze so successfully that a young fellow named John Price arranged a partnership with him for double flights, and they made a public appearance at a London music-hall as the

Brothers Price. Shortly afterwards Price acquired, by heritage or bequest, a large fortune—20,000*l*. I have heard—and thereupon gave up his somersaults in mid-air from one trapeze to another. Welsh then took his late partner's name, and, as the single flying trapeze had been familiarized to the public by the feats of Leotard, Julien, Verrecke, and Bonnaire, he invented a novelty—the long flight, in which he mounted a perch in front of the gallery, holding a pair of stirrups suspended by cords from the centre of the ceiling, and swung off, loosing his hold of the stirrups on reaching the other end of the hall, and catching a fixed trapeze by the legs.

Some professional changes of name are very curious. After Jean Price, otherwise Welsh,—why Jean, I know not—the long flight was done at several London music-halls, and afterwards in a travelling circus in America, by a married couple named Haynes. To make it a double performance, the feat was varied from the flight performed by its originator, and, instead of catching the trapeze with the legs, being caught by the hands by her husband, who hung from the trapeze by his legs. The pair adopted the name of Senyah,—their real name spelt backward, as the London costermongers make their peculiar slang, in which, for an instance, the phrase "fat of the land" is translated "taf of the nal."

CHAPTER XVI.

The return of sunshine—Writing for a periodical—What is a "penny dreadful"?—Writers for the penny periodicals—Lady novelists—"Bob Lumley's Secret"—Another attempt at dramatic writing—Shepherd, of the Surrey—Managerial courtesies—Townsend, the dramatist—Anecdote of Yates.

THAT portion of my life which I have described in a former chapter as a Dead Sea voyage came to an end about the period to which these reminiscences have now been brought down, and once more the best influences that sweeten life made for me such happiness as I had not known for years, brightening even the dingy walls and uncarpeted floor of a second story in a back street of Lambeth.

Material sunshine followed that which had been revivified in my heart. A spinster aunt departed this life, in which her final trouble was concerning the possibility of meeting in the next the murderer, Franz Muller, having bequeathed to me one-fourth of the residue of her personal estate. She was the old lady mentioned in an early chapter of these reminiscences as presiding over the consumption of a bottle of hollands smuggled by a long-deceased relative. This bit of good fortune enabled me to remove from the slums of Lambeth to a cottage in the vicinity of Battersea, to furnish it with a degree of comfort and refinement to which I had of late years been unaccustomed, and to add somewhat to my income by an investment in Turkish bonds, afterwards disposed of at an advance of 5⅜ per cent.

My connection with the *Shrewsbury Chronicle* ceasing temporarily in the early part of 1869, I had to cast about for other occupation for the time which, for several years previously, had been devoted to writing leaders and leaderettes for that journal. Newspaper employment not being immediately available, I wrote half a dozen chapters of a sensational story of London life, and took them to the proprietor of one of the most largely circulated of the illustrated popular periodicals. I am unable to say whether this publication is one of those which we sometimes hear spoken of as "penny dreadfuls," because I have never heard that term defined, or any publication assigned by title to that category. I once asked a Sussex clergyman for titles of the publications he had referred to in a letter to Dr. Macaulay, the editor of the *Leisure Hour*, as "pernicious," and was informed by him that he intended his remarks to apply to penny novelettes. But why should a story be pronounced "pernicious" because it is published at a penny? I will venture no farther than to say that the periodical in question was a penny publication, with an immense circulation, aiming at instruction as well as amusement, and harmonizing with the shilling magazines, as well as with the older half-crown miscellanies which they have superseded, in giving a very little of the former element with a good deal of the latter.

Apropos of "penny dreadfuls," I cannot refrain

from relating a conversation which I had at this time with a City gentleman who shared his office with the stockbroker who transacted my own small financial operations.

"Do you write for *Chambers's Journal?*" he asked. Receiving a negative reply, he observed, "That is a very poor story now running in it."

The story referred to, I may observe, was one of Mr. James Payn's.

"I have not read it," I returned. "But the journal has never been very brilliant in the department of fiction. There are better stories in the *London Journal.*"

"That is a 'penny dreadful!'" he exclaimed, elevating his eyebrows.

"I don't know what constitutes a 'penny dreadful,'" I rejoined. "It is a kind of literary ware we often hear of when an errand-boy has robbed his employer, but as the titles of the publications supposed to be included under that head are never given, I don't know to which the character is supposed to apply."

"But are there not some horrid stories in those publications?" he asked, in a manner which showed that he knew them only by repute.

"There are horrid stories in Shakespeare, and Shelley, and all the great writers," I replied. "If you mean stories of a demoralizing tendency, I must say that, in my opinion, the stories in the penny periodicals are far more moral than one-half of the novels on Mudie's shelves, especially those written by ladies."

He looked surprised, and the entrance of the gentleman for whom I was waiting put an end to the conversation.

Among the contributors of fiction to the penny periodicals at this time were Harrison Ainsworth, Watts Phillips, Edmund Yates, and Mayne Reid. It is a curious circumstance, for which I am unable to account, that feminine fictionists are, as a rule, greater offenders than male writers in the matter of plots which derive their interest from infractions of the seventh commandment of the Decalogue. This applies equally to the authoresses of three-volumed novels and to lady contributors to the popular periodicals which are read almost exclusively by the fair sex.

"Do you object to seduction?" was the startling question very gravely put by one of the latter class to the proprietor and editor of the publication for which her services had been retained.

"That," he replied, "depends upon the manner in which the incident is treated. It should not be made too prominent, nor be related with too much detail, or too great warmth of colouring."

"Would you object to two seductions in the course of the story?" the lady asked.

"Pray do with one if you can," replied the editor. "It is to be hoped such incidents are not so common in real life as two in the same story might lead its readers to suppose."

I have before me a month's numbers of a periodical read exclusively by ladies, and which is edited by a lady. I cannot positively assert that all the serial tales are written by ladies, but I believe so from internal evidence. There are five stories in different stages of progress in the four numbers, and in every one of them a laxity of moral principle is developed in the principal female characters which, if shown in stories written by my own sex, would cause the writers to be stigmatized by the reviewers as men whose knowledge of the feminine portion of humanity had been gathered among its worst examples. The heroine is, as a rule, remarkable for filial obedience, which is exemplified by jilting at the parental command the man whom she professes to love, and marrying, or engaging to marry, one whom she despises or hates. In some cases, the heroine, having married to please her parents, chooses to consider herself a victim, and consoles herself with a lover who pleases herself; but, as a rule, she stops short of the marriage bond, though the engagement to the scoundrel or fool favoured by the parents is only broken when the parties stand before what novelists, in common with newspaper reporters, call the "altar." Then the discarded lover, after a year's wandering on the Continent, renews his acquaintance with the young lady who was so ready to prostitute herself, and they are married, and "live happily ever afterwards."

Who are the young ladies who read stories of this character? Apparently, not work-girls and domestic servants, as some persons seem to suppose; for a very large proportion of the answers given in the correspondence columns relate to questions of etiquette and precedence, presentations at Court, wedding breakfasts, and like matters of interest for young women in the higher grades of the middle class. The consideration how far such stories reflect the moral standard of their authoresses and readers is a very serious one, and I commend it to the attention of moralists and social reformers of both sexes.

Returning to the masculine purveyors of imaginative reading to the millions, I remember among them Townsend, the veteran dramatist, who had written in his time many dramas for the minor theatres, some of which, as the "Orange Girl" and the "Sea of Ice," had long runs, and had been revived with success at several subsequent periods; Ross, the editor of *Judy*, and author of the transpontine drama, "Clam;" Hildyard, who wrote some tolerable stories at that time for the *Boys of England;* Stagg, the editor of that publication, and formerly connected with theatricals in Birmingham; Stevens, the original editor, I believe, and afterwards a contributor to the *Gentleman's Journal;* Suter, the editor of the *Penny Miscellany;* the St. Johns, Percy and Vane, the latter editor of the *Young Men of Great Britain;* and Greenwood, "the Amateur Casual," so called from the celebrity he had achieved a few years previously by undergoing the ordeal of a night in the casual ward of Lambeth workhouse in order to qualify himself to relate his experiences in the columns of the *Pall Mall Gazette*. The narrative created a great sensation, and not only gave a considerable impetus to the *Gazette*, then in its infancy, but also had a large sale when reprinted in a separate form. The writer being then unknown, it was rumoured that he was a young nobleman who had subjected himself to the ordeal of the casual's bath and a night's association with some of the most degraded vagabonds in existence in order to win a wager. Writers for the *Pall Mall* were munificently remunerated at the time, and "the Amateur Casual" was well paid for the disagreeable experiences of that night. He afterwards went to Ireland for the same journal, to observe the life and manners of the "unfortunates" who haunted the camp on the Curragh, of which he produced as graphic a narrative as that which related the incidents of " A Night in a Casual Ward."

Percy St. John I had known fifteen years previously, when we were both on the staff of Cassell's publications. Stagg I met very frequently; and with Townsend I became acquainted somewhat later, when the success, at the Britannia, of a dramatic version of "Bob Lumley's Secret," my first story in the *Boys of England*, encouraged me to dramatize a story I had written in 1852 for the *National Instructor*.

I made a fair copy of my play when I had written and revised it, tied it up in a neat roll, and called with it at the residence of Mr. Shepherd, then the senior partner with Mr. Creswick in the management of the Surrey. Not finding him at home, I left the manuscript at his house, with a note, referring him to my published works in the department of fiction. A fortnight elapsing without any communication reaching me from Mr. Shepherd, I called his attention to the matter by letter, thinking that he might have laid the manuscript aside, and forgotten it. But though I wrote again and again, and called several times at his house, no reply did I ever succeed in eliciting from him. As a last resource I wrote to Mr. Creswick, who certainly favoured me with an immediate reply, but only to refer me to the notification at the stage-door of the theatre, that the management would not be responsible for manuscripts left *there*. Subsequently, however, I received a communication from Mr. Dalton, the stage-manager, informing me that the manuscript would be returned to me on application at Mr. Shepherd's residence.

Having succeeded in recovering my manuscript, I was unwilling to risk its loss by another exhibition of misplaced confidence. I offered it by letter, therefore, to some half-dozen managers, only one of whom accorded me the bare courtesy of an answer. This rare exception to what was *then* the managerial rule was afforded by Mr. Hollingshead, who had not had the management of a theatre long enough to have forgotten the amenities of professional life, and whose unique courtesy deserves to be recorded, even though his inability to read my drama was conveyed to me in the concise form of three words on a memorandum form: "Full at present."

It occurred to me that I might succeed in getting the play read by getting Townsend to revise it and associate his well-known name with my own. So one day I walked up to Kentish Town, and broached the idea to him, at the same time relating my recent experiences of managerial courtesies.

"It is their way," he observed. "They will accept a play from Mr. Boucicault or Mr. Byron, without reading it, and risk a failure that may oblige them to close the house in the midst of the season, rather than read a play offered them by an author who has produced nothing that has been acted."

"But an author cannot get a play acted if managers will not read it," said I.

"Just so," he rejoined, "and it is because managers have not realized the consequences of their short-sightedness that they are reduced now to dependence upon three or four authors, against whom an unknown writer, whatever his talent may be, has no chance unless he is in a position to make the acquaintance of half a dozen managers and the leading actors, and to treat them to champagne suppers."

"Has this always been the case?" I inquired.

"Always, I fancy," replied the veteran dramatist. "It has been so as long as I have known anything about the stage. Managers are great sticklers for the traditions of the profession, and this seems to be one of them. I will give you an instance. Many years ago, when Yates had the Adelphi, I left a manuscript there, which, just as you found it, I could get no answer about, nor its return. After repeated inquiries, I one day planted myself at the stage-door, and said I should remain there until I obtained an answer. So, after waiting an hour or more, the manuscript was brought to me by a boy, with the question, Mr. Yates says, is that your rubbish?"

"Worse than I was served," I remarked.

"Well, that play," he continued, "was afterwards produced, with great success, at the Pavilion; and, in the midst of the applause which testified the gratification of the audience, a literary friend observed to me, 'You should have let Yates have this; it would have been just the thing to go at the Adelphi.' Then I told him how Yates had treated me. 'Just like Yates!' said he, with a shrug; and it's just like all of them."

"They will find out their mistake before long," I ventured to predict. "Such treatment of authors may have been safe for managers when theatres were fewer, and stock-pieces were played so much more frequently; but now there are more theatres, a greater demand for new dramas, and actually fewer authors whose productions the managers will look at. Already they are obliged to pay large sums for 'new and original' dramas adapted from the French and German; what will they do when Robertson, and Boucicault, and Byron are gone?"

Townsend read the manuscript, and thought it would not do, owing to the scene being laid in Russia, which would render Russian costumes necessary.

"The plays that go now," he observed, "are Robertson's comedies, which have taught us the fine-drawn distinction between the new and the original, and Byron's, which go by force of sparkling dialogue, such as one never hears in real life; and these require only ordinary evening dress."

There has been a change since that time, or we should not have had "Mardo," "Fedora," and "The Danicheffs." Nor is this the only change that has come over the spirit of the managerial dream during the last twelve or fifteen years. Managers were beginning even then to see the insufficiency and short-sightedness of "their way." The weakness of their defences was exposed when the *Daily Telegraph*, taking up the cudgels for them, met the complaints of the unacted dramatists with the argument that an unknown author might ask a friend to ask somebody else to ask a manager to read his play, and quoted the rapidly-attained success of Mr. Albery as a proof that the prize is well worth the winning, and the interest even in excess of the capital of labour and anxiety invested. This involves the assumption that only the industry and perseverance with which the *Telegraph* credited Mr. Albery are necessary to enable any dramatist who can write as good a play as the "Two Roses" to achieve the same degree of success. But how could it have been with Mr. Albery if he had not been so fortunately situated?

There was another contributor to the *Boys of England* whose name I never heard, and am not sure that it was even known at the office. Before I had ever seen him, or heard anything concerning him, I was one day asked for my opinion of a story which had been commenced two or three weeks previously, without the author's name.

"There are some good characters in it, and some of the incidents are told with great force," I replied. "But the plot is too intricate for me to follow it. I cannot understand."

"I am not surprised at that," rejoined my interlocutor. "The author does not understand it himself. He is mad."

The next time I visited the office, I found in the ante-room to the proprietor's *sanctum*, besides Townsend and Hildyard, a tall, gaunt individual, who sat apart from the others and in silence, enveloped in the stained and worn cloak of a trooper of the Life Guards. His throat was destitute of collar or necktie, and, when a movement disarranged the ample folds of his capote, I caught a glimpse of a bare and hirsute chest, rendered visible by the absence of a vest and the fact that his not over-clean shirt was minus all the buttons. I never saw him again, and never could learn anything more concerning him. No one knew who or what he was, or where he lived. That was the mad author.

CHAPTER XVII.

The London letters of the *Albion*—Blunders of Mr. Grant—Mr. Kelly—Death of Charles B. Bean—Controversy with Sir Howard Douglas—Article in the *United Service Magazine*—A mysterious individual—Another dishonest publisher—Contributions to *Et Cetera*—Arthur Raggett Cole.

THE London correspondence of the *Albion* was written at the period to which these reminiscences have been brought down by a gentleman named Kelly, the contributions of my old and esteemed friend, Mr. E. B. Neill, which had for so many years reproduced so pleasantly for the Liverpoolians the gossip of the lobby and the clubs, having ceased some time previously. Mr. James Grant, in his work on the newspaper press, makes the strange mistake of calling the latter gentleman Mr. B. O'Neil, and adds the further blunder, writing in 1872, that "about ten or twelve years ago he received an appointment connected with a foreign government, which led him to cease his connection with the *Albion*, to the great regret alike of the proprietor of that journal and its readers." The fact is, that the appointment of the gentleman in question to the consul-generalship of the republic of Uruguay was almost as ancient as his connection with the *Albion*.

Towards the close of 1870, Mr. Kelly threw up his

post as London correspondent at the briefest notice in order to join the headquarters of the Saxon army as special correspondent of the *Times*. Owing to the suddenness of this change, the *Albion* was for several weeks without a London letter, two or three writers being tried in the meantime, but failing to exhibit the qualities to which its readers had been so long accustomed to in the gossipy letters of Mr. Neill. Charles Birch Bean dying at the commencement of the following year, and the direction of the journal passing into the hands of his brother, Mr. Thomas Bean, an approach was made towards an arrangement between that gentleman and myself; but I only added another to the "failures," and the negotiations came to nothing.

I continued, however, to write most of the *Albion* leaders, Charles B. Bean having written to me, no very long time before his death, "I have always had more confidence in articles written by you than in any others." Social questions had to be alternated at this time with the collapse of imperialism in France and the crowning of the edifice of German unity. In the Franco-German war, my sympathies had been entirely with the Germans, not through any national or individual partialities, which coloured the views of so many at that time, but for the several reasons that the French were the aggressors, that they aimed at the appropriation of German territory, and that their defeat would involve the dawn of freedom for themselves as well as the consolidation of the liberty and unity of Germany.

I had another motive for watching the movements

of both armies at the beginning of the war with deep interest. At the time when Lord Palmerston, while throwing cold water on the volunteer movement, asked for a vote of ten millions for the construction of coast defences, I had opposed him stoutly in the *Albion*, contending that coast and frontier defences had stopped invaders only when they were foolish enough to knock their heads against them. In 1866 I had seen the Prussian generals in Bohemia, deliberately ignoring the formidable fortresses relied upon by the Austrians for stopping an invader's progress, and the Italians crossing the Po, and thus turning the Quadrilateral, from which they had been hurled back with such heavy loss in the previous attempt to liberate Venetia.

Once more I saw, with curious pride in my ideas of military tactics, the invaders disregarding the French fortresses, and pushing on for the capital. The views set forth by me in the *Albion* began to force themselves upon the consideration of military men, and to find expression in the organs of military opinion. An officer wrote in the *United Service Magazine* for December, 1870, as follows: "A great deal has been already said respecting the advantage and disadvantage of fortresses in the event of invasion. So far as France is an example, they have been of little use in arresting the march of a victorious army. Toul was simply brought into notice because it commanded the direct route from Germany to Paris. All the others were easily turned or invested, and when the worst came to the worst, all that the invaders had to do was to drive their beaten enemy like a flock of sheep into a penfold and there hold them as in a trap, punish them with a little well-timed hunger, and, if necessary, some shot and shell, and then quietly march them off as prisoners of war."

This was not the only military question upon which I had written articles for the *Albion*, for I had had, some years previously, a controversy in the columns of that journal with Admiral Sir Howard Douglas on the value of rockets in war. I have forgotten how it originated, but remember that I drew some of my data from the Peninsular War, and later instances from hostilities in the Platine region, and that I was thought not to have had the worst of the argument. The confirmation of my views upon the inutility of frontier defences which was afforded by the results of the Franco-German War, coming as they did so soon after the rapid march of the Prussians through Bohemia and Cialdini's passage of the Po, prompted me to a more ambitious effort, and I sent to the *United Service Magazine* a lengthy article on the subject. It was inserted, and I was paid for writing it; though military men would probably have pooh-poohed it if they had been shown the article in manuscript, and been told that the author had never smelt gunpowder or wore epaulettes. How I came by the ideas which Count von Moltke was the first to apply to the operations of war I scarcely know. They were, I think, the results of careful reading of modern history, growing slowly in my mind until I was led to make an application of the fruits of my studies to the hypothetical case of an invasion of England when Lord Palmerston asked Parliament to vote ten millions for the defence of places which it seemed to me that an invader would carefully avoid.

The interest which I felt in the matter did not arise from any proclivity for the military profession. I can imagine circumstances in which I might have been disposed to play the part of a Garibaldi or a Mieroslawski, but I have never been placed in them, and, if I had been, should have regarded the change from a general's charger to an editor's stool as promotion. The sword is too often a dire necessity, but it must, now and in the future, always be subordinate to the pen in all countries having any valid claim to be regarded as civilized.

To Count von Moltke belongs the glory of having introduced a system of tactics which, while it tends, by the celerity with which it hurls ruin upon the defeated, to make ambitious rulers count the cost of war before provoking it, mitigates the miseries and horrors of international strife by reducing the duration of hostilities to a few weeks. There are no signs yet of the Millennium, and it is something, in the meantime, to have the means of compressing into so brief a space the operations which were formerly spread over as many years.

One day, in the summer of 1871, when I had called upon Mr. Brett, for whose various publications I had written about a dozen serial stories since the spring of 1869, that gentleman handed to me the last packet of manuscript I had submitted to him, with an intimation that he had fiction on hand, in manuscript, to the value of 600*l*., and could not accept another from any contributor for some months.

"You are doing too much," he added. "You had better take a holiday for two or three months."

Circumstances not permitting me to allow myself the amount of recreation which he so considerately suggested, I considered myself released from the obligation to write for no other publications than those belonging to him so long as I remained upon his staff. I took the manuscript at once, therefore, to the office of another publisher; and, as a precaution against the not improbable contingency of having to wait a month or six weeks before I received the editorial decision upon it, I immediately commenced another story, having no doubt that, having renewed my repute as a writer of fiction, I should be able to dispose of it to the proprietor of one or another of the numerous periodicals then in existence.

When I had completed my story, I left the manuscript at an office in the Strand, with a note for the editor, who, as usual, was "invisible," except by appointment. So long a time elapsed without any communication from the editor, or the return of the manuscript, though I had repeatedly written and called at the office, that I at length insisted upon seeing either the editor or the proprietor. Neither, I was assured, was on the premises.

"Oblige me, then, with the proprietor's name and address," said I, for the imprint gave only the name of the publisher, who was merely an *employé* of the proprietor.

"I am forbidden to communicate his name or address to any one," was the reply.

"The editor's name and address, then," said I.

"That would be the same thing," returned the publisher. "It is edited at the residence of the proprietor."

"Then," said I, with an air of stern decision, "I shall apply to the Court of Queen's Bench for a rule calling upon you to declare the name and address of the proprietor."

I had not the slightest idea as to the existence of such a remedy; but the menace had the desired effect. The man communicated to me the name of his employer, though, as if doubtful of the propriety of what he had done, and desirous of a compromise with his duty, he refused to add the address. The name sufficed, however, for it was well known in the news-offices about the Strand, though no one seemed to know where the individual who answered to it had his residence. The first person of whom I made inquiries informed me that the gentleman I wished to see had a villa a few miles from town, naming the locality; but he did not know his address, which, however, he thought might be procured, either from a bookseller in the locality indicated, whom he named, or at the office of a weekly newspaper, which was believed to be the property of this seclusion-loving gentleman.

At the newspaper-office I could learn nothing. The gentleman inquired for was not on the premises, and the clerk whom I saw declined to furnish me with his address. I had, therefore, to follow back upon the clue already in my possession. From my then residence a walk of less than an hour took me into the locality indicated as the place of abode of the gentleman who, for some reason or other, was so extremely desirous of hiding himself. Without going so far as the shop of the bookseller to whom I had been referred for further information, I had the villa pointed out to me by the first person of whom I inquired its whereabouts, and in a few minutes I was ringing the bell at the front-door. The servant who responded to the summons showed me into a room which appeared to be the editor's study, and in which I was presently joined by a lady, who, informing me that Mr. —— was too ill to see me, first inquired my business, and then referred me to the publisher.

"I have been to the office half a dozen times," I returned. "The publisher informs me that the manuscript is here, and that all the letters I have written on the subject have been sent here."

"Did he tell you where to find Mr. ——?" inquired the lady.

"No," I replied. "He declined to give me any information."

"Then how did you find out?" the lady asked, with an air of mingled curiosity and anxiety.

"I received a clue from a gentleman I am not going to name, and I followed it to this house," I replied.

"We don't undertake to return rejected manuscripts," said the lady, after a pause, during which a cloud passed over her countenance. "There is a notice to that effect over the answers to correspondents."

"But," said I, "the proprietor cannot rid himself

of a liability which exists in law by giving notice that he intends to repudiate it. If he desires to receive no manuscripts from authors outside his staff, he has only to instruct his publisher not to receive any; but the publisher informs me that his instructions are to forward all manuscripts to this house. That being so, the case is the same as with goods left with a tradesman on sale or return; and the manuscript, like the goods, must be returned or paid for."

The lady seemed to see that she must yield. She hesitated for a few moments, and then informed me that, if I would call at the office any day after the morrow, the manuscript should be there.

Upon that understanding I withdrew; but the explorations of the night were not at an end, for on leaving the house I found that a thick fog was gathering, and that I could not see the light of one lamp at its distance from the next. The obscurity that prevailed presented no difficulty, however, to my progress until I reached a large common, across which lay the nearest way to my home. In the confidence proceeding from familiarity with its features, I plunged into the darkness, knowing that a diagonal line from the point at which I had left the road would strike a road on the other side which I had to cross, taking me clear of all dangers. For there were dangers—"ponds to the right of me, ponds to the left of me." I must have diverged gradually from the line I thought I could keep, for I was brought up suddenly by a splash, as if of some small creature, a frog or a water-rat, dropping into water. I stood still for a few moments, straining my eyes into the grey vapour, and seeing nothing; and then I made a few cautious steps forward. Then I stopped again, for my feet were in mud, and it was probable that beyond the mud there was water. I drew back, wishing that I had a stick, and, turning off at a right angle to the line which led me to the pond, went cautiously forward again. Not knowing how far the pond extended in that direction, I now and again made a step or two to the left, and, finding mud or water, went on until I seemed to have turned that extremity of the pond. Then I went on again, hoping I was not far from the line I wished to travel on, and trusting that I should, at the worst, strike the road at some point.

After some time I became doubtful and perplexed. I could not see my watch, but a longer time seemed to have elapsed than should have enabled me to reach the road. I stood still and listened, but no sound reached my ears, the fog deadening the sound of wheels and horses' hoofs, if any were on the road. Presently I head a detonation which I knew to be a fog-signal on the railway which was parallel with the road I wished to reach. Guided by the sound, I went on again, and in a short time discerned the lamps along the road glimmering through the fog.

The promise of the lady of the villa was not kept, and I had to threaten legal proceedings for the recovery of the manuscript before it was returned to me. Then the editor's communication, declining it, was most unwarrantably endorsed on the last slip, which I had to re-write before sending the story to the office of the periodical in which it eventually appeared.

Ill-luck followed that manuscript to the end of its wanderings. As in the first instance, I had to write several times to the editor, and several months elapsed before I received any communication as to its fate. One day, as I was making inquiries about it at the office, a man whose appearance would have presented nothing remarkable in the midst of a group of workmen going to their daily labour came in, and began to ascend the stairs.

"There's the editor," said the man of whom I had been making inquiries, "you had better ask him about it."

I did so, springing up the stairs, and soon catching him.

"I am not the editor," he returned, "but I shall see him in a day or two, and I will remind him of the matter."

I knew not what to think of his repudiation of the functions assigned to him by my informant below; but I had no other course open to me than to receive his promise that I should be communicated with by post. A fortnight passed, however, and no letter came. The affair began to look fishy.

Once more I called at the office, and was shown into a small room, almost bare of furniture, and without a fire, though it was a cold day. When I had waited there about an hour, the not too respectable-looking individual whom I had seen before came in, regarding me with an expression which might have been natural to him, but which seemed to me to have been called up by the unwelcome object of my visit.

"Why, your story has been running these six or seven weeks," said he, in a surly tone. "A deal of interest you must take in the publication not to have seen it."

"I take no interest in it at all," I rejoined, in my iciest tone.

"Well, you had better see the governor," said he.

Being of the same opinion, I followed him into a well-furnished office, at a desk in which sat a stout, middle-aged man, sleek of exterior, and oily of manner, who listened with polite attention to what I had to say, and then informed me, in his blandest manner, that the firm did not pay for the first story they accepted from an author, but, if it proved acceptable to the readers of the publication, they then made an arrangement with him for another.

"But you seem," said I, "to have overlooked the important fact that you have used my story without acquainting me with that singular condition."

"Oh, it is our invariable rule!" he rejoined, as if he thought the rule ought to be as well known as an Act of Parliament. "We never deviate from it."

"You will have to do so in this case," said I. "I have no wish to take advantage of the situation in which you have placed yourselves by using an article without ascertaining what you would have to pay for it; but I shall expect to receive payment at the rate paid on other publications for which I have written."

"I think," returned Mr. ——, after a brief pause, "you can only claim to be paid at the rate and in the manner we are accustomed to pay. We never pay for a serial story until the whole of it has appeared, so that we can see how many columns it makes. When yours has run to the end we will have it cast up, and send you a cheque for the amount."

Against this strange and hitherto unheard-of system I protested, but in vain; and, as half of the story had already appeared, I at last consented to await the result of the casting up. The five or six weeks' delay did not, however, improve the situation. On my next visit to the office, the sleek individual with the oily tongue expressed regret that he had been too much occupied to cast up the matter, but assured me that he would do so at his earliest leisure, and immediately send me a cheque. Contenting myself with a reminder that the amount of that cheque could not be finally at his own discretion, I again waited.

After a further delay of two or three weeks, I received a letter requesting me to call at the office on a day and hour therein fixed, at which time, punctuality being one of the virtues I have specially cultivated, I presented myself, and was ushered into the little fireless room in which I had waited before, the "governor" being engaged, as I was told. I sat down, but was soon glad to tramp the bare floor to warm my feet. After more than an hour of this exercise, I grew rather savage, and sallied into the passage, where I met a boy, from whom I learned that the "governor" had gone out, and would not return for several hours.

Indignant at this treatment, and weary of the man's shuffling proceedings, I wrote to him rather sharply on reaching home, threatening legal proceedings if my claim, at the rate I had received on other publications, was not immediately paid. In reply, I was informed, without a word of apology, that the sleek individual was merely the printer of the publication, and that he had no funds in hand with which to meet my claim. Here I must record an act of generosity on the part of a solicitor which is unexampled in my experience of the legal profession. There was living at that time at Surbiton a gentleman of that profession, whose offices were in the neighbouring town of Kingston-on-Thames. I refrain from mentioning his name only because I might thereby direct to him the attention of a flock of clients who might expect to be treated as generously as I was. A letter from this gentleman procured the immediate remittance of the sum which I had claimed, and for this service the solicitor declined to accept a fee.

During the progress of this dispute I had removed from Battersea to the pleasant village of Long Ditton, about a mile from Kingston, and one of the most rural spots now to be found within a much greater distance from London. My literary undertakings at this time affording me more leisure than I could command while engaged solely upon newspaper work, I was now able to indulge my love of rambling as far as possible from towns and dusty roads, which for sixteen years I had been able to gratify only while taking my annual week's holiday, and also my proclivity for gardening. There was a miniature lawn and flower-garden before my cottage, and a larger plot in the rear, which sufficed to supply my table with all the vegetables and fruit that were required. Round the rear of the house there was a rustic arcade, covered with American creeper; and between the kitchen and the fence was a narrow space which I converted into a fernery, covering the black fence and the wall with ivy and American creeper, and screening the dust-bin from view by constructing a miniature rockery.

When the garden did not require my attention, and I felt that I should be the better in body and mind for exercise in the open air, I rambled through the fields and woods, and over the breezy commons, often as far as Croydon, or Epsom, or Leatherhead, and upon one occasion reaching Dorking. I always avoided the highroad as much as possible, and sought my goal by devious routes, by field and woodland paths, meandering green lanes, and tracks across commons, half hidden by furze and broom, and brambles and bracken.

About this time the problem of the sources of the Nile was attracting considerable attention in literary and scientific circles, and, having read the latest books on the subject and the controversial articles in reviews and newspapers, I studied old and new maps of Africa, and formed my own conclusions on the question. The map drawn by Juan de la Cosa, the pilot of Colombo, satisfied me that the great lakes were known in the fifteenth century, and the modern maps led me to the conclusion, since proved to be the correct one by the explorations of Stanley and Cameron, that the Lualaba was not, as Livingstone supposed, the Nile, but the Congo. I wrote an article embodying these conclusions, and sent it to the anonymous editor of a new magazine which had lately made its appearance, with the singular title of *Et Cetera*.

I expected a cheque to follow the appearance of this

article in the magazine, but instead I received a letter from the editor, accepting a short story I had sent him, and promising to pay for both contributions on the publication of the number containing the story. On his failure to fulfil this undertaking, I called at the publisher's office and asked for his name and address. Failing to learn them, and my application for payment receiving no attention, I had recourse to stratagem. Though the communications I had received from the editor had all been dated from the publishing office in London, they were posted at Micheldever, in Hampshire, and to that address I sent an application for payment by postcard. In reply to this I received a furious letter, signed " Arthur Raggett Cole," informing me that the postcard was a libel, and that he had placed the matter in the hands of his solicitor. Close upon this communication came a letter from his legal adviser, enclosing a cheque for the amount due to me, and requiring me to apologize to his client. I realized the cheque, but I did not apologize. I wrote instead an explanation of the matter, and, instead of notice of action, received an apology from the man of law.

CHAPTER XVIII.

Editorship of the *Gentleman's Journal*—A misunderstanding about a presentation—Experiences of writing for the magazines—The fortunes of a farce—Mr. J. S. Clarke and Mr. Joyce—A Durham journalist's experience—Cessation of my connection with the *Shrewsbury Chronicle*—Mr. B. H. Grindley and the *Albion*—Mr. William Hind—At a loose end again.

I HAD just returned one afternoon from a delightful stroll over the wastes and woods between Claygate and Chessington, when I found a cab at my gate and a gentleman at the door, in conversation with my wife.

"You have returned most opportunely," said the stranger, turning to me as I approached, and he learned that I was the person of whom he was in quest. "I should not have liked to have been obliged to return to London without having seen you, as I am only in town for a few days."

He proceeded to introduce himself as one of the proprietors of the periodical for which I had destined the story written before the one which I had had so much trouble about. When we were seated in the drawing-room he informed me that he had read the manuscript, and found it very interesting; but it could not be used for some time, and the object of his present visit was to offer me the editorship of the publication.

"It has not, I am sorry to say, been a success," he

added, "and it has been a question with my partner and myself whether it should be discontinued at once, or be entrusted, experimentally, to another hand. Mr. H— was for giving it up, but I am disposed to try the alternative; and my view has prevailed."

As the work would leave me more than sufficient time for the fulfilment of my newspaper engagements, only the question of remuneration remained to be considered; and, this being settled to my satisfaction, I accepted the offer at once, and it was arranged that I should commence my editorial duties with the commencement of the ensuing month.

As the greater part of the contents of this publication consisted of serial stories, my new duties were more varied than those of my former editorship, from which, in other respects, they differed very much. The heaviest were reading manuscripts and correspondence, and writing replies to questions upon an infinite variety of subjects for the correspondence page. Besides these duties I had to correspond with contributors, write articles on games and amusements, and hold conferences with draughtsmen and engravers. As much of the work could be done at home as well as at the gloomy office in one of the narrow lanes between Fleet Street and the river, I attended at the office only on the last day of each week, when I conferred with contributors, draughtsmen, engravers, and the printer, and made the necessary arrangements for the next number. Every Saturday I found upon my table several rolls of manuscript and a pile of letters, which I placed in my bag on leaving, and took home for quiet perusal in my study.

I had been some months installed in the editorial chair, *vice* George Frederick Pardon, when Mr. Viles—the gentleman who had visited me at Long Ditton—gave me one day a brief notice of a presentation to the editor from the contributors of enigmas, charades, and the like, for insertion in the *Journal;* and, at the same time, invited my attention to the testimonial, which had taken the form of a very handsome inkstand and a portrait-album, containing the photographs of the contributors. As I was personally known to only two or three of the ladies and gentlemen whose portraits adorned the album, I concluded that it was intended for my predecessor; but, some months afterwards, when the cessation of the publication had made me eligible for enlistment in the corps of "frozen-out gardeners," I received a letter from one of the donors, informing me that Pardon had not received it, and requesting information on the subject. As I had not received it, I communicated the substance of this letter to Mr. Viles, to whom I had referred the writer; but neither the donors nor myself received any reply.

While casting about for similar employment, I wrote several short stories and papers of the kind readers of fiction only irreverently term "padding;" but, contrary to what is said to have been the experience of many of my literary brethren, I found this department of work more unsatisfactory and less remunerative than any of which I had had any experience. Perhaps I have been exceptionally unfortunate; but I believe I am within the bounds of fact in stating that of every half-dozen manuscripts which I have sent to the editors of magazines only one has been accepted, while three have been returned, and two neither returned nor accepted. It is sickening work to devote two or three days to gathering materials for an article and weaving them together, and then to have the manuscript returned some months afterwards, when the freshness of the subject has been worn off, and it is as useless as an old almanack. Still more unsatisfactory, if possible, is it to find that the editor has lost your manuscript, and, as a matter of course in that case, either remembers nothing about it, or is positive that he returned it by post as soon as he had read it.

What becomes of manuscripts which thus drop out of the knowledge of their authors? Is there any international agency for their production in magazines issued on the other side of the Atlantic? Or are they "annexed" and re-named, as mutineers and pirates re-name and disguise with paint the vessels they have seized? I had a strong suspicion of such a trick when the publisher mentioned in a preceding chapter refused to return my manuscript, which could have been of use to him only for the lighting of fires unless he had resorted to some such dishonest device. A very candid editor once admitted to me that he sometimes kept usable manuscripts for several months, if their return was not applied for; and then, when a sufficient time had elapsed to render it probable that the author had forgotten them, or abandoned all hope of their return, sent them to the printer. I have heard, too, of an instance in which the manuscript of a drama was kept for years by a London manager, and produced after the author's death, under another title, with great success and corresponding gain to the treasury of the theatre. I give this story for what it may be worth, as a bit of theatrical gossip repeated to me by an actor, who asserted that he had heard it mentioned in the profession on more than one occasion.

True or not, it reminds me as I write of the loss which I experienced about this time. The remark of a critic that the story of "Dr. Doremer's Hobby," which appeared in *Et Cetera*, seemed to have been founded upon a dim recollection of an old farce suggested to me the idea of working up the characters and incidents into a farce, a mode of treatment to which they lent themselves very readily. As the action of the story, with the exception of a single incident, passes in the study of an enthusiastic, but rather eccentric, votary of science, and within a period of twelve hours, while the incidents are of a decidedly farcical character, the transformation was easily effected. After offering the manuscript to Mr. Hollingshead, and receiving from him a polite assurance that the number of manuscripts awaiting his perusal precluded the possibility of his looking at it, I sent it, with a note, to Mr. J. S. Clarke, who had then recently opened the Charing Cross Theatre.

After an interval of several weeks, during which I had written four letters to Mr. Clarke without receiving any reply, I was informed by Mr. Walter Joyce that he had no recollection of my farce, and that its title was not in his list, in which he entered every manuscript received before handing it to Mr. Clarke. As every manuscript sent to the theatre passed through his hands, he was sure that mine could not have been received. I reminded Mr. Joyce that the loss of postal matter is a very rare occurrence, and that the loss of both letter and manuscript would be a most remarkable coincidence; while, if the letter had been received, Mr. Clarke should have immediately informed me that the manuscript had not reached him. Further correspondence ensued, extending over three months, but I never recovered my manuscript, concerning which Mr. Clarke himself could only assure me, in the only letter I received from him, that he had never seen it, and expressed his regret at its loss.

Theatrical managers seem to be peculiarly liable to the loss of letters and manuscripts in transit through the post. Not very long after the loss of "Dr. Doremer's Hobby," a brother journalist in the city of Durham made the following statement:—"Some time ago, meeting with the manager of a comedy company, travelling on the northern circuit, I mentioned to him that I had just completed an original comedy-drama, and the result was that, by his desire, I posted a printed copy of it to him at the Sunderland Theatre. The copy was accompanied by a letter. Hearing nothing from him, after a time I went to Sunderland, and saw him (Mr. Y—) at the theatre. He said he had received neither the comedy nor the letter. I have never heard from him since. I afterwards posted a copy of the same comedy to a London manager (Mr. H—), also accompanied by a letter. Hearing nothing from him, I wrote to inquire about the matter, and the reply that I received was that he had no knowledge of either comedy or letter! He promised to look into the matter, but I have heard nothing from him. Now, in my profession—I am a newspaper editor—I post and receive several thousand letters per year, and I cannot call to mind any case in which both book parcels and letters have disappeared in transit through the post. Theatrical managers' correspondence should be as safe as other men's, but it does not appear to be so, at least not for one side."

My own experience agrees with that of my brother in misfortune, the Durham journalist. Of the thousands of letters and hundreds of manuscripts, proofs, books, &c., which I have posted, only my unlucky farce and another manuscript lost since have been lost in transit, or alleged to have never reached the persons to whom they were addressed. Surely theatrical managers must have very bad memories.

Misfortunes, it is said, never come singly. My connection with the *Shrewsbury Chronicle* ceased soon after the loss of the farce. The competition in the newspaper trade, which had become more and more keen since the abolition of the stamp duty, had obliged the proprietors of the old journals to increase their expenditure in a greater degree, in many instances, than the extended circulation augmented their profits. A heavy advance in the price of paper took place in the spring of 1872, and diminished the annual profits of the *Chronicle* by 250*l.*; and this addition to the cost of producing the paper, coming close upon the increased cost of composition, consequent upon the concession of shorter hours, obliged the proprietor to reduce his expenses in other directions. He would now have, he told me, to write the leaders and leaderettes himself. My contributions ceased, in consequence, a month after the rise in paper.

This was not all. Charles Bean had died at the beginning of 1872, and the paper had passed into the hands of Mr. B. H. Grindley, who had been curator of the Walker Art Gallery, located at St. George's Hall, Liverpool. Then a change took place in its politics and its fortunes, and from being the best weekly paper in the town it became the poorest of the dailies. The new proprietor being a Conservative and the other weekly journals having become dailies, or having a morning issue in connection with them, he determined to follow the example, and convert the *Albion* into a morning organ of Liverpoolian Conservatism. Mr. William Hind was selected to edit it, and he arranged with me for two articles weekly, warning me at the same time that, in the event of their not being used, they would be neither returned nor paid for. These terms were not satisfactory to me, but I determined to give them a trial, rather than reject them without experience of their working. Of course I expected to receive the paper regularly, as I had when it belonged to the Beans; but I never received it after the change of owners, and did not, in consequence, know whether my articles were used or not. On this point I was expected to confide implicitly in the statements of Mr. Hind; and so many articles were, according to those statements, either found inadmissible in a Conservative journal or squeezed out by pressure of news, that I found the pecuniary results less by thirty or forty per cent. than they had been when the paper was issued weekly. I declined, therefore, to contribute any more articles under that arrangement.

The *Albion* was not such a success under Mr Grindley's management as it had been while in the hands of the Beans. Politics of the order it now purveyed were so much better supplied by the *Courier*, that it went to the wall as a morning paper, and underwent another transformation. As an evening paper it was carried on with better success until the close of 1882, when it underwent another change of proprietorship, passing into the hands of a limited company, and being converted into a morning paper again, with Mr. Grindley as managing director and editor. Recently, however, that gentleman has resigned both appointments, and undertaken the editorship of the *Birmingham Gazette*.

In the first draught of the work now before the reader, written at intervals prior to 1875, I find the following passage, which I preserve only because it records what was the state of my mind with regard to journalism at this period:—" I have not written a line for any newspaper since. Probably I never shall write another. It is a grand thing to aid in forming the opinions of the people, or to direct the organ of a popular movement, and give an impulse to humanity that will be felt through many generations. But there are few journalists who are so happily placed as to be able to pursue the independent course which alone can make the position satisfactory to a conscientious and honourable man. Most of them have to regulate the views which they express by the Procrustean standard established by their employers, so as to further the aims of some small section of the community, so far as that course can be pursued without injuring the circulation. Mr. Grant's revelations of journalism show that this state of things is not peculiar to provincial editors and leader-writers. Some of the glimpses of journalistic woes which he has given to the world are sadder, indeed, than any troubles that have fallen to my own lot in connection with newspaper work; but my eighteen years' experience of journalism do not inspire me with any very ardent longing to continue them."

Towards the end of the summer of 1872 I found myself once more without a single journalistic or literary engagement of any kind, or income from any other source. Just after my Liverpool and Shrewsbury engagements came to an end, the proprietors of the *Gentleman's Journal* gave me a month's notice of their intention to discontinue the publication, which I had failed, as Pardon had done, to make a success. Thus I was "at a loose end" again.

CHAPTER XIX.

A batch of literary projects—"Half-hours with the Early Explorers "— The " pot-boiler " that became a great success—A friendly hint —Dr. Manning—On the staff of the Religious Tract Society— George Belmore and the Cookes—Charlie Keith, "the roving English clown "—"The Old Showmen and the Old London Fairs "—" Circus Life and Circus Celebrities "—A reviewer's error—Mistake in a railway-carriage.

To a steady worker like myself, having, moreover, always half a dozen literary projects ready to be selected for realization, a month is worth a great deal. I had collected a pile of materials for the present work, in the form of old letters and memoranda; and had on my study table some notes relating to the second Lord Lyttelton, the outlines of a projected work on certain historical puzzles and judicial mysteries, and two or three short narratives of maritime explorations in the sixteenth century, intended to have formed part of a series to be commenced in the next volume of the publication now so near its end. These manuscripts I looked over on my return home, after learning the decision reluctantly arrived at by my employers.

" Autobiography ? " I said to myself, as I passed my literary projects in review. " Too doubtful a subject, and would take too long to prepare for publication, even if I was sure of a publisher. And the time has not come for it, if there was no other reason. Lyttelton? Might be made an interesting book, I think; but the materials have yet to be gathered, and I don't even know whether they exist. That must wait. Historical puzzles and judicial mysteries? Would make a good volume for Nelson or Routledge, and I will hear what they have to say to the idea. Half-hours with the early voyagers? Three of the series done. Why not make it 'Half-hours with the Early Explorers'?"

My cogitations upon this question led to the adoption of the idea which it embodied. I had written for the last volume of the *Journal* a series of short narratives of travel previous to the middle of the seventeenth century, and I determined to revise and partially re-write the earlier of these, and add to them, in chronological order, the contemplated narratives of maritime explorations during the same period. So I passed a few days in the reading-room at the British Museum, diligently reading the folios of Hakluyt and Purchas, and making notes and extracts; and the result was the profusely-illustrated volume published in the following year by Messrs. Cassell, Petter, and Galpin.

While this work was in preparation—typographically—I was living upon the surplus earnings of the previous year, eked out with the proceeds of an occasional magazine article and the interest of a small investment in Turkish bonds. I had been unfortunate in my endeavours to find a publisher for the narratives of certain unsolved mysteries of history and judicature, and was casting about for another editorship, when I received a friendly hint as to the probability of literary employment from an unexpected quarter.

I had called upon a gentleman on the staff of a publishing firm east of Waithman's obelisk, and we were talking of my present position and future prospects, a subject which prompted the question from him, had I ever tried the Religious Tract Society?

"I hear," he said, on receiving a reply in the negative, "that they are reorganizing their literary staff, and would be glad to infuse a little new blood. I think it would be worth your while to try them. Don't mention my name, but write to the chief editor, offering your services, and referring to your past work."

I acted upon the suggestion, and in a few days received a letter from the Rev. Dr. Manning, asking me to call upon him, at the offices of the Society, the next time I was in town. Taking care that the opportunity should not be long in coming, I ascended three flights of stairs in the rear of the publishing office, and tapped at the door of a room which had been indicated to me as that of the chief editor. A pleasant voice invited me to enter, and I found myself in the presence of a stout, full-bearded, jolly-looking man, with nothing about him to denote a clerical character, who was sitting at a desk covered with books and papers.

"What I have been thinking you might do for us," said he, when I had introduced myself, and taken a seat, "is a story of travel and adventure, such as boys delight in, and which we purvey for them without the vicious sensationalism which renders so objectionable a large portion of the cheap periodical literature of the day. I believe that, with the majority of lads, the craving for such stories is natural, and also that it may be safely gratified, if care is taken to combine the incidents with a healthy moral tone, and to make them subservient to the teaching of the Gospel."

I signified my assent to this view, and, after refreshing his olfactory organ with a pinch of snuff, he went on, leaning back in his easy-chair, and playing with a gold watch-guard.

"We have many writers who are very good in domestic subjects,—stories of home life,—but none who have shown the capacity for treating subjects of the kind you select in the manner we are bound to require them to be treated. If you avoid an excess of sensationalism, and keep always in view the aims of the Society, I shall consider you a desirable acquisition to our staff."

This was encouraging, and when the number of sheets to which the story should extend had been settled, and I had been informed that the book would be illustrated, and the *honorarium* twenty guineas, I took my leave, well pleased with the results of my application.

Well practised as I was in the composition of stories for boys, I could not, however, feel so much confidence of success in my present undertaking as I should have done if the commission had been given to me by a publisher who had to cater for a quarter of a million of readers, and performed the task on purely commercial principles. To avoid the deprecated excess of sensationalism without degenerating into tameness, and to impart to my work the requisite religious tone without offending against orthodoxy, was to incur the proverbial risk involved in steering between Scylla and Charybdis in a double degree. But, as I had always kept the sensational element of my stories within the bounds of the natural and the probable, the former desideratum was much more easy of attainment than the latter. In both directions I worked carefully and conscientiously, however, and my endeavours were rewarded by success.

The story was completed in a fortnight. Dr. Manning was very much pleased with it, and at once gave me a commission for another. Again I succeeded, and this second story, entitled "Saved from the Wreck," was the first published, it being found that the first, "The Land of the Mammoth," was much too long for a shilling book, and could not, therefore, be produced in the series for which it had been intended. It did not appear, in consequence, until 1877, when a further cheque for 10*l*. was forwarded to me. "Saved from the Wreck" was followed by "A Sailor Boy's Adventures in the Land of the Sun," founded on the strange adventures of Andrew Battell in West Africa, which had formed one of the narratives in "Half-hours with the Early Explorers." The last-named work had, in the meantime, made its appearance, profusely illustrated; and I may here remark that the book which I had regarded as what artists call a "pot boiler" has been, commercially, the greatest success of all the works I have produced, 18,000 copies having been sold down to the present time.

I produced a fourth story for the Religious Tract

Society, entitled "The Wreck of the *Raven*," a story of Arctic adventure, which was accepted by the copyrights committee, but never published, the manuscript having been destroyed in a fire at the offices in the Row. Fortunately for me, it had been both accepted and paid for before that event. Besides these books, I produced for the Society the narrative of Arctic exploring voyages and land journeys comprised in "The Realm of the Ice King," of which two or three editions have been printed.

In the intervals of leisure between the completion of one of these stories and the commencement of another, I was working on a history of circus entertainments. While I was conducting the *Gentleman's Journal*, a conversation which I had with Mr. Viles and one of the sons of his partner, on the morning after a visit to the Holborn Amphitheatre, resulted in my being asked to write an article or two on the history of circus entertainments in this country; and with a view to their preparation I wrote to the proprietors of the principal circuses for information concerning the history of their respective establishments. I found them, however, disposed to be reticent on the subject. Charles Hengler, who was then at the Palais Royal, London, declined to accede to my request on the ground that he thought the subject was one in which the public felt no interest. George Sanger and Eugene Cooke made no reply. James Newsome alone gave me the desired information, forwarding from Aberdeen, where his circus was then located, full particulars of his career, first as an equestrian, and later as the proprietor of a circus.

At the British Museum I was scarcely more successful. The autobiography of Wallett, the clown, a few passages in Elliston's memoirs, and a collection of the bills of Astley's, from 1819 to 1845, constituted all the material I could find. Gleanings from these, with my own recollections of circus performances and some anecdotes of Ducrow supplied by a friend of the artist who furnished the illustrations, were the raw material of the few pages which I was able to produce at that time, and which formed the nucleus of the volume subsequently published by Messrs. Tinsley Brothers, under the title of "Circus Life and Circus Celebrities." When, in 1873, the idea occurred to me of producing that volume, I saw that its realization in anything like a satisfactory manner would be impracticable unless I could procure a supply of material from sources as yet undeveloped; and I knew by experience that the working of such sources was a matter of considerable difficulty.

Further researches at the Museum resulted in the discovery of some good matter for my purpose in Fitzball's memoirs and a French memoir of Adah Isaacs Menken. To the history of circus entertainments thus constructed, I added the interesting reminiscences of the Brothers Francisco, put together from conversations with them and letters from Willie Francisco; and the chapter on the habits, manners, and peculiar dress and slang of circus performers.

"I take some interest in circus performances," said Mr. William Tinsley, when we first met in his office in Catherine Street, "and nothing like your manuscript has ever come under my notice before. I don't suspect you of being an old acrobat, but, knowing a little about circus business, I can see that you have a more intimate knowledge of it than I should have expected to find a literary man possessed of. May I ask how you acquired it?"

The question was readily answered by reference to my reminiscences of my sojourn at York in 1865, and my acquaintance with the Brothers Francisco. Mr. Tinsley desired, however, that the work should be as complete and exhaustive as possible, and measures were taken for procuring further supplies of raw material. The difficulties which I had experienced in 1871 were encountered, however, in every direction, and were in most cases insurmountable. George Sanger was again applied to, but with no better result. George Belmore, the popular comedian, gave us hope of a memoir of the Cookes, the data for which was to be furnished by John Henry Cooke, an equestrian of cosmopolitan fame, to whom he had become related by his marriage with Miss Emily Cooke; but the fulfilment of the promise was postponed from time to time, and the manuscript was never received.

A correspondence with Charlie Keith, known all over Europe as "the roving English clown," resulted in another disappointment. Charlie, who has some claim to be numbered among the small fry of the literary world, having been for some years a correspondent of the *Era*, could have supplied a narrative of his wanderings and adventures that could not have failed to be amusing, and also an interesting chapter on the continental circuses; and he did, indeed, forward from Germany, where he was then travelling as a leading member of the Salmansky *troupe*, a very interesting narrative of his career, from his earliest acrobatic performances at a " gaff " in the vicinity of the City Road to his latest professional experiences at St. Petersburg and Moscow. Unfortunately, however, he insisted upon the publication of his contribution without abridgment or alteration; and with this condition it was impossible to comply. The manuscript was equal in bulk to the whole of the matter that I had in hand, and many pages were occupied with arguments intended to show that a circus performer— or *artiste*, as Charlie would have insisted—was as good a member of society as any other man, a proposition which no one had controverted, and other matters in which readers of the book could not be expected to feel a very lively interest.

The travelled clown's manuscript had, therefore, to be returned to him, though I was sorry to part with his interesting narrative of his early adventures and his professional wanderings, which have extended from the Tagus to the Volga, and from the Baltic to the Alps. The incidents of his " pitching " tour in Spain, consequent upon the breaking up of a circus company of which he and the veteran John Ryan were members, and his descriptions of the great fairs of Seville, St. Petersburg, and Nijni-Novgorod were very amusing, and would have formed capital companion chapters to those containing the reminiscences of the Brothers Francisco. But Mr. Keith preferred the return of his manuscript to the omission of any portion of it, and still cherished the hope of its publication in a complete and separate form when I last heard from him. It still lies, however, at the bottom of his travelling trunk, and I doubt very much whether it will ever be submitted to the public, unless time should abate the rigour of his stipulations.

I was not, however, entirely unsuccessful in my endeavours to obtain additional materials. Mr. Montague, who was then Mr. Newsome's manager, and had formerly been Mr. F. Ginnett's, contributed some interesting anecdotal matter; and Mr. Henry, who was Mr. Newsome's manager when I met some members of the company at York, and then held a similar position at Hengler's, furnished the material for the memoir of the Henglers, and the record of the later movements of the establishment owned by the Sangers. For the material of the chapter relating to the American circuses I was indebted to Mr. Barnum, the world-renowned showman, who happened to be then in London.

While this book was in the printer's hands I was working upon another of a similar kind, namely, "The Old Showmen and the Old London Fairs," much of the material for which I had collected while engaged upon "Circus Life," and which was completed before that work was ready for publication.

"I think I'll rush this out at once," said Mr. Tinsley, when I submitted the manuscript to him. "It may help to make the circus book go."

And so it came about that "The Old Showmen," though written after "Circus Life," was first submitted to the verdict of the critics and the public. The *Athenæum* gave it a very favourable notice, and of the numerous reviews which it elicited I do not remember one that could be called unfavourable.

One of my reviewers surmised that I had been all my life in the habit of wandering from one fair to another, making the acquaintance of acrobats and circus-riders. I was much amused with this mode of accounting for a knowledge of the subject-matter of the two books, "Circus Life," and "The Old Showmen and Old London Fairs," which seemed to be regarded as exceptional, for I had really not seen a fair from the time I left Croydon, in 1853, until I visited Kingston fair, in 1874, as related in the concluding chapter of the latter work. The reviewer's surmise came back to my mind in an amusing manner a few days afterwards, as I was travelling by rail to Surbiton. A middle-aged man, of respectable appearance, who sat opposite to me, and had regarded me with a glance of half recognition when I took my seat, leaned forward a little and said, " Have I not the pleasure of speaking to the Rev. —— ? "

"That is not my name," I replied, " Nor have I any right to the prefix of Reverend."

"Dear me!" exclaimed my fellow-passenger, looking as if he could scarcely credit my disclaimer. "You are remarkably like that gentleman, and, but for your appearing not to recognize me, I should have felt assured of the identity."

The resemblance must have been striking, indeed, for there was nothing clerical in my appearance, my attire consisting of a suit of black, with a soft felt hat and a black neck-tie. I looked as little like a minister of religion as like a circus-man. As regards the reviewer's error—I forget now whether he was the critic of the *Pall Mall* or the *St. James's*—it is a great mistake to infer the character and habits of a literary man from the books he has written. I trust our lady novelists are not to be so judged. When " The Secret Societies of the European Revolution " was published, the *Times*, in a lengthy review of the book, hinted that I was a modern Guy Fawkes; so that, as I have since been more correctly described in the *Athenæum*, and other journals, the reviewers have, among them, made of me, as Mrs. Malaprop says in the comedy, " three gentlemen rolled into one."

CHAPTER XX.

An old volume of letters—A literary mystery—Researches at the Museum—Study of the letters—Correspondence with Lord Lyttelton and Lord Edmund Fitzmaurice—Help from Hagley—The statement of Combe brought to light—A banshee story—"The Secret Societies of the European Revolution"—Opportune references to the subject by Lord Beaconsfield and Cardinal Manning.

THAT part of my education which was received in my pupilage was of a somewhat desultory character, all the instruction of my early years having been given under the supervision of an elder sister until I attended the school at Lower Norwood mentioned in an early chapter of these reminiscences. During those years I read with avidity every book that came in my way, whatever might be the department of literature to which it belonged. My uncle, the master of Archbishop Whitgift's school at Croydon, lent me a life of Nelson and the memoirs of Baron Trenck before I was ten years old, and before I was fourteen I was admitted to the use of a few books belonging to my maternal grandmother, which reposed undisturbed in that long, low-ceiled parlour at Norwood, the walls of which were adorned with those black-framed engravings of the Harlot's Progress which furnished me with the plot and some of the incidents of my first work of fiction. My grandmother's books were, for the most part, not very lively reading, and my mental hunger, keen as it still was, was content to nibble here and there only at Hervey's "Meditations among the Tombs," Flavel's "Husbandry Spiritualized," and Zimmerman's "Reflections on Solitude." These books, calf-bound and large-typed, contained matter much less to my taste than was that which I found in the paper boards and smaller type of the "Spectator," "Guardian," "Adventurer," and "Persian Letters," and I scarcely need say that the judgment of maturer years confirmed the choice of my youth.

But the book of my grandmother's which I read at that time with most interest was a small volume printed in 1806, being the latest edition of the letters of the second Lord Lyttelton, and containing all those in the two volumes published respectively in 1780 and 1782. The attraction which this book had for me consisted, I believe, in the tinge of scepticism to be found in several of the letters, and the metaphysical questions argued, lightly and cleverly, in others. I was beginning to assert for myself freedom of thought, and to rebel against custom and convention; and there was naturally much in common between the writer and the reader. At my grandmother's death, her books, with the rest of her personal effects, became the property for life of a spinster sister of my mother, and after my aunt's decease, which took place in 1868, as already related, the volume in question passed into my possession. It is now, I believe, a rather scarce work, the copy in my book-case being, with the exception of another in the library of the British Museum, the only one that has ever come under my notice.

I dipped into the volume again when it came into my possession a few months after my aunt's death, and after I fixed my abode at Long Ditton I availed of the opportunity afforded by a ramble to Epsom to view the scene of the wonderful story of the last days of Lord Lyttelton's life which had passed current for ninety years. I was not then aware that the genuineness of the letters had ever been questioned; and when, in reading for a Junius narrative, to be included in my projected series of historic and judicial mysteries, I came upon an article in a *Quarterly Review* of 1851 upon that literary puzzle of the last century, I first became aware of the fact that their authorship had been ascribed to Combe. I found at the same time reasons adduced by the reviewer for rejecting the hypothesis which satisfied me that the letters were the genuine productions of Lord Lyttelton.

The subject had an interest for me which grew with the study of it. Subjects of an occult character always possessed a peculiar fascination for me; and hence my selection of the social ideologies, pagan mysteries, and the secret societies for my contributions to the "Papers for the People." While reading and working at the Museum upon works for which I had commissions, or which I saw my way to producing and selling, I gathered, therefore, every scrap of matter relating to the second Lord Lyttelton, or which could help to elucidate the mystery of his life, that which I have called his dual existence, or throw light upon the question of the letters. I gathered evidence from a variety of sources that the spiteful stories told of Lyttelton by Horace Walpole were, in some instances, false, in all others exaggerated or distorted. I found that the Lyttelton family had pronounced spurious many of the posthumous poems of the second lord as confidently as they had the letters, though the former were edited by his friend Roberts, who was one of his executors; and that the evidence adduced by Mr. Robert Cole for the spurious character of the letters, and relied upon by the late John Camden Hotten, was so flimsy that it would not bear the slightest examination. The farther I extended my researches, the stronger became my conviction that the letters were genuine epistles of Lyttelton to his friends, and that the noble writer, though far from being a virtuous man, was not a worse one than many of his contemporaries who enjoyed better repute, while he possessed abilities which, if he had lived a few years longer, might have assisted him to a leading place in the conduct of the State's affairs.

The estimate which I formed of Lyttelton's character from the results of my researches and study of the letters is set forth in the preface to the work published by Messrs. Tinsley Brothers in 1876. "It seems to me," I said, "that the motive for the general desire to ignore or depreciate Thomas Lyttelton may be found in the independence of party of which he was almost an unique example in his day, and which must have rendered him to his contemporaries a political anomaly. Though he held office under a Tory minister, his speeches, equally with his letters, evince a regard for civil and religious freedom greater than was felt by some even of those who sat on the benches of the Opposition. There was no one among the Whigs who spoke more strongly against the North Ministry than he did whenever he believed them to be in the wrong. As that political phenomenon, an independent member of a Ministry, he could not fail to be misunderstood, suspected, reviled, even if he had been the most virtuous man in the kingdom.

"He was suspected, moreover, of holding the sceptical views of revealed religion which were then beginning to prevail among the educated classes of continental Europe. There is not only no proof that he held such views, but the strongest reasons for believing that, inconsistent with the requirements of a Christian life as his conduct often was, he entertained the most profound respect for the Gospel. He certainly always professed such a respect, and there seems no reason to doubt that he felt it. No one ever accused him of being hypocritical or dishonest; but he read the works of deistical authors, and that was sufficient for his condemnation. The hands of his pious father and right reverend uncle were held up in horror, and, as the semblance of piety was fashionable in those days, than which none have been marked more strongly with corruption and immorality, society shrank from him as a matter of decorum, if not of loyalty.

"Thomas Lyttelton was not a virtuous man. Virtuous men were scarce in those days, and it cannot be claimed for the subject of this biography that he was one of the comparatively few exceptions to the general rule. But it may fairly be doubted whether his character has not been unfairly blackened. Some of the scandals associated with his name, which have been repeated by successive writers, without inquiry, have proved on investigation to have no other foundation to rest upon than the idlest rumour. Others have been so variously related by different narrators as to sufficiently testify, by their variations, to their mythical character. It was the common belief of that generation that a man or woman who was sceptical on the subject of revealed religion must necessarily be abandoned to every kind of wickedness; and such scepticism being unfairly attributed to Thomas Lyttelton, he became the dog with an ill name, whom it was an evidence of piety and respectability to abuse."

I have quoted this passage for the benefit of those who have not read the work it prefaces, to show that the subject was really, from my own point of view, worth writing about. I felt that "the wicked Lord Lyttelton," as he was called by some of his contemporaries, was not understood. When I informed a literary friend that I was engaged upon his life, he said, in an interrogative tone, and with the air of seeming to recall all that he knew of the subject, "The one who saw the ghost? Do you think anybody cares about him?" he added, dubiously, when I had replied.

"Not for the traditional 'wicked Lord Lyttelton,' who saw the ghost, as you observe," I returned.

"But I believe that the reality was something much worthier of preservation in men's minds than the traditionary hero of that ridiculous ghost story, which is all that most people seem ever to have learned about him, beyond his bad repute as a gambler and a libertine."

I said much more that seemed entirely new to my friend, who acknowledged that his reading enabled him to give me no other suggestion as to materials for my work than the hypothesis of the *Quarterly Review* that Lyttelton was Junius. That I had already convinced myself could not be advanced beyond mere conjecture, and I think I have given sound reasons for its rejection.

There was one important matter upon which I was very anxious to obtain information which I had vainly sought for in the published letters and memoirs of the last quarter of the eighteenth century. That was, the relations existing between Lyttelton and the Earl of Shelburne at the time when the former made his speech on the Earl of Bristol's motion for the dismissal of the Earl of Sandwich, speaking for the first time from the benches of the Opposition. He had then resolved upon an independent course, and it appears from Hansard's "Parliamentary History" that he had taken a seat near the Earl of Shelburne and the Duke of Richmond. In the course of his speech he observed that, in the then state of public affairs, which he regarded as critical, party should be forgotten, and men of ability consulted, without reference to their political sentiments. He indicated the Earl of Shelburne, the Duke of Grafton, and the Earl of Bristol as desirable members of such a Ministry. On the reassembling of Parliament in November, Lord Lyttelton again sat next the Earl of Shelburne, and spoke and voted against the Government. He was to have spoken again, on a motion of the Earl of Shelburne, but before it could be made he had departed this life.

Now, the Earl of Shelburne, who held the same position towards the Whigs as Lord Lyttelton did towards the Tories, favoured such a combination as the latter had shadowed forth, and realized the idea when entrusted with the formation of a Cabinet, three years later, on the death of the Marquis of Rockingham. I was very desirous, therefore, to obtain evidence of an understanding that Lord Lyttelton was to have held a Secretaryship in the Shelburne Ministry, if he had lived; but none could be found. The late Lord Lyttelton very kindly sent me a packet of letters from Hagley, but most of them referred to the earlier period of my subject's career, and none of them contained a sentence relating to politics. Lord Edmund Fitzmaurice, who was then engaged upon his biography of the Earl of Shelburne, with equal kindness promised me the benefit of any discovery he might make concerning the relations between his subject and mine; but nothing was discovered.

Along with the faded letters written by Thomas Lord Lyttelton to his father, Lord Westcott, and others, there came to me from Hagley an unexpected contribution to the history of the published letters, in the form of a letter from Major Cockburn to Mr. J. Lyttelton, of Wimbledon Park, Surrey, written in

1818, and embodying a very circumstantial statement made to the writer by Combe, that he really was the author of the letters! This communication, which covers several sheets of paper, will be found in the preface to my "Life of Thomas Lord Lyttelton," wherein I have set forth my reasons for rejecting the testimony of Combe, and adhering to my original conviction that the letters were genuine, an opinion which I now found was, according to Combe, held by the second Lady Lyttelton, widow of the first lord.

This work I offered, when completed, in the first instance, to Messrs. Hurst and Blackett, by whom it was declined, for the strangely insufficient reason that they had published, some years previously, the memoirs and correspondence of the *first* Lord Lyttelton! I had previously turned over the leaves of that work at the Museum, and in the four volumes of which it consists I found Thomas Lyttelton mentioned just twice, and then in the most casual manner. After the acceptance of the manuscript by another firm, I one day had some conversation with Mr. William Tinsley on the subject of the Lyttelton ghost story, the various versions of which by different persons, in letters communicated by the late Lord Lyttelton to *Notes and Queries*, I was, by the kindness of Dr. Doran, enabled to introduce in the last chapter of the work. The conversation flowed naturally into supernaturalism.

"Well, I am not superstitious, as you may suppose," said Mr. Tinsley, leaning back in his easy-chair, with an air of thought, "but I am willing to admit that there may be, as Hamlet says, 'something more in heaven and earth than is dreamt of in our philosophy.'

I never saw a ghost, even of the most questionable character; but I once heard something which, in the circumstances, was so strange as to be utterly inexplicable upon any natural or rationalistic hypothesis."

He paused a moment, and then proceeded to tell the story, which, as I cannot pretend to repeat his precise words, I take leave to tell in my own way, though without the slightest deviation from the original.

A large party of ladies and gentlemen, himself being of the number, were assembled at the house of a friend who lived a few miles from London. The occasion was a joyous one, for on that day their host had taken to himself a wife, with every prospect of a large amount of connubial felicity. The happy couple were young and in good health, and on this occasion in the highest possible spirits, over which nothing during the day had occurred to cast a cloud. The gas had just been lighted, and the festivity of the evening was at its height, when a peculiar tapping was heard at the drawing-room window, which opened upon a small lawn, forming a portion of the charming garden and shrubbery surrounding the house. The sound was such as would be produced by a person tapping sharply and repeatedly on the glass with the tips of the fingers, supposing the fingers to be furnished with long and strong finger-nails. The strange and unexpected sound caused the conversation that was going on to be immediately suspended, while every eye was turned towards the window. Mr. Tinsley, who was seated near the window, drew aside the curtain, and looked out, but no living creature, human or otherwise, was in sight.

"Some one is playing a trick upon us," said the bride's father, rising from his chair. "Let us go and see who it is."

Mr. Tinsley and others of the gentlemen accompanied him, and they looked all round the house, peeping among the shrubs, and into every spot in which an intruder could be concealed; but no discovery was made. No living being was visible, not the faintest sounds of retiring footsteps could be heard, nor could any traces of such be found on the damp turf of the lawn or the soft earth of the flower-beds. They all agreed that the incident was a strange one, and there was a general concurrence in that opinion among the guests who had not left the drawing-room when they returned and related the negative result of their search; but it was not allowed to damp their spirits or mar the festivity of the evening.

Little more than a month afterwards the bride was no longer of this world. She contracted a severe cold, fever supervened, and in a few days she was numbered with the dead.

Time passed, and the bereaved husband did not prove inconsolable. In little more than a year after the death of his first wife he contracted another marriage under circumstances which promised to be as conducive to his future happiness as those of the first union had been. On the first anniversary of the wedding-day, however, the mysterious tapping which had been heard on the night of the first marriage was again heard by the guests assembled to celebrate the occasion. The host became pale as he listened, and those of the guests who had been present on the former occasion looked at each other in mute consternation. For a moment no one moved or spoke; then the host sprang to his feet, and rushed out, followed by several gentlemen of the party.

As on the former occasion, the search was in vain. The searchers ran round the house, dashed in and out among the shrubs, scoured the grounds on every side, vaulted over the fences, and ran hither and thither; but without finding any solution of the mystery.

On the following day the wife of the giver of the feast was seized with an illness which, within a month, proved fatal.

"What do you think of it?" I asked the narrator of the story.

"It is quite beyond me. I have told you what occurred, but I have no hypothesis to offer by way of elucidation. It is a mystery! Explain it who can."

I can only, with regard to what the late Robert Dale Owen called "footfalls on the boundaries of another world," echo the remarks of the publisher. I am neither a believer nor a sceptic, as, while I am disposed to be sceptical as to the supernatural character of the ghost stories I hear, I am, as a believer in the immortality of the soul, unable to deny the possibility of such spirit manifestations.

As my regular income at this time was limited to the interest of a small investment in Turkish bonds, I was obliged, as soon as one literary venture was launched, to put another on the stocks. Before the "Life of Thomas Lord Lyttelton" was completed, I was busy collecting materials for my next book. I thought, at first, of writing an elaborate and exhaustive history of the social ideologies which I had treated briefly in one of my contributions to the "Papers for the People." But Utopias had much less interest for ordinary readers in 1876 than in 1850, when the disciples of Cabet, and Constant, and Proudhon, and Weitling had so recently forced them upon public attention; and, upon consideration, I abandoned the idea, and began to collect materials for the history of the political secret societies of the last hundred years.

These also had formed the subject of one of the papers written by me for the series just mentioned; but I had now to treat them in a more elaborate manner, and to amplify my thirty-two pages into a couple of volumes. The writing of the first of these was a comparatively easy task, for histories of the Illuminatists, the United Irishmen, the Philadelphians, and the Carbonari, which, with the Tugendbund, the Associated Patriots, and the Communeros, are comprised in the first volume, had been written by other hands. The production of the second volume was a very difficult task. The materials for the history of the Hetairia, the United Sclavonians, the Polish Templars, the various societies founded by Mazzini, the Families, the Communists, the Fenians, the Nihilists, and the Omladina existed, but they had to be gathered, collated, and examined before they could be made available. Scores of books, English and French, and translations of German and Italian authors, had to be read before the history of the Carbonari, from the period of the Neapolitan and Piedmontese revolutions to the decline of the society, could be written, and the chapters on the Hetairia, the United Sclavonians, the Templars, Young Italy, and the Families produced.

The nearer I brought my work to the present day, the harder became my task. The materials for the histories of Young Germany, Young Poland, Young Switzerland, and the Communists had to be gleamed, in great part, from letters, and from papers which came into my possession during my management of the *Communist Chronicle*, and my subsequent connections with the Fraternal Democrats. There was much which I had learned orally, which I now would have been glad to have confirmed or amplified, and passages in the epistolary matter which it was desirable to have explained. But thirty years had elapsed since I had received the letters and had the conversations to which I am referring. Where were the men who had reported the progress of Communism in Germany? What had become of the refugees whose bond of union in a foreign capital had been the motto: " All men are brethren "? Some had fallen while fighting under Hecker and Mieroslawski, others in the fusillades of Rastadt, many more during the terrible June insurrection in Paris. There was not one whom I now knew where to find. Julian Harney, whom I had supposed to be in Jersey, proved to be in the United States; and he seems never to have received a letter which I wrote, asking for information concerning certain of our old associates of the " White Hart " in Drury Lane.

I was forced, therefore, to make the most and the best of the matter in my possession; and in using this some care was required, as I was unwilling to make any statement upon authority that was doubtful, or to supply by conjecture gaps that I could not fill with facts. Though by this conscientious method of working I somewhat reduced the amount of matter which I might otherwise have produced, I had the satisfaction of knowing that I had admitted no statement which I had not every reason to regard as the truth.

While the work was going through the press Lord Beaconsfield, in a speech which he made at Aylesbury on the 20th of September, 1876, drew attention to the subject in the following words:—"In the attempt to conduct the government of this world, there are new elements to be considered which our predecessors had not to deal with. We have not to deal only with emperors, princes, and ministers, but there are the secret societies—an element which we must take into consideration, which at the last moment may baffle all our arrangements, which have their agents everywhere, which have reckless agents, which countenance assassination, and which, if necessary, could produce a massacre."

I saw at once the use that might be made of this passage as an advertisement for the book; and I was pleased to find Cardinal Manning speaking, a week or two afterwards, in a similar strain. "The secret societies of the world," said his Eminence, "the existence of which men laugh at and deny in the plenitude of their self-confidence, as men laugh at and deny the existence of Satan himself—the secret societies are forcing their existence and their reality upon the consciousness of those who, until the other day, would not believe that they existed. In the year 1848 they shed innocent blood in the city of Rome; in the year 1871 they shed innocent blood in the city of Paris. They are again as widespread and as active at this moment."

Nothing could have been better for my purpose than these utterances of the Minister and the Cardinal; though, as a matter of fact, it was the priests, and not the Mazzinians, who procured the assassination of Count Rossi in 1848, the motive of the crime being the reforms which he had advised the Pope to introduce into the administration of the civil affairs of the Papacy. The two extracts were printed on the back of the title-page, and form the best answer that can be given to the allegations of certain critics, that the secret societies were powerless, and had always been so, and that I had exaggerated their importance as an element of the European revolution that has been in progress for the last hundred years. This is not the place to argue that question; but, in the present state of affairs in the East, the quotation of the concluding passages of the work may be excused.

"There can be no doubt that the dream of a Sclavonic Confederation will some day be realized, and that day may not be far distant; though the precise manner in which the new political edifice is likely to be raised is not foreshadowed in the pamphlet of Mr. Gladstone, or the letters of Mr. Grant Duff. No one acquainted with the under-currents of foreign politics, and with the policy which Prince Bismarck has been steadily pursuing since he saved Germany from revolution by binding up the aims of the people with the fortunes of the House of Hohenzollern, can fail to perceive, firstly, that the Eastern Question cannot receive its final solution without the disruption of the Austro-Hungarian Empire, as well as the extinction of Ottoman rule in Europe; and, secondly, that it is from Berlin, and not from St. Petersburg, that the signal will be given for the crowning crash. The Austrians are now the only Germans not included within the new German Empire; and German unity will not be complete until the south-eastern frontier is extended to the Carnic Alps and the border-line of Hungary. It may be confidently anticipated, therefore, that when the Eastern Question is ripe for solution, and Austria is brought face to face with the imminent formation of a Sclavonic Confederation, the Court and Cabinet of Vienna will have to choose between the loss of the south-eastern provinces of the empire, and the incorporation of the adjoining provinces of Turkey within its limits. It will be truly a choice of evils; but it will have to be made, the interests of both Germany and Russia requiring them to put the strongest pressure upon Austria, to prevent her from remaining neutral.

"The annexation of Bosnia and Herzegovina will be the alternative recommended at Berlin and St. Petersburg; the interests of Germany demanding the incorporation of Austria proper with the German Empire, and those of Russia being opposed to the formation of a Sclavonian Confederation. As the rejection of this course would involve a revolt of her Sclavonic population, aided, openly or secretly, by Germany and Russia, she may be expected to accept what seems inevitable, and drift eastward, with the hope, perhaps, of recovering on the Lower Danube the prestige and influence which she has lost in Germany since Sadowa was fought and the Treaty of Prague signed. The change will produce discontent among the German and Magyar subjects of the Kaiser; there will be agitation among the former for incorporation with their Fatherland; and Prince Bismarck, or his successor, will demand the cession of Austria proper as compensation for the extension of the Kaiser's dominion south-eastward. The cession will be made sooner or later, and the separation of Hungary will follow, leaving the Sclaves to shape their own destiny, free from the influence alike of Vienna and of Pesth; while the dreaded domination of Russia will cease with a solution which will reduce her to isolation. The Sclavonic Confederation may not be founded upon the lines laid down by the Omladina, any more than the Germany and Italy of to-day realize the aims of Young Germany and Young Italy; but its formation may be as confidently anticipated as the unity of those countries might have been thirty or forty years ago."

CHAPTER XXI.

Removal to Croydon, where I find myself forgotten—Mr. Frederick Baldiston and the *Croydon Chronicle*—" Recollections of an Old Croydonian "—Another flitting—Rural rambles, and their literary results—An Irish Colenso—An extraordinary project—Correspondence concerning literature for boys.

My mother died, within three months of her eighty-seventh birthday, in the latter days of 1875, having survived my father, who attained exactly the same age, about three years and a half. A small estate at Upper Norwood thereupon became divisible between my two sisters and myself, my only brother having died in Canada soon after my father. Lest my readers should suppose that this event placed me in a position to live at ease, free from the cares and anxieties which attend through life those who are not born "with a silver spoon in their mouth," I had better state at once that my share of the income of this property is about sixty pounds per year.

Shortly afterwards I removed to the neighbourhood of Croydon, where I found myself as completely forgotten as if I had never lived there. My fellow-apprentice passed me in the street without recognizing me. Former neighbours and fellow-workers in the Chartist movement and the Parliamentary reform agitation which succeeded it were, with one or two exceptions, dead or had left the town. The town itself was changed. It had grown in every direction. South Croydon had come into existence, where I remembered only a roadside public-house, called the "Surrey Drovers," in the lane leading to Sanderstead, and a beer-house called the "Red Deer," on the high-road southward, where the chalk ridge of the North Downs begins to rise. Westward the houses extended to the verge of Waddon Marsh, and the meadows between the Old Town and the southern portion of the High Street were the site of several new streets. Lines of villas covered the district known as the Common, which, when I left it in 1853, consisted of gardens and pastures, dotted sparsely with cottages; and a similar eruption of bricks and mortar had broken out all over the hamlet of Addiscombe, where I remembered only a few cottages and a public-house called the "Black Horse," which, or rather a new and larger house with the same sign, remains there still. Lord Ashburton had fled before the irruption of the builders, and a portion of his park had been sold in building lots, and the grounds of the military college formerly maintained here by the East India Company had been similarly appropriated.

I was endeavouring at this time to obtain the editorship of a Liberal journal; but, though I expended several pounds in advertising, and answered many advertisements, I was unsuccessful. I have often asked myself, when conning the advertisements of journalists in the *Athenæum*, whether success ever does attend those who thus announce their wants, my own experience being decidedly of a negative character. As these reminiscences have so far shown, and will continue to show to the end of the last chapter, I have never obtained journalistic or literary employment of any kind by means of the press.

There had been no newspaper published in Croydon when I left the town. There were now two. The older of these, the *Chronicle*, had been started by Mr. Frederic Baldiston soon after the remission of the last penny of the newspaper stamp duty, and was now a good property.

"It was up-hill work to establish it," he told me one day, at my house, where he visited me on a matter of business presently to be mentioned. "How many copies do you suppose I sold the first week?"

"Fifty?" I returned, at a venture.

"Two," said he. "All the rest were given away, and all the advertisements in that issue were inserted gratuitously. I carried it on for the first year at a loss; but the loss grew less and less by degrees, and in the second year the turning-point was reached, and it began to pay."

It had paid so well since that he had removed from his old premises, bought the building in which the butter-market used to be held, in one of the best positions in the town, and converted it into a printing-office. The success of the *Chronicle* had induced some members of the original staff to secede from it and start the *Advertiser*, which had also become a paying concern; and in the summer of 1877 another paper, the *Guardian*, was started, under favourable auspices, with Mr. Basil Young, the well-known entertainer, in the editorial chair.

Soon after my removal to Addiscombe I had introduced myself to Mr. Baldiston, with a suggestion that I should write for his paper a series of articles under the title of "Recollections of an Old Croydonian." He invited me to his house, one of a line of villas which stretched for nearly a mile along a road which, twenty years before, had been bounded by hawthorn hedges, and then called Middle Heath Lane. I found that, though he had not known me personally during my former residence in the town, he recollected me and the active part I had then taken in the Chartist movement. He regarded my suggestion very favourably, and the reminiscences with which I supplied him were so well received by the public that I was induced to extend the series beyond the length which I had originally intended.

As Mr. Baldiston was the only person in the town, or in the neighbourhood, to whom I had made myself known, I had many opportunities of hearing the "Recollections" spoken of; and I was much amused with the inability of any one to guess who was the writer of them. Old inhabitants recognized their truthfulness, but no one recognized me, and I was so much forgotten that even persons who knew my name, and the connection of one of that name with the Chartist movement in 1848, never surmised that I was the same individual. Mr. Baldiston told me once that, in the course of a conversation in his publishing office on the subject, an old resident remarked that there was a printer living in Surrey Street in 1848 whom that part of the narrative seemed to point to, but he could not be the writer, for he left the town in that year, and nobody knew what had become of him!

Flattering, was it not? Here was one of their own townsmen, whose name had become known in the literary world, and whose works had been criticized in the reviews and the newspapers, living in their midst, and they knew it not, never thought of associating with the authorship of books which bore his name on the title-page the man with whose form and face they had been familiar on public platforms, and in the business life of the town thirty years before.

I did not prolong my residence at Addiscombe beyond the year, removing at Christmas to the little town of Southborough, about two miles north of Tunbridge Wells. The surroundings of this pleasant and healthful place, which many visitors prefer to the larger and gayer town in its vicinity, are more picturesque than those of any other in which I have ever resided. It is situated on the ridge which divides the valley of the Medway from that narrower valley through which runs the brook which divides Kent from Sussex. Its common, though smaller than that of Tunbridge Wells, is one of the most beautiful in England. It slopes from the highway towards the west, and its lower part is clothed with a mixed growth of furze, broom, and juniper, dotted with clumps of oak, beech, and birch. Wood-anemones and dog-violets spangle the verdure of the spaces free from shrubs, wild thyme perfumes the air in summer, the feathery fronds of the male fern adorn the sides of the gullies worn by water, and the hard fern grows profusely under the trees.

East and west of the little town are lanes and byways leading to villages of historic interest, up hill and down hill, through varied scenery, here cut through sandstone rock, there overhung by old oaks and beeches, with glimpses now and again of the fir-woods of Pembury, Frant, or Broadwater, which have in most spots replaced the ancient forests of oak, or the blue ridge of Crowborough, distinctly seen from the higher parts of the locality, rising above the remnants of Ashdowne Forest. Within a circle of five or six miles are Penshurst, rich in historic and poetic associations, with its grand old mansion and extensive park, and its old cottages, notably the "church houses" at the entrance of the churchyard; Chiddingstone, where more old houses of the Tudor period may be seen; Hever, with its castle, haunted by memories of Anne Boleyn, and its church, the registers of which record generations of Boleyns, with the name spelt in every conceivable way; Rusthall, where the sandstone rock of the adjacent common crops up above the verdure in a variety of strange forms, and on the western side forms an escarpment as abrupt and steep as the chalk cliffs of Thanet; Eridge, with its ivy-clad castle and its aromatic fir-woods; Frant, near which are the ruins of Bayham Abbey; Lamberhurst, called by Cobbett the prettiest village in England; Pembury, with its ancient church almost buried in the surrounding woods.

Solitary rambles amid the beauties of nature have always had a great charm for me, and I indulged in them as much here as in the neighbourhood of my former abode at Long Ditton. I made considerable additions to a series of descriptive sketches, interspersed with notices of bird and insect life, which I had commenced in Surrey, and when I had written as much as would form a portable volume for the pocket of a nature-loving rambler I endeavoured to find a publisher. Messrs. Marshall Japp and Co. were then commencing the issue of a series of "Half-holiday Hand-books," and they suggested that I should divide the matter so as to form three of these, respectively relating to the neighbourhoods of Croydon, Kingston-on-Thames, and Tunbridge Wells. To this I assented, and, some necessary addition and revision being accomplished, they were issued in that form, with maps and illustrations, and have commanded a steady summer sale ever since.

The books published with my name on the title-page between the years 1876 and 1880 represent a portion only of my literary labours during that period. On looking through my journals for those years, I find entries respecting a mass of correspondence with publishers and editors on a variety of subjects, some of which I had forgotten until my recollection of them was thus revived. I wrote several serial stories for a Sheffield newspaper, another for the periodical which received most of those written in 1869 and 1870, and one of the "Crystal Stories," edited by Mr. F. W. Robinson, besides producing a mass of manuscript which still lies on the top shelf of one of my bookcases. In turning over the correspondence to which these entries refer, I came upon the following curious letters, the first of which seems to have been written in response to an advertisement for literary employment.

"SIR,—Seeing in the *Athenæum* of last week your advertisement, I write, hoping you will undertake the editorship of my (or the) *original chronology of the Holy Bible*, which I am preparing to *print* and publish in NUMBERS, as soon as I can. My calculations are based upon the generations recorded in Genesis, and proves the creation therein chronicled was the work of SIX DAYS such as we know days to be, A.M. 1, B.C. 10,000. Your notice speaks of 'great and varied experience in every department' of literature, and I can assure you the sustaining arguments will require every kind of knowledge within the great circle of universal information. For we will have to prove not only our 10,000 B.C., but to show the 4004 B.C. is the head and front of all the fashionable philosophers of the present day,—in a word, we must sustain the word of God as we find it in holy writ, to whom 'there is nothing hard or impossible,' and consequently all His commands concerning the peopling and subduing of the earth were fulfilled some 3500 years before the flood.

"Who need wonder just now at the rapid spread of scepticism and infidelity, when Christian literates teach that interminable confusion existed previous to the Mosaic creation, that the first, second, and third chapters of Genesis are mere allegories, that man only attained knowledge by long experience, that God, notwithstanding His INFINITE WISDOM, destroyed the creatures He had made *in one lifetime and a half*, and yet we read 'His mercy endureth for ever.' But we will show His MERCY did endure [here three words which I find undecipherable] 2820 years. At last mercy was staid at the *cry* of the *Poor*. Then came the judgment, but, lo! mercy gave 100 years' truce, and it was laughed to scorn. So came the hour of execution, but, lo! no torture,—'The door was shut no more. Crash went the world, and all was o'er.'

"After the flood we hear that God blessed Sem, Ham, and Japheth, and made a covenant with them. See Gen. ix. Yet, according to the commentators of our Bibles, this special blessing had very little effect, for they tell us Sem, Ham, and Japheth had only sixteen sons between them, although they lived in or about 500 years after the flood. Again our commentators say the sons and grandsons of these SPECIALLY-BLESSED fathers grew so wicked that God was forced to afflict them with the confusion of tongues in HALF a lifetime, 144 years after the flood. Again, we read '*all the Laws of God are eternal*,' but, lo! our commentators declare 'tis no such thing, for they tell us Abraham MARRIED HIS SISTER, and Amram married HIS AUNT; yet the eternal law says very differently. *See Leviticus*. Again, God says to Abraham, 'Thy seed shall sojourn in a land not their own, and they shall bring them under bondage and afflict them 400 years,' which, with thirty years of friendship, gives 430 years for the sojourn; but no, says our commentators, the sojourn only lasted 264 years. Now, when we consider these things, we need not wonder at the rapid spread of infidelity and scepticism. Now, sir, you will see by this outline the nature of the work you would have to edite, for along with theology all the other *sciences* will have to be introduced. Say, then, will you undertake the editorship, and inform me how we could get on together? Money I have none, and only expect or hope the sale of each number would enable us to *devote our whole time to the subject.* What say you?"

The italics and small capitals are the writer's. The offer of the impecunious Milesian Colenso did not attract me, but I have no copy of my reply. I answered his letter on the day I received it, but I presume he had not received my reply when, two days afterwards, he wrote again as follows:—

"Seeing in the *Athenæum* of last week your advertisement, I wish to inform you I have discovered the chronologers of the Holy Bible have made a *monstrous error* in their calculations of past time, amounting to 6000 years. Nor can we doubt but to this most erroneous calculation must be attributed the present widespread scepticism and infidelities of the world, its pride, its pomp, its extravagance, and its political and social tyrannies.

"After telling us the work of each day, we read, 'so the heavens and the earth were finished, and ALL the FURNITURE of them,' that is, in six days. *No such thing*, cries our commentators and chronologers. There was a pre-Adamite age, counting billions of years, during which countless myriads of FORCES were working pell-mell—upon what? Why, upon the disorderly matters which lay scattered about through space during billions and trillions of other years, long previous to the action of *the forces*, for this period, it seems, was the reign of Chaos. But who reigned before Chaos our philosophers sayeth not. In a word, the sustaining arguments of 'the original chronology of the Holy Bible' will, at one and the same time, prove the creation recorded in Genesis was perfected in six regular days, A.M. 1, B.C. 10,000 years; THAT only one man and one woman, Adam and Eve, were made by God for this globe on which we live; THAT Adam and Eve were intuitively gifted with every knowledge, as parents, teachers, rulers; THAT all the commands of God relating to the peopling of the earth and its subduation were fulfilled in or about the birth of Cainan A.M. 1879; THAT, notwithstanding all the BOAST and BRAG of this 19th century, its PROUDEST PHILOSOPHERS HAVE NOT YET ATTAINED THE FIRST RUDIMENTS of the SCIENCE, ART, and literature known to 'the mighty men of old, the men of renown,' a few stray waifs of which enabled the wise men of Egypt to cope with Moses and Aron, and aye in later times enabled the OLD WOMAN of *Endor* to make the dead appear and speak, scientific feats of which our modern philosophy knows nothing. Here, then, in the original chronology of the Holy Bible, you will have work not only for yourself as editor but for many other writers—not for awhile, but for years to come, for according to the *plan* of the work, every INCIDENT referring to a date will have its own *sustaining argument*, while the dates themselves must be likewise sustained by proofs drawn from the generations, besides the *criticisms* which must follow, showing the [here a doubly-underlined word which I have not been able to decipher] ABSURDITIES and CONTRADICTIONS of the present received chronology of western Europe, of Christendom. One word more. With the dogmatic creeds of any church we will have nothing to do; but we will have everything to do in sustaining that glorious being whom some call God, as being in power almighty, in knowledge boundless, in wisdom infinite, and in mercy most enduring. All honour, praise, and glory be to His holy name for ever.

"P.S.—Up to this I have only the direct line worked out by the generations from Adam to the exodus, bringing in all the branches from Heber to Jacob. My date for the first year of the sojourn is A.M. 8000, and for the exodus A.M. 8430, for the death of Moses and the sole leadership of Joshua A.M. 8470, and 8475 for the conquest of Chanaan. As the period in which Job flourished is a mixed question, I give it as I find it—Job, b. 7962 A.M., Job's affliction A.M. 8014, made king A.M. 8030, died A.M. 8154, the ages of his three friends being—Eliphaz, b. 7913, was in the year of Job's afflictions 102 years of age; Baldad, b. 7940, was 75 years; Sopher, b. 7960, was 55; and Eliu, b. 7992, and so was only 22 years the year of Job's afflictions."

Two days afterwards, having in the meantime received my reply, my correspondent wrote again, as follows:—

"SIR,—The candour and courtesy of your reply more than ever make me anxious to win you over to my *views*. You say, 'If the work had been of a more promising nature, I should not have objected to waiting for payment.'

"But I only gave you one view of the work, the scriptural, which has only reference to the dates, as they turn up by *computation* of the generations, while the EVENTS connected with those dates will, as a matter of course, bring in SCIENCE, history, politics,—I say *politics*, for in our *arguments* to sustain man, religion, government, and this fair earth *co-eval* I mean to prove that government was a ROYAL REPUBLIC, the people princes all, and GOD their king. Aye, and we shall prove 3000 years that first royal democracy delighted heaven and blessed the earth. And three times the royal republic will come under discussion, under Adam, Seth, Enos, Cainan, Mahaleel; secondly, under [a name undeciphered here] Sala, Heber; and lastly under the Judges, Jered, Henoch, and Mathusalem. Three times, too, will royalty come under discussion, in the times of Mathusalem, Lamech, and Noah, to the flood; secondly, in the Nimrod; and lastly under Saul. As for history, we'll have enough when we open the records enclosed in the notable names recorded in Genesis. And as for SCIENCE, why, my dear sir, we will have far more than the Secularists will bargain for in the *very first chapter of Genesis*, after which will come the Ark, another grand scientific work, followed by the FLOOD, and its testimonials, those wondrous fossils to be found ALL OVER, aye, aye, and down, down into the very bowels of the earth. No, no, my dear sir, this work will only introduce theology twice or thrice, and each time we shall prove to ALL churchmen it is their *crude ideas* of the Deity that has just now so filled the world with scepticism and infidelity. ONE WORD FOR ALL. The original chronology of the Holy Bible shall be not only original in name but in the treatment of its subjects, consequently, as the work is not confined to theology, and has nothing to do with the uncertain dates of bygone dynasties, you may yet change your mind, no doubt provided the line of politics I have glanced at meets your approbation, for I mean to put forward a *royal democracy* as the only fairest form of government. What you may think I know not, but I do know some forty years ago England had a FROST who *thought, wrote,* and *suffered* in the cause of democracy, and I can't see, with a *constitution* to guide a man, what difference there can be between a KING and a PRESIDENT. Again, we find leading officers of republican governments HONOURABLES; why not style them PRINCES? Why, man alive, in no time KINGS AND PRINCES would be *common as ditch-water.* But enough of this gossip.

"P.S.—Is it possible that some thirty pages of printed matter would be, even if a failure, such a heavy loss? I think 5*l.* would cover all expenses."

I could not discern a promise of either fame or fortune in my correspondent's projected undertaking, and the certainty that I should have had most of the work to do and all the risk to bear would, under any circumstances, have prevented it from being realized, so far as the result depended upon myself. I again expressed to him by letter the impossibility of giving him any assistance, and so the correspondence closed.

There was at this time much talk about the "pernicious literature" purveyed for the perusal of boys, and, though there was much nonsense talked and written on the subject, it was undeniable that much of the periodical literature provided for the rising generation was of a very trashy character. I was led by what I heard and read of the desirability of providing mental *pabulum* of a higher order for boys to ask myself the question, "Would it pay? Would the boys take the better if it was provided?" I remembered that Mr. Wilkie Collins had, nearly twenty years before, announced his discovery of "a reading public of three millions which lies right out of the pale of literary civilization," and expressed the opinion that it was "perhaps hardly too much to say that the future of English fiction may rest with this Unknown Public, which is now waiting to be taught the difference between a good book and a bad. It is probably," he added, "a question of time only. The largest audience for periodical literature, in this age of periodicals, must obey the law of universal progress, and must, sooner or later, learn to discriminate. When that period comes, the readers who rank by millions will be the readers who give the widest reputations, who return the richest rewards, and will therefore command the services of the best writers of their time."

Had the time come? The experiment was worth trying, but few publishers care to risk capital in experiments of this description. It was so certain, too, that the something better that was to be provided must be something like the article which it was intended to supersede, that the way was not so clear to me, who was so well acquainted with the periodical literature of the day, as to those who, without that knowledge, were quite convinced that the penny publications read by boys were of an exceedingly demoralizing character. The more I thought about it the more clear it became to my own mind that, if anything was to be done, it must be by providing literature of the same kind, but of a higher quality.

I found a publisher who was willing to move in

the required direction if he could be shown some very original feature which would prove an unfailing attraction to some 150,000 or 200,000 boys. But I had no such feature in my embryo scheme, and I saw that such a very simple idea as giving similar matter, but of higher quality, would not commend itself to his mind on commercial grounds. The negotiations fell through, therefore, and I then cast about for literary associates in the enterprise who could bring to its aid the required capital. At the first step in this direction, however, I found that a provisional committee was in existence with the same object I myself had. Mr. J. Macgregor wrote me,—"We have numerous offers of aid in various ways, but a good working capital would be needed as a foundation."

That was in November, 1876. A month later I received the following letter from a gentleman residing in the neighbourhood of Birkenhead:—

"DEAR SIR,—As one who takes the greatest possible interest in the matter of a periodical for boys, might I ask how your idea is succeeding? It is a question over which I and a barrister friend have had long consultations, but we could never see our way clear. The last attempt in which we both helped came to grief. If your plan promises better success, perhaps something might yet be done; and really it is the greatest need of the day in the literary line.

"You have my sympathy, for it is an up-hill task; and, if you care about telling me anything of your plan and progress, I might be most willing to help you, if it was a thing that commended itself to my mind."

My correspondents saw their way no clearer than I did, or they were met by the same difficulties; for two years passed before I heard any more of the matter. Then, in the last week of October, 1878, I received the following letter from Mr. W. H. Hutcheson:—

"Kingsbrook House, Leytonstone, E.

"DEAR SIR,—The widespread mischief wrought by the sensational trash now so largely circulated amongst boys has impelled the committee of the Religious Tract Society to resolve to try, at all hazards, if something effective cannot be done to drive the bad from the market by providing the better.

"They have desired me to take charge of the matter for them, and the design is to produce immediately a boys' weekly illustrated paper,—to be essentially a boys' journal, bright with 'fun' and 'go,' adventure and instruction. Can you help us? Already the names of some of the best known and most honoured writers of the age have been secured, and we hope to start with good promise.

"Do you happen to have by you any stirring story of adventure on the lines of 'The Realm of the Ice King,' &c.? If not, and especially as we have no time to spare in the getting out of the initial number (particularly as regards the illustrations), I would suggest that you work up a good chapter of adventure, so as to be able to bring in one of the best cuts from 'The Realm of the Ice King,' say that facing page 87, or 101, or 275. Your narrative accompanying the latter cut would do, perhaps, with very little amplification, should you not see your way to send us anything else you thought better.

"I am sorry thus to seem to hurry you, but the committee, having laid their plans, are most anxious that not a day should be lost; and I want to get as much variety as possible into the first number.

"Waiting the favour of your early reply,
"I am,
"Yours truly,
"W. H. HUTCHESON."

I complied with Mr. Hutcheson's request without loss of time, entitling the narrative suggested by him, "Wrecked on a Floe." It duly appeared in the first number, issued at the beginning of 1879. I was, of course, then under the impression, derived from Mr. Hutcheson's letter, that he was the editor of the *Boys' Own Paper*; but from that time he dropped out of the undertaking and all the correspondence relating to it, and Dr. Macaulay was announced as the editor. This arrangement, whether or not it was a dislocation of the original intention of the Society, affected me only so far as my understanding of Mr. Hutcheson's letter was concerned. As my previous position on the Society's staff had been that of a contributor of fiction, I had anticipated an arrangement for a serial story, but in this I was doomed to disappointment, Dr. Macaulay would take no fiction from me, but was open to receive a narrative of personal travel or adventure abroad! It was in vain that I contended that, as a writer of fiction, my engagement by Mr. Hutcheson as a contributor could only mean that I was to contribute fiction. The only reply the doctor could make to this was, that some fifty writers had been communicated with, and they could not all expect to supply serial stories! Of course my contention was nothing so absurd. I only objected, as a round man, to being put into a square hole; and I submitted to Dr. Macaulay, and ultimately to the committee, that to require a writer of fiction, who had never been out of England, to contribute narratives of personal travel and adventures abroad was as unreasonable as to ask a writer on chess to supply a serial story. I suppose the committee failed to see the matter in that light, for the correspondence went on through the year without resulting in any change in the situation.

CHAPTER XXII.

"In Kent with Charles Dickens"—Letter from a lady—"Forty Years' Recollections"—How publishers' readers sometimes read manuscripts—Letter from Mr. John Morley—Reviews—Dr. Mackay's protest—My reply, and a friendly comment—Mrs. Victoria Woodhall.

"In Kent with Charles Dickens" appeared at the beginning of 1880. It did not receive much notice from the reviewers, the only paper in which I remember seeing anything about it being the *Graphic*, whose remarks, though brief, were favourable. It elicited, however, the following complimentary letter from a lady entirely unknown to me, who was contemplating a Dickens' pilgrimage such as I had described:—

"Dear Sir,—Next week I am going to Gravesend, Rochester, &c., for Dickens' sake, taking with me 'In Kent with Charles Dickens.' Will you add to the happiness I anticipate by according to me this favour —your autograph? I am so much obliged to you for your book that I covet the autograph of one who has given me such pleasure.

"I am, dear Sir,
"Yours truly,
"—— ——."

Of course a few lines were sent to the lady, and the

reference to a book and certain magazines in the letter in which she acknowledged the receipt of the coveted autograph indicates something Dickensian in the literary world which I brought under her notice.

"My dear Sir,—Accept my thanks for your autograph; I have put it opposite to that of Dickens in my collection. I am also much obliged to you for naming the book and magazines, neither of which have I seen, but both of which I have ordered. My tour was nearly perfect. We followed the course in your book, but, in our case too, Cooling was 'voted impracticable.' I was sorry, for 'Great Expectations' is almost my favourite of Dickens' works, and my dog is named Pip, but it could not be helped. I shall try for it another time. Again thanking you for your courtesy to a stranger,

"I am, my dear sir,
"Yours truly,
"―――― ――――."

"Forty Years' Recollections" was published towards the end of the same year, after encountering the too frequent difficulties raised by publishers' readers,—publishers, as Mr. William Howitt somewhere remarks, being the only tradesmen who do not consider themselves competent judges of their own wares. The manuscript lay several months with Mr. Henry S. King in 1872, when I received the following letter relating to it:—

"65, Cornhill, 25th June, 1872.

"Dear Sir,—We have to acknowledge the receipt of your letters of the 12th and 24th inst.

"We should have written long since respecting your autobiography, but we have had such contradictory and somewhat unsatisfactory reports on the book, and we were desirous of giving it our fullest consideration before coming to an ultimate decision.

"As a piece of autobiography there is a good deal of interest in it, but we think there is not sufficient of *public* interest to warrant the expectation of a successful publication.

"The memoirs of Samuel Bamford have to a certain extent occupied the ground, and if we are called upon to determine finally at this moment we think our decision must be adverse to undertaking its publication.

"If you would like, however, that we reconsider the subject at a later period, we have no objection to doing so.

"We are, dear Sir,
"Yours faithfully,
"Henry S. King and Co."

The paragraph about Bamford must surely have been prompted by one of the readers whose reports are said to have been "contradictory." We shall see presently that the manuscript had at this time been read by two of them, and, as their reports were "contradictory," one of them must have been favourable, the other being that of the gentleman who blundered in such an extraordinary manner about Samuel Bamford. The political career of that representative of the Radicalism of the nineteenth century was ended before mine began, and was running, indeed, before I was born! How, then, could his memoirs to a certain extent occupy the ground? I allowed the manuscript to remain with the Cornhill firm, however, and four months afterwards received the following intimation of its rejection:—

"65, Cornhill, October 17th, 1872.

"DEAR SIR,—We have now received the MS. of your autobiography from the hands of the third judge to whom we had confided it for perusal and advice.

"We regret to say that an entire agreement in our readers on the main point, viz., that the book is not likely to interest the public sufficiently to make its production remunerative, compels us to decline its publication.

"We should have been glad if we could have found grounds for a more favourable decision; and with our best thanks for the opportunity you have given us of considering your book,

"We are, dear Sir,
"Yours faithfully,
"HENRY S. KING AND CO."

Where there was contradiction in June there appears to have been agreement in October, unless I was to understand that the agreement applied to the personal matter, and the contradiction to the political history in which the autobiography was set. However this was, the season was now lost, and, as I found plenty of occupation for my pen during the next three years, the manuscript lay for a long time on the top shelf of a book-case. It was seen in the following year, however, by Mr. John Morley, who, in returning it to me from Puttenham, wrote,—"I have read your manuscript with much interest, for many of its incidents are beyond my memory."

The work subsequently underwent some revision, and in its new form was accepted and published by Messrs. Sampson Low, Marston, Searle, and Rivington. The first review of the book which came under my notice was in the *Literary World*, and commenced as follows:—

"Mr. Thomas Frost, a gentleman who has mixed considerably in the political history of the country, and not a little with its periodical literature, has written his recollections of what he has seen and heard. . . . Mr. Frost seems in the days of his youth to have conceived a strong liking for progressive social and political ideas. Familiar through his circumstances with the thoughts of the lower middle and working classes, his mind was astir, while young, with some new ideas which were then taking shape in a large number of minds."

Next came the *Athenæum*; and in respect of these reviews let it be observed that I quote only what relates to myself, and that only for the purpose of giving completeness to these reminiscences without trenching upon what was given in the book under notice.

"Mr. Frost has done a great public service by printing these 'Recollections.' The second half of his volume, readable and often amusing as it is, does not tell much that is new or important to know, but the earlier chapters, giving an evidently truthful account of his participation in the Socialistic and

Chartist movements of the second generation of this century, are a really valuable contribution to the history of opinion in our own day.

* * * * * *

Even while he was dabbling in these Owenite projects, Mr. Frost appears to have been much more of a Chartist than a Communist, and his volume concisely tells the story of the Chartist movement almost from its commencement to its close. Beyond some personal details, there is nothing very fresh or important in Mr. Frost's narrative; but it furnishes, at any rate, a quite satisfactory vindication of his own share in the movement. It is now well known that the Chartist leaders were by no means such desperate characters as they were supposed to be when people who at present rejoice in the triumph of the political views they advocated shuddered even at the mention of their names; but at the same time it is now generally acknowledged that the objects which the Chartists aimed at would have been attained all the sooner had they gone to work more prudently and wisely. In Mr. Frost's case, at any rate, Chartism was nothing very terrible. He was able to work zealously for the reforms it aimed at without being anything but a peaceable and steady-going citizen. His Chartism, in fact, seems to have been only useful to him in what is known as 'getting on in the world.' It certainly helped him to become a successful journalist."

I am not aware what data the reviewer had before him for the formation of the judgment given in the last sentences, or what his idea of success was in connection with journalism. But I am not aware that my political antecedents had any influence whatever on my career as a journalist, as I believe they were completely unknown, so small had been the part I had played in the arena of politics, until the publication of the " Recollections." As to the degree of success which I have achieved in journalism, tested by its results to myself, I shall have something to say upon that point before these reminiscences are closed.

The *St. James's Gazette* was merely amusing in its notice of the book, much of the matter of which was distorted, as in the opening passages :—

"Mr. Frost's story of his political and literary career is instructive and entertaining. He allows us to understand that from his earliest years he was influenced by a love of novelty and a desire to upset established institutions. With all the generous impulses of the youthful reformer, he had that want of judgment which usually accompanies those impulses. If as a young man Mr. Frost sought by a variety of absurd methods to effect the regeneration of society, greater men have done the same thing. There is a time, however, when the wise man no longer clings to even generous illusions; but how far Mr. Frost himself has gained wisdom by experience is not evident. Mr. Frost confesses that in early life he wished to agitate for ' the reconstruction of the entire fabric of society.' . . . A wilder set of enthusiasts than the men with whom he seems to have associated at this time it would be difficult to find, even in America."

The ascription to me of " the love of novelty and the desire to upset established institutions," so expressed as to convey the idea that I desired changes for the sake of novelty, and to destroy for the love of destruction, is a common delusion, or device, of Conservatives. It is of a piece with their constant application to Republicans, Socialists, and (if they are Russians) Constitutionalists of the term Anarchist, which truly describes no man outside a lunatic asylum. The only other notice I shall quote appeared in *Lloyd's Newspaper*, and concluded with the following sentence:—" We may confidently say of it that it is the record of a long life of work and of thought—a truly democratic life, which embodies a lesson of its own, to those who will learn."

I was at this time endeavouring to obtain regular and sufficiently remunerative employment on a newspaper, and after the publication of the "Recollections" I advertised as the author of that work, thinking that it should be a recommendation. In point of fact, it has never proved so, any more than my work in the Chartist movement; for, though Mr. Moy Thomas recommended me once for an editorship on the score of having written that book, without knowing me personally, I did not get the appointment. I mention the advertisement referred to because it elicited from Dr. Charles Mackay the following protest in the *Athenæum*:—

"An advertisement appears in the *Athenæum* that the author of 'Forty Years' Recollections' solicits employment as editor, sub-editor, or literary adviser, &c. I shall be obliged if you will state that in the year 1876 I published, through Messrs. Chapman, Hall, and Co., a work entitled 'Forty Years' Recollections of Life, Literature, and Politics,' that I have not issued the said advertisement, that it does not refer to me in any way, and that I have no knowledge whatever of the person who seeks employment as author of a book with that title."

To this I replied, through the same medium, as follows:—

"Will you allow me to state, for the information of Dr. Mackay, that I am 'the person who seeks employment as author of a book' bearing the title 'Forty Years' Recollections;' and that, as my book has been before the public only as many months as Dr. Mackay's has years, and my advertisement is signed with my initials, I had no reason for supposing that the announcement would be attributed to Dr. Mackay, which could only be done by those (if such there are) who would suspect him of having used the initials of the author of a similar work to his own."

The next issue of the *Printing Times* contained, under the head of "Two Richmonds in the Field," both the protest of Dr. Mackay and my reply, with the following comment, in which I traced the friendly hand of Mr. Charles Wyman, by whom a copy of the publication was forwarded to me by post:—"Mr. Frost is an old typo, and we need hardly say quite incapable of acting shabbily in this or any other transaction."

The only response to my advertisement which afforded even the glimmer of a prospect of employment was a brief note from Mrs. Victoria Woodhall, an American lady, whose name I remembered as a lecturer on "The Human Body the Temple of God," a title suggested by a passage in the Apostle Paul's first epistle to the Church at Corinth,—" Know ye not that ye are the temple of God, and that the Spirit of God dwelleth in you?" (c. iii. v. 16). No intimation was conveyed in the note of the purpose for which Mrs. Woodhall desired to see me; and though our subsequent interview took place by appointment, the lady was from home when I presented myself, with my usual punctuality, at her residence in Brompton, and I waited for her the greater part of the afternoon. Mrs. Woodhall's absence procured me, however, the pleasure of a very agreeable conversation with a young lady,—her daughter, I believe,—the chief topic being a comparison of English and American manners and customs, so treated, as under the circumstances it could not avoid being, as to convey information to both.

When Mrs. Woodhall returned, she plunged at once into business, speaking with great readiness and fluency. She was about, she informed me, to issue a publication for the double purpose of disseminating the views propounded in her lectures on the connection between morality and the knowledge of human physiology, and of refuting a scandalous rumour which had followed her from America, that she had been connected with the propagators of the gospel of Free Love. She had made arrangements for printing and publishing, she told me, but had not yet engaged an editor. Before making any arrangement with me she would like to see how I could write upon the subjects with which I should have to deal if she decided to employ me. Then she gave me some newspaper cuttings,—reports of her lectures,—and the interview was at an end.

Two days afterwards I posted to Mrs. Woodhall an article which I thought would be suitable for the paper she contemplated, according to her own exposition of her views and aims; but I never heard from or of her again.

CHAPTER XXIII.

Mr. H. H. Murphy and the *Sheffield Evening Post*—First impressions of Sheffield—Mr. Murphy prosecuted for libel—Mr. J. E. Bloomer—Result of the trial—Sheffield sewage—The children of Thomas Miller, the poet—Letter from Lord Wharncliffe.

WHILE I was seeking journalistic employment, and, in the meantime, collecting materials for a "Life of Feargus O'Connor" and "Chronicles of Tunbridge Wells," I received an offer of the sub-editorship of the *Sheffield Evening Post*, which the Press Directory informed me was an "independent" journal, established in 1873. There was some difficulty in arranging the terms, owing to a very wide difference of ideas as to what the remuneration of the sub-editor of an evening journal should be; but it was absolutely necessary for me to obtain employment, even the small supplies I had derived from the Ottoman Government having stopped, and the bonds themselves been sold, and I was forced to accept Mr. Murphy's terms.

I had been a contributor of serial fiction to the weekly issue of the *Post* from its commencement, finding it a good medium for the disposal of manuscripts which I could not succeed in placing with the periodicals. I knew something of the history of the paper, gleaned from my correspondence with Mr.

Murphy during that period, and we had some time before exchanged photographs. The present proprietor had been a reporter in Edinburgh, and afterwards at Sheffield, where he was employed on a journal which had a somewhat brief existence. Mr. Murphy and Mr. Dunbar, also a reporter from the Land of Cakes, then started the *Post* in partnership, and as a weekly journal. They did not get on well together, however, and agreed to dissolve the partnership. It was then found that, by some strange oversight, the deed of partnership had not been signed; and the affairs of the firm had, in consequence, to be wound up in Chancery. The paper was sold, and Mr. Murphy bought it, his late partner then joining the staff of the *Sheffield Daily Telegraph* as chief reporter, which position he still occupies.

The photographic *carte de visite* of Mr. Murphy, which I had in my possession, represented him as a pleasant-looking, rosy-cheeked young man, with very little hair about his face. It had been taken some years before he presented me with it, when he was a reporter in Edinburgh. I failed, therefore, to recognize him when, on my arrival in Sheffield, I was met on the platform at the railway station by a stout, middle-aged man, with a heavy moustache and abundant whiskers. He received me very cordially, conducted me to his office, inquired for lodgings for me, and, after some conversation, sent a man with me to the tramway station, to carry one of my bags. I obtained a bedroom, and the partial use of a sitting-room in what I described to my wife in a letter written the same evening as "a quiet street in one of the most elevated parts of the town, right out of the smoke, and with green trees and green hills in sight at one end." In fact, as I was not long in discovering, I was located within five minutes' walk of the picturesque scenery through which the little river Porter runs before entering the town.

Circumstances prevented my family from joining me until three months afterwards, and some extracts from the letters I wrote to my wife during that interval record my first impressions of Sheffield, and may interest those who are unacquainted with the peculiarities of South Yorkshire, where everything was as strange to me as if I had been in a foreign country.

" Among the peculiarities of the place are the *white* frocks worn by the butchers, the clean white aprons and little coloured shawls over the heads of the factory women, and the practice among the women of the working-class of cleaning the doorstep in the evening." " Among the peculiarities of Sheffield, coals are delivered by shooting them on the path from a cart, and then shovelling them into the cellar. All the bread I have seen has been tin-loaves, besides rolls and flat cakes. Women's stays are all black, red, or striped. [This I state only from observation of the shop windows, mind.]" " Hairdressers, instead of displaying toilet requisites, fill their windows with walking-sticks and fishing-tackle. Bakers' shops are very few; I know only one, and Mrs. Whike [my hostess] can count only four or five. Baking at home is very common, and grocers and pork-pie and polony shops sell bread. Pork-pies and polonies are sold by weight." " Many of the private houses have the edges of their doorsteps and window-sills whitened. Some of the poor people have a taste for colour, and, instead of hearthstone, use yellow ochre or indigo blue." "I saw a milkman ringing a bell yesterday morning, like a muffin-man. Many strange beverages are sold at little shops in the suburbs, such as 'treacle beer,' 'sugar beer,' 'herb beer,' 'sarsaparilla beer,' &c." "Sheffield is worse provided with coffee and dining rooms than any town I have ever been in. I shall amuse you some day with my dinner and tea experiences, though I am afraid I shall not be able to make them as amusing as Sala's search for beef while in Paris."

My first day at the office made me acquainted with the fact that, though I had been engaged as sub-editor, it was the intention of Mr. Murphy that I should be also editor, leader-writer, and reader, for he did nothing himself, and the staff consisted of myself, a single reporter, and a gentleman named Bloomer, who was canvasser, collector, and book-keeper, but had lately contributed a series of scandalous papers entitled, "Unburied Manuscripts," written in the style of Eastern narrative, and divided into numbered passages, like the Bible. For one of these papers Mr. Murphy was under prosecution by a brewer named Richdale at the time when he invited me to Sheffield, but the particulars did not become known to me until after I had commenced my duties. He had been bailed for trial at the Leeds Assizes, but he then seemed confident of acquittal. Of that result there seemed to me very small hope when I had read the incriminated narrative.

New as sub-editorial duties were to me, I got through the first day's work so well that Mr. Murphy, who was not in the office more than an hour that day, told me next morning that he could now go to Leeds with an easy mind, satisfied that everything would be done promptly and well. I had only been three weeks in my new position when the trial came on. Here I shall quote a letter which I wrote to my wife on the following day.

"I had an anxious day yesterday. Fisher was at Leeds, and was to have sent a full report of the trial. He says he did; but it did not reach the office. Murphy telegraphed three times, and the first two were in time for the first edition, but they were very short. The second ended with Mr. Digby Seymour, senior counsel for the prosecution, reading the libel, 'as follows.' As the 'Manuscript' had been stereotyped, I told the overseer to put it in. While the first edition was being worked off, the third telegram arrived. The defence had broken down, and Murphy, by the advice of his counsel, had withdrawn the plea of justification, and pleaded guilty! I rushed downstairs, stopped the machine, and had the libel taken out; for, as sentence was deferred till this morning, the republication of the libel would have been an aggravation of the offence, and probably increased the severity of the sentence. There was only one thing to be done, viz., to delay the publication while other matter was got up to replace the libel. This threw us behind an hour with the first edition, and half an hour with the others. As Fisher's report did not arrive, I sent out for each edition of the *Evening*

Star as published, and used their report for our later editions. Turner brought up a girl who had been subpœnaed for the defence, and who had called at the office on her return from Leeds; but she added nothing to what I knew, beyond enabling me to contradict the *Star's* statement (made to sell the next edition), that the sentence would be passed after the adjournment of the Court for luncheon. Bloomer came an hour later, and confirmed what the girl had said. We are all in the dark, and (except myself) in a state of bewilderment and dismay."

After this there were no more "Unburied Manuscripts." Mr. Murphy was sentenced to six months' imprisonment and the payment of 100*l*., the judge telling him that the plea of justification was an aggravation of the original offence. I now became editor in name as well as in fact, and a little incident occurred soon afterwards which enabled me to strengthen my position. A great meeting on the Transvaal question was held at the Cutlers' Hall, and I told Fisher, the reporter, to attend. Next morning, just as I had commenced writing a leader on the subject, the overseer brought me the proof of an article which he said had been given in by Fisher. For the three reasons that it was very fairly written, that I had plenty to do, and that, being short-handed in the composing-room, the composition could not well be sacrificed, I allowed it to pass rather than cancel it; but I called Fisher up from his desk in the publishing office, and asked for an explanation, for he had written no report, and it had to be cut out of one of the morning papers. He said he had had instructions from Mr. Bloomer. On that gentleman coming to my room in the afternoon, I told him what had happened, and what Fisher had said. He said Fisher must have misunderstood him. I let the matter drop, without any unpleasantness arising out of it, but I wrote to Mr. Murphy, asking him to define my position, as I could not do my best for the paper, as I wished to do, if there was to be any division of authority. The proprietorial response was,—" You are in sole charge, and, as my representative, I authorize you to write all political leaders, and discharge any man or boy in the place."

The paper soon began to improve, but, as the circulation had been materially increased while Mr. Bloomer was disinterring imaginary chronicles of the " City of Soot," and fell off when they ceased to appear, there was a considerable amount of lee-way to make up. Mrs. Murphy made a holiday trip to the Isle of Man, satisfied that the paper was in good hands. Fisher, after a second reprimand, was brought into due subordination; and Bloomer and I settled into our proper grooves without the slightest bickering, he tacitly recognizing me as editor, and assisting me with the sub-editorial work (as he had Mr. Murphy before my advent), and I leaving him all the business of management.

There was a little difficulty—a very small one—about politics. Mr. Murphy was a Conservative, and had conducted the paper on Conservative principles. I was not surprised, therefore, when Mrs. Murphy came down to the office one afternoon, and informed me that their friends thought my leaders were not Conservative enough.

"I am not a Conservative," said I. " Mr. Murphy

knew that when he engaged me, and that all my previous engagements had been on Liberal papers. Moreover, the *Post* is described in Mitchell's Press Directory as Independent, and that description must have been furnished by Mr. Murphy himself."

To this Mrs. Murphy could only rejoin that she thought journalists adopted the politics of the papers on which they were employed. I told her that, however that might be in some cases, I could not be a renegade to the principles I had held through life, and reminded her that Sheffield had been Radical, and that the political creed of a very large number of those who now called themselves Conservatives would be Radical again as soon as the hopes of the "Fair Traders" were disappointed, as they assuredly would be, by the failure of the Conservatives, when again in office, to return to the policy of protective duties. I had found, in fact, that "Fair Trade" was the only article of the Conservative creed that was held by most of those with whom I had had any conversation on politics, men who were Radicals on every other point, and some even Republicans, calling themselves Conservatives, simply because the craze of the time was associated with Conservatism in their minds.

I decided, however, to refrain from touching political questions on which parties were divided, and to confine my attention as much as possible to social questions. This I had no difficulty in doing, Sheffield, though one of the largest towns in the kingdom, being also one of the least advanced in civilization. I had never seen streets so dirty, or such a pall of smoke continually hanging over a town. The water supply, though abundant, was not good for drinking, being the surface water of the moors, and therefore of the same composition and quality as rain-water. The system of sewerage and sewage disposal was the worst I had seen in operation since my boyhood. The liquid sewage ran into the Don when the drains were not choked, and was absorbed by the soil when they were; while the solid constituents were dealt with by the old "night cart" system, and deposited at depôts out of the town, where the accumulations constituted a yearly increasing nuisance, and a standing menace of an epidemic.

I combatted this evil so vigorously in the columns of the *Post*, that when an inspector was sent down from the Local Government Board, I got the credit of having been in communication with that department. This was a mistake; but it is probable that a copy of the paper had been sent up by one of its readers. However this may have been, an inspector came down upon some other business, and, when that had been disposed of, startled the Corporation officials with the unexpected question, "What are you doing with your sewage?"

"We are waiting for a scheme," replied the town clerk.

The truth was that the Corporation and the authorities of Mexborough and Doncaster were each waiting to see what the other would do.

"You can soon get a scheme," said the inspector. "Tell your surveyor to put his brains in steep."

Conversation ensued, and the Corporation officials had it forced in upon their minds that something must be done. I did not remain in Sheffield long enough to see the scheme carried out, for there was a long delay, dilatoriness being one of the prime characteristics of Yorkshiremen.

In the autumn of this year I received from Mr. E. B. Neill some printed slips of an appeal on behalf of the orphans of Thomas Miller, the poet and novelist, accompanied by the following request: "Kindly aid in this urgent case of sore distress by inserting, and getting inserted, wherever you can. Perhaps you could enlist some local literary or other benevolents to make a little whip, to ever so small a degree. Nothing too insignificant, as it is really a matter of starvation to two people, one an imbecile." The appeal set forth the claims of Miller on those whom his poetry had delighted, and the fact that Lord Beaconsfield, who had given him a pension during the last few years of his own life, had died without making any provision for its continuance. The poet died soon afterwards, and his family were now in a state of destitution.

I need not say that I gave prompt insertion to this appeal in the *Post*, and sent copies of it to Messrs. Leader, the proprietors of the *Independent*, and Mr. Leng, the proprietor of the *Telegraph*, enclosing with each a brief note, expressing a hope that they would open a subscription in aid of the object at their own offices, and forward the amount collected to Mr. B. H. Grindley, proprietor of the *Liverpool Albion*, who had kindly undertaken the duties of treasurer to the fund. I also wrote letters to a large number of the men whom I hoped might be induced to give something. But the *Post*, I am sorry to have to record, was the only local journal in which the appeal appeared, and the responses I received to my epistolary communications numbered only two. The first was from the Earl of Wharncliffe, and ran as follows :—

"Wortley Hall, Sheffield,
"Sept. 25th, 1881.

"Sir,—I am sorry to say that I have not seen the appeal to which you allude, nor is the name of Thomas Miller known to me. But, as I gather from your letter that the case of the two children of Miller is one deserving of charity, and as you are good enough to say that my name will be useful, I will send you 1*l.* when you apply for it. I remain,

"Yours faithfully,
"Wharncliffe."

The case being one of urgency, I wrote immediately for the promised subscription, which was duly received, and remitted to Mr. Grindley. A similar sum was received from Mr. Mappin, M.P., and, with my own contribution, expended in postage and other expenses, completed the sum of Sheffield's efforts to keep the orphans of the best descriptive poet of the century from the workhouse. I find in my next letter from Mr. Neill the following passage: "Cannot sufficiently thank you in *re* Miller. The affair is a wretched failure thus far. Several people have written me long letters, telling me how they had applied *elsewhere*, but not giving a penny themselves, though well able to give pounds, and daily giving them in the most wasteful manner for the paltriest purposes." A week later he wrote, "You have done *uncommonly* well in *re* Miller, equal to the best that has been done single-handed, for, alack! the thing has been an abortion thus far, with small prospect of proving otherwise." I believe the nearest amount to the subscription received by myself was a sum of 1*l*. 14*s*. received by a member of the typographical staff of the *York Herald*.

CHAPTER XXIV.

Barnsley journalism—Reporting in the country—Lost in a fog—Zigzagging in a swamp—"Life and Times of John Vallance"—John Hugh Burland—Thomas Lister, the Barnsley poet and naturalist—Yorkshire dialects—Reuben Hallam and Charles Rogers.

THE six months for which I had been engaged expired in the beginning of January, and, though Mr. Murphy had then three weeks longer to remain in the county gaol at Wakefield, my engagement was not renewed, and my offer to conduct the paper until his liberation was not accepted. I received an offer, however, of the sub-editorship of the *Barnsley Times*, and, though the remuneration offered me was very little more than I had received in Sheffield, circumstances constrained me to accept it.

The *Barnsley Times* was described to me by Mr. Bloomer as a Conservative journal, and such I found it to be; but its proprietor had described it in the Press Directory as Independent. Such it may have been originally, if not non-political, for it was the oldest journal in Barnsley, having been started in 1855 by a Mr. Pybus. It subsequently passed into the hands of a company, by whom it was made the organ of the Conservatism of the district, not a sufficient force, it must be said, to sustain a newspaper, the population being mainly engaged in mining and manufacturing industries, and imbued with Radicalism from generation to generation. The enterprise was not a success, therefore, and the paper passed into the hands of the present proprietor, Mr. Joseph Wood, who had been the manager for the company. The change of ownership produced no improvement in its fortunes. The extreme cautiousness of Yorkshiremen, which passes with those who have not lived among them for astuteness, and their reluctance to part with money for any purpose which is not absolutely certain to result in immediate profit, paralyzes, when it does not altogether prevent, any enterprise of this description. I shall have said enough on this point when I add that it was a maxim of the proprietor that the week's expenditure should always be covered by the income of the preceding week, a Procrustean standard which must cripple any enterprise, however promising and well devised.

Added to this drawback was the fact that, with the exception of one comparatively brief period, the paper had never been well edited. In the early days of the company's rule it was edited by a gentleman named Cowan, who was described to me as a young man of considerable ability; but he was so harassed and hampered by the constant interference of the editorial committee, who knew no more of journalism than a pig does of geometry, that he threw up the editorship in disgust, and obtained a better position on a Leeds journal. Since it had been in the hands of Mr. Wood, who was a music-seller and stationer, without any experience of journalism, he had been always nominally, and sometimes actually, the editor; it being a too common practice of newspaper proprietors at the present day, when they require the services of an editor, to advertise for a sub-editor, who, when installed in the office, finds that he has to be also editor and leader-writer, his employer, by this device, securing an editor for the salary of a sub-editor. Under these circumstances, there had been a succession of sub-editors in the *Times* office, none of whom had remained long, some proving incompetent for the duties thrust upon them, and those who were better qualified taking the first opportunity of leaving that was presented by a better opening elsewhere.

The only other journal in the town was the *Barnsley Chronicle*, which was started three years after the other by Thomas Lingard, originally a shoemaker, who had been a prominent worker in the Chartist cause, and in 1839 received the distinction of imprisonment in York Castle, with John Vallance and others, some of whom were still living when I became a resident in Barnsley. The paper was at first printed at Wakefield, but the success resulting from its announcement as the organ of the local Liberalism encouraged Lingard to set up an office of his own in the centre of Barnsley. When he died the management of the paper, and of the printing and stationery business connected with it, devolved on his sons, the editorship remaining in the hands of Mr. Alexander Paterson, who had been seventeen years the occupier of the editorial chair when I assumed the editorship—I beg the proprietor's pardon, the sub-editorship—of the *Times*. Liberalism being the predominant political creed of the town and district, of a moderate type among the trading portion of the community, and more advanced among the dense industrial population, chiefly miners, the *Chronicle* had a very much larger circulation than the *Times*, and I was not long in discovering that there was no prospect of lessening the difference.

My experience at Sheffield of the duties supposed by some newspaper proprietors to pertain to the office of sub-editor had prompted me to seek an explanation on this point before completing the negotiation with the proprietor of the *Barnsley Times*. I was reassured by his statement that this was not a nominal editorship, but that he required a sub-editor who was competent to relieve him. I understood this as meaning that I might be called upon to act as editor and leader-writer in his occasional absence from Barnsley, or when prevented from acting by an unusual pressure of business. I found, however, that the only difference between my new duties and those I had performed on the *Sheffield Evening Post* was, that I had to assist in the reporting department, and was subject to almost daily interference, in which appeared to consist the proprietor's whole understanding of editorship.

As a matter of course, in these conditions, the same difficulty presented itself as at Sheffield. Mr. Wood, though he knew that I had always, as a leader-writer, been engaged on Liberal journals, expected me now to write Conservative leaders, though I had been engaged only in the subordinate capacity of sub-editor. To write leaders I had no objection, and I evaded the difficulty as much as possible by making foreign politics and social questions the subjects of my pen, not venturing at first to deal with local topics; but this could not always be done, and on occasion we came into collision. One of the earliest leaders in which I ventured beyond the domain of what I had told Mr. Wood were my specialities was on the question of Mr. Bradlaugh's admission into Parliament, which I was careful to treat on constitutional grounds, without any reference to the religious grounds involved in the question. Mr. Wood refused to allow the article to appear, however, observing that the readers of the paper would not discriminate, in which he was perhaps right, being, as a Conservative himself, better able than I was to measure their mental capacity.

My extra-Parliamentary reporting had hitherto been limited to two meetings for the *Birmingham Journal*, and one for the *Liverpool Albion*, the three occasions being the annual dinner, at the Freemasons' Tavern, of the Iron and Hardware Trades Pension Society; a meeting of watchmakers at a public-house in Clerkenwell to oppose Sir John Bennett's scheme for the employment of women; and the indignation meeting at the London Tavern to condemn the mismanagement of the war in the Crimea, which, being held on a Saturday afternoon, I was able to give in the *Albion*, then published on Monday morning, before the London papers could reach Liverpool. Now I had to report the proceedings in the police-court on the days when both borough and West Riding courts were held, and meetings of every description, in the town or within six or seven miles of it, whenever there were two engagements.

My experiences of country reporting commenced, it must be remembered, on the last day of January, when snow lay deep on the ground all round the town, and the evenings were dark. Readers who are unacquainted with South Yorkshire require a little information as to the superficial features of that part of the country to enable them to understand the disagreeablenesses, and even dangers, to which strangers are exposed in traversing the by-roads, and some portions of the highways, during the hours of darkness. As results of the unwillingness of the people to incur any expenditure for improvements, the constant cry of "keep down the rates," and the innate conservatism in matters not political which makes them cling to whatever they have been accustomed to, the region abounds in perils to the traveller by night. Railways cross the roads on the level; roads are carried across depressions ranging in depth from a few feet to forty, from a fall into which there is only the protection of a dilapidated stone wall, often in ruins, and in some instances rising only eighteen inches above the footpath; streams running through fields intersected by footpaths are crossed by wooden bridges destitute of a hand-rail; trains of coal-trucks glide in the darkness along colliery tramways crossing public roads.

I had been only a week in Barnsley when it fell to my lot to report the monthly meeting of the Local Board of Darton, a half-mining, half-agricultural township, three miles distant. The Lancashire and Yorkshire Railway—waggishly denominated the Loungeshire and Yawnshire—is about the worst in the kingdom, and the station at Darton is, I trust, the worst on the line. There are two approaches from the road—both bad. One is an unlighted lane terminating at a dark railway arch, under which the traveller has to pass, then turn under another dark arch, and follow the line to an uncovered platform. The other is by a dark lane which conducts him to a narrow wooden bridge over the River Dearne, beyond which bridge it skirts the unfenced river, which roars and foams ten or twelve feet below, between perpendicular banks of sandstone, fragments of which lie at all sorts of angles in the bed of the stream, making a fall as dangerous in dry seasons as in times of flood. The bridge crossed, a track across a pasture-field leads to a little, broken-backed stone bridge over a "cut" from the river, and thence into the other approach.

It was six o'clock in the evening when I reached the station, and so dark that nothing was discernible beyond a few yards. Two girls who had travelled with me from Barnsley directed me from the lane to the school-house at which the Board met, and the lights of which I could see across the intervening distance. I could scarcely see the path or the bridges, but I reached my destination safely, and was there joined by a reporter from the *Chronicle* office. When we left the darkness had become absolute blackness, the effect of a cloudy sky and a thick fog, so that we could not see a yard before us. My companion took my arm, and hurried me down the lane towards the bridge, for we had only just time enough to catch the train. We ran against the fence two or three times, and were presently admonished to pause by the knowledge that we were near the bridge, and that if we missed it we should probably be precipitated into the river. We groped for the hand-rail of the bridge, but could not find it. I thought afterwards, when I had seen the spot by daylight, that we must have gone beyond it. We could hear the water rushing and splashing, and knew that we must be close to the brink. My companion declined further exploration in that direction, and we hurried back into the road—that is, what he knew to be the road, but what was to me only a black void. Presently I dimly made out a railway arch, and then my companion, hearing the train coming, dropped my arm, and ran off as fast as he could, leaving me in the darkness, without the remotest idea of my surroundings.

I ran forward, however, in the direction he had taken, and on the other side of the viaduct saw the lights at the station on the left, and ran towards them. My companion was already lost to sight and to hearing, having passed through the next arch in the contrary direction. I could dimly discern the viaduct on my left, and knew there was a low stone wall on my right, for I had run against it. Presently I missed the wall, and had only the lights at the station to guide me. The path, if there was one, was uneven and muddy, and when within twenty yards of the railway I stumbled, and fell, with a splash, into some standing water. Scrambling to my feet, I ran on, and found myself brought up by iron railings fencing the line.

Over these I clambered, but the train was then in motion, and there was not another for nearly three hours. A porter took me into a room, where I washed my hands and face, scraped the mud from my trousers, and dried them by the fire. On consulting a labourer who had missed the train as to the road, I was advised to wait, as being preferable to tramping three miles in the mud and fog, especially as I did not know the road. So I resigned myself to circumstances, and made the best of the situation by smoking a cigarette, reading a newspaper lent me by the civil and obliging porter, and writing out my report.

The School Board of this delectable place meets at the schools, which are situate in the neighbouring hamlet of Mapplewell, which is much more populous than the village which gives its name to the township. The distance from Barnsley is about the same, but there was at that time no communication by railway with Mapplewell, except *viâ* Darton. A fortnight after the adventure just related I visited that village again, and found, on getting into the road, that I had a mile and a half, or more, to walk. It was already dark, and the road was not much lighter where, at a little distance beyond Darton, I saw a red flame casting a flickering glare upon the mud, and on reaching it found that it proceeded from a coal fire in an iron basket, where a colliery tramway crossed the road on the level. A sound as of an approaching train reached my ears, and, on looking in the direction whence it proceeded, I discerned a distant red light. I paused for a moment, but the train seemed to be moving slowly, and I ventured to cross.

I did not go that way again, however, for I found the distance from Darton to Mapplewell was more than half the distance from Barnsley to the latter place, and preferred the highway. On the occasion of my first visit by the latter route, I was about to return by the same way, when the reporter who had been my companion in the adventure at Darton suggested that we should save half a mile by crossing some fields into the Huddersfield road, instead of following the Wakefield road. At the end of the hamlet, therefore, we turned into a lane which descends into the valley of the Dearne, and, though the evenings were still dark, and the ground after the first quarter of a mile very rough, we reached the river without encountering any obstacle, and crossed it by a wooden bridge. Between the river and a shallow, sedgy stream which flows into it a little lower down, and is crossed by another wooden bridge, unprovided with a hand-rail, a swampy pasture-field intervenes, often impassable in winter, when much of it is under water.

"We must go carefully now, Mr. Frost," said my companion. "The ground is worse than I expected to find it. You had better let me go first, and keep close behind me, treading where I tread."

Slowly and in single file we zig-zagged across that dismal swamp, now curving to the left, now to the right, seeing here and there the glimmer of water through the fast-increasing obscurity, until at length the second wooden bridge was crossed, and we began to clamber up a steep path, strewed with pieces of sandstone.

"Now we are on the canal bank," said my companion, as we again saw water glimmering before us, and heard it rippling among the flags along the bank. "The towing-path is narrow, mind, and we shall presently be at the high bridge, where you must mind not to step into the canal."

A pleasant walk, to save half a mile, was it not? A few yards brought us to the bridge, which loomed blackly through the obscurity like a scaffold. It is approached at either end by an ascent of fifteen steps, and at the end opposite to the towing-path the approach is by a strip of land not more than a yard across, with water on each side. The bridge crossed, we struck into a footpath across the fields, and I soon had the satisfaction of seeing the lights of Barnsley before us.

The dangers of the district are not always escaped with no worse result than a little excitement. During the last four years three or four fatal accidents have occurred at level crossings; one man tumbled over a broken wall, and was killed; another stumbled against a wall not more than a foot above the level of the road, and was precipitated into a garden, with the like result; besides several minor casualties. Among the latter, a reporter whose ill-fortune it was to have sometimes to go to Darton, on one occasion narrowly escaped a plunge into the Dearne at the spot where I turned back in the fog on my first visit to the place, and on another stumbled at the stone bridge, hurting one of his knees so much that he was temporarily incapacitated for duty.

I have mentioned John Vallance as one of the

fellows in misfortune of Thomas Lingard in 1839, when both suffered imprisonment in York Castle. Vallance was still living at the beginning of 1882, but before I had an opportunity of becoming acquainted with him I heard of his death, and immediately announced "The Life and Times of John Vallance," which was continued in the columns of the *Times* for about three months. He was a local notable, though only a hand-loom weaver, and long past labour of any sort, being supported in his latter days by the aid of a few benevolent persons. He had been implicated in the march to Grange Moor, near Huddersfield, of the Yorkshire Radicals, in 1820, on which occasion he had been convicted of treason and condemned to death, a sentence never intended to be carried into execution. It was mitigated to fourteen years' transportation, which in the case of his companions was actually suffered, but Vallance, after four months' sojourn aboard the convict hulk at Gosport, received a pardon. He was in his eighty-eighth year at the time of his decease, and such was the respect in which he was held by his fellow-townsmen that a large concourse attended his funeral, a county magistrate and several members of the Town Council joining the procession.

Another old Chartist, who has since joined the majority, was John Hugh Burland, who was a frequent contributor of both prose and verse to all the newspapers of the district. I became acquainted with him soon after my coming to Barnsley, though, as he then resided at Hoyland, we seldom met. He was entirely self-educated, and claimed to have taught himself grammar—a rare attainment in Yorkshire, even amongst what are usually regarded as the educated classes—history, and mathematics. He began to figure as a Radical in 1838, and when the Northern Political Union was formed he became a member; there he found his old schoolfellows, Amos Maudsley, author of "Roland: a Masque," and John Widdop, and made the acquaintance of Joseph Crabtree, William Ashton, John Vallance, and Peter Hoey. He delivered speeches and moved resolutions, was sometimes elected chairman, and was placed on the general committee and the committee of public safety. Isaac Lister, who was treasurer to the Northern Union, introduced him to his brother, Thomas Lister, the author of the "Rustic Wreath;" and the intimacy thus formed was maintained through life. On the 12th of August, 1839, when the great demonstration was held on May-day Green, he read from the hustings the memorial to the Queen for the mitigation of the punishment of the Birmingham political offenders. In three days after this he absconded to escape imprisonment, and for three months found refuge amongst his maternal kin at Great Driffield.

On his return to Barnsley he assisted in the establishment of the Franklin Club, for the mutual improvement of the education of the members by means of classes, lectures, and discussions. In 1844 he became a schoolmaster in Barnsley, and, three years afterwards, having qualified in a training-school at York, he obtained the appointment of head-master of an elementary school in the county of Durham. The Duke of Cleveland, who was a patron of the school, employed him to write a catalogue of the library at Raby Castle, in a legible hand, in a book provided for the purpose, which was intended to show from a glance where any particular volume might be found, as books were deposited in different parts of the castle. This employment gave him an extensive knowledge of books. He returned to Barnsley in 1849, and became the local correspondent of the *Leeds Times* and the *Wakefield Examiner*. In the following year he was selected for the mastership of the township school at Stainborough, a scattered and thinly-populated place about three miles from Barnsley, which appointment he held for eighteen years. In his leisure hours he wrote sketches of local "characters" for the *Barnsley Times*, and contributed many specimens of his verse to the columns of every journal in the district. His poetry is not above mediocrity, but verse-making seems to be regarded in Yorkshire as the highest exercise of the intellect, even though rhyme and metre may both be defective. Hence every one who aspires to literary fame, such as can be made in the columns of a newspaper, writes verses, which are not always entitled to be regarded as poetry, even upon the most charitable construction. There is more real poetry in the "Roland" of Amos Maudsley than in all the productions of all the rest of the so-called Barnsley poets put together.

In 1868 Burland left Stainborough, and during the next four years was in business at Rotherham, as a grocer and provision dealer, removing in 1872 to West Melton, where he carried on the same business four years longer. While at Rotherham he contributed numerous essays and reviews to the *Rotherham Advertiser*, and in 1873 commenced the publication in the *Barnsley Chronicle* of the " Annals of Barnsley and its Environs," which extended over several years, and would be a very useful work for reference if the manuscript, which, bound in four volumes, is in the library of the local Mechanics' Institute, was more readily accessible; but the librarian only attends for an hour or so in the evening. He also contributed to the same journal memoirs of Amos Maudsley and Charles Rogers, *alias* Tom Treddlehoyle, the *nom-de-plume* under which the widely known and quoted *Bairnsla Foaks Olmenack* was produced.

In 1875, accompanied by Dr. Payne, of Newhill Hall, he made a survey of Roman camps and roads, and other places of antique and historical interest in South Yorkshire, which appeared in " Historic Notices of Rotherham." In the following year he was unanimously elected school-warden of Hoyland Nether, and he removed from West Melton to that place, where he died in June, 1885. Many gentlemen of the district attended his funeral, assembling for the purpose at the Town Hall, Hoyland, whence they walked in procession to the cottage of the deceased, and there fell into the rear of the mournful *cortège*, and accompanied it to the place of interment. These friends included the vicar and several members of the School Board and a party from Barnsley, comprising Joseph Wilkinson, author of " Barnsley Worthies " and a " History of Worsborough;" Thomas Lister, author of a collection of poems entitled " The Rustic Wreath;" John Grimshaw, president of the Radical Association;

two officials of the Corporation, the editor of the *Barnsley Chronicle*, and myself.

My esteemed friend, Thomas Lister—more frequently called Tom Lister, in the familiar manner common to Yorkshiremen, who abbreviate the first names of the squires in the same manner—must not be overlooked after saying so much about Barnsley. Lister is now in his seventy-sixth year, having been born in 1810. His parents were highly respected and well known in the neighbourhood for their industrious lives and practical Christianity. Thomas Lister was educated at the Friends' School, Ackworth, where, besides receiving a good English education, he became famous among his schoolmates for athletic feats and physical courage; and those early exercises, with the thoughtful element at all times pervading his mind, developed that great love of natural objects and robust outdoor life which forms so striking a part of his vigorous intellectual work. After leaving school, he went to work with his father, a gardener and small farmer, and several years were passed in that employment.

In 1832, having already earned a local literary reputation, Mr. Lister was introduced to Lord Morpeth (afterwards the Earl of Carlisle), who nominated him for the situation of postmaster then vacant at Barnsley. But it was necessary for him to take an oath before entering upon the appointment, and this act, contrary to the principles of his sect, the young Quaker poet declined; the position was consequently given to another. Two years later, Mr. Lister was induced to publish a little volume of poems, under the title of "The Rustic Wreath," of which 3000 copies were quickly sold. In the summer he visited Derbyshire, the Lake district, and the Highlands of Scotland, travelling chiefly on foot, and walking from thirty to forty miles per day. James Simpson, author of "The Philosophy of Education," introduced him to the late William Chambers and Dr. Robert Chambers, and his sonnet on entering Scotland appeared in their *Journal*. He also visited Professor Wilson at Hawthornden. He had previously been introduced to Ebenezer Elliott by Charles Reece Pemberton, the dramatist and elocutionist, and to Robert Nicoll by James Battison, who was then in the office of the *Leeds Times*.

Early in 1838, Mr. Lister lectured at the Barnsley Institute on the scenery, institutions, and manners of Scotland, and in the following summer set out for a tour on the continent, which he accomplished partly by diligence and partly on foot. His travelling companion was George Bayldon, a brother bard, who penned some fairly good descriptive poetry. Lister visited Paris and Lyons, crossed Mount Cenis, traversed the great valleys of Piedmont, and the plains of Lombardy, entered Milan, Turin, and other Italian cities, saw the classic lakes of Como, Lugano, and Maggiore, re-crossed the Alps, explored Switzerland, and returned by the Netherlands. The scenery which met his eye, the authors and philosophers he met, and the antiquities and works of art he examined, greatly stimulated his genius; and his impressions found utterance in such poems as "Sonnets, written in the Valleys of Piedmont" and "Sunset Musings in Milan." He translated from the German, "The Herd Boy of the Mountains;" from the Italian, "The Gardener and the Shepherdess;" and from the French, "The Dream of Joan of Arc in Prison," Beranger's "Holy Alliance of Peoples," and his "Visions of Peace." Several of these compositions and translations appeared in *Tait's Magazine*, to which they were forwarded by Ebenezer Elliott, unknown to the writer, who was pleasantly surprised at this mark of appreciation.

To "A Casket of Sonnets," which appeared this year, Mr. Lister contributed eighteen and Elliott four, one of which is addressed to the Barnsley poet. Others were contributed by Bayldon. On the subject of his continental travels Mr. Lister delivered gratuitous lectures in different towns in Yorkshire, repeating in them the poems written during his wanderings, by which means numbers of persons were made familiar with them. Many of the poems were also inserted at different times in Leeds, Wakefield, Doncaster, and Sheffield newspapers. In 1839, the office of post-master at Barnsley again became vacant, and Mr. Lister was offered and accepted the situation, a simple form of declaration having been substituted for the oath in all post-office appointments. Unlike his brother Isaac, the Barnsley post-master had no predilection for politics; but he frequently mounted the platform to advocate social reforms or elucidate literary questions. In 1845, when John Holland, with unexampled generosity, published "The Poets of Yorkshire," the posthumous work of William Cartwright Newsam, a sketch of the Quaker poet appeared in it, accompanied by his "Sunset Musings in Milan." Elliott thus spoke of him at this time, in a letter to

George Tweddell, the editor of the *Yorkshire Miscellany*:—"You will find him in many respects remarkable: a courageous, energetic, gristle-bodied man, with a bump of 'I'll have my own way' bigger than a hen's egg on his summit ridge; his face is handsome, except the eyes, or rather their position, which is cavernous; the eyes themselves are keen and characteristic. If there is truth in phrenology, his observant faculties should be strong and active, which his writings seem to prove. Had I known such a man forty years earlier, I should have climbed Ben Lomond with him."

In the early part of 1850, Mr. Lister delivered a course of lectures in the Mechanics' Institute, on modern English poetry. On the evening of the 12th of March, when the last had been delivered, Mr. Inns, the president, said he had something better to present him with than a vote of thanks, and gave him a silver inkstand and a gold pen, which had been subscribed for by several members as a token of their appreciation of his services. Mr. Lister was agreeably surprised by this testimonial, of which he had received no hint, though living in the centre of news. In a long letter to "January Searle," written about this time, Mr. Lister described the literary life of Elliott, and this sketch was printed in the appendix to Searle's memoirs of the Corn Law Rhymer, which appeared two years later. Searle also inserted in the same appendix a sketch of the Barnsley poet.

To the members of the Franklin Club, Mr. Lister delivered a lecture on the Genius and Character of Elliott, on the 25th of November following, in the course of which he said, that a work containing fuller information about Elliott had for some time been announced, by John Watkins, Elliott's son-in-law. The completion of this work was followed by the death of the author. The poet and his biographer sleep side by side in the churchyard at Darfield. The two widows now reside at Hargate Hill. On the 2nd of December, Lister lectured again to the Franklins, on the subject of Elliott.

Mr. Lister was an occasional contributor to the *Naturalist*, a publication conducted at one time by Mr. B. R. Morris, and afterwards by his brother, the Rev. F. O. Morris. In January, 1857, he read a paper on the mineral beds and coal workings of the Barnsley district before the members of the local Naturalists' Society; and in June of that year, when he accompanied the society to Walton Hall, a copy of Waterton's natural history essays was awarded him as a prize. Soon after this he read a paper on the natural history and fossil remains of the Barnsley district before the West Riding Geological and Polytechnic Society, in the Barnsley Court House. In 1862, Mr. Lister produced "Rhymes of Progress," illustrating the advantages of education, temperance, and economy. Many years before he had been urged by Ebenezer Elliott to make the question of education the subject of his muse; in fact, to become the "Educational Rhymer." Picturing the beneficent results likely to be obtained thereby, and stimulating his friend for the glorious mission, Elliott wrote as follows to Mr. Lister:—"What a name you may win, and what good you may do by writing short pieces on education!

What a world of pathos, beauty, hope, humour, and sarcasm is within your reach! Let education be your text, to be expounded in a thousand ways, with a thousand sad and beautiful elucidations! From natural ignorance results not drunkenness only, but all other public evils. When you conquered the rare power of expressing every-day and common life-thoughts in rhyme, you bent the bow of Ulysses. This power, and your love of the beautiful, with your knowledge of the people, and your graphic power to paint them, all point you out as the man who is to be the Education Rhymer. What felicitous opportunities you will have of introducing your fine pictures of rural scenery, and what might be and ought to be happiness! What a universe of sorrowful thought and sweet contrasts, and heavenly anticipations." Mr. Lister's subsequent engagement at the Barnsley Post Office in a measure prevented him from any systematic attempt to poetically realize Elliott's idea.

The inauguration of the statue of Joseph Locke, in 1865, led to the composition of one of the poet's finest lyrics, which was set to music by Mr. Joseph Wood, and sung at the public dinner on the occasion. Mr. Lister had several interviews with Baron Marochetti, from whom he received a small bust of Wellington in token of the sculptor's appreciation of the poems on his native land. As a member of the British Association, Mr. Lister has annually attended the gatherings in different parts of England for many years; and, at Southampton meeting, August, 1882, he read a valuable paper on the distribution of Yorkshire spring migrants. He had read similar papers at Bradford, Belfast, and York meetings, in previous years. Mr. Lister is president of the Barnsley Naturalists' Society; and his sympathies and labours have been earnest in the promotion of mechanics' and similar institutions throughout his native county. Mr. Lister retained the position of postmaster until 1870, when he retired upon a pension; and the inhabitants of Barnsley, rightly viewing his long and faithful services as worthy of recognition, presented him and his wife with a handsome testimonial, at a large public meeting, presided over by the mayor.

Charles Rogers had departed this world before my appearance in Barnsley, but I may mention here a circumstance which is probably little known, namely, that he was once interviewed by no less a personage than Prince Lucien Buonaparte, who was desirous of a specimen of the Barnsley dialect, in which the *Bairnsla Foaks Olmenack* was produced. Yorkshiremen are proud of their dialect, which flourishes vigorously all over the county, though in the southern counties of England the old provincial dialects have died out, the only trace of them that remains being some slight peculiarities of pronunciation. I once heard a Barnsley churchwarden preface a speech at a public meeting with the remark that he could only speak Yorkshire and the Barnsley dialect; and on another occasion a Barnsley clergyman, presiding at an entertainment given by the members of a mutual improvement class, announce a recitation "in the dialect we all love so well." There are variations of this dialect peculiar to different districts. The dialect used by the working classes of Sheffield differs in some respects from that of Barnsley, and Reuben Hallam, whose acquaintance I made while in the capital of Cutlerdom, is said to be the only man who perfectly understands it. He is the author of a story written in that dialect, entitled "Wadsley Jack," which, first in the weekly supplement of the *Sheffield Independent*, and afterwards as a volume, attained immense local popularity. Once, when reporting in the Barnsley police-court, I heard a witness from Skelmanthorpe, a village between Barnsley and Huddersfield, say, in reply to a question, "Ah took na gorm of it."

"Took no what?" said one of the magistrates.

"He means, your worship, that he took no notice," observed the inspector.

I had never heard the word before, and have never heard it since, but I lately came across it in one of the novels of Charlotte Brontë.

CHAPTER XXV.

A disappointment and another change—First impressions of Liverpool—The *Evening Albion* and the *Telephone*—My Italian host—A priest in search of relatives—Transfer of the papers to a company—Letter from Mr. Moy Thomas—Return to Barnsley.

THE six months for which I had been engaged on the *Barnsley Times* expired in August, and I expected that the promise of an increase of salary after that period would then be realized; but I was disappointed, and resolved at once to take the first opportunity of leaving. This presented itself in October, when Mr. Grindley offered me the sub-editorship of the *Evening Albion*, with a salary which would have exceeded what I could expect on the *Barnsley Times*, even if I had got the promised advance. I accepted the offer at once, therefore, and, leaving my family at Barnsley for the present, proceeded to Liverpool.

The city of the mythical marsh-bird which figures in the municipal arms impressed me very favourably. I had imagined it something like the east end of London, and to my surprise found broad streets of shops rivalling those of the west end and a display of architecture at one end of Lime Street more than rivalling Trafalgar Square. At one end of the city I found two fine large parks, one exceeding in picturesqueness anything to be seen in the public parks in the suburbs of the metropolis; and at the other a broad expanse of sandy beach, commanding a fine view of the sea and the opposite coast of Cheshire.

The contrast with Barnsley was very striking, and I felt this as much in the office as when six o'clock p.m. released me for the day. There was no interference with my duties, no fault-finding for the sake of it; but the utmost geniality and the fullest appreciation on the part of both Mr. Grindley and his partner. I found that Mr. Hind had left the staff three or four years previously, and the only link remaining between the past and the present was the overseer, who, though nothing of mine had been in the *Albion* for more than ten years, recognized my caligraphy as soon as my "copy" again came under his notice. The *Evening Albion* was, as Mr. Grindley had told me, still struggling, but the proprietors had, a few months before I joined the staff, started a new morning paper, the *Telephone*, which, being published in time to catch working-men on their way to work, was said to be doing well, and likely to prove a success. Mr. Grindley edited this new venture, and the *Albion* was left to me as entirely as the *Sheffield Evening Post* had been.

I lodged at the house of an Italian named Zanetti, with whom I one evening had a pleasant conversation about Garibaldi, of whose enthusiastic reception in London I had been a deeply interested and sympathizing witness. Happening to speak of the manner in which Carlo Gatti, the proprietor of the music-hall in Westminster Bridge Road, formed the tail of a magnificent procession in his little pony-chaise, I found that my host knew him; and then, having some slight knowledge of the Rev. V. Zanetti, the priest of St. Mary's, Westminster, and knowing that the name was not a common one, I inquired if he was in any way related to the *padre*.

"Now that is curious," said Zanetti. "It is about a year ago that Father Zanetti came here, all the way from London, to ask that same question. He had only one relative in the world, he told me,—a sister, who, I think he said, was in a convent. He had accidentally come across my name in some way or other, and thought it probable that there might be some relationship. We had a long conversation, and the discovery, at the outset, that we both came from Lombardy, and from the same district, increased the interest with which he pursued the inquiry. But, though we each brought all our knowledge of our respective families to bear upon it, not the slightest relationship could we trace."

All the circumstances considered, this was a result which could scarcely have been anticipated, and I could not but sympathize with the disappointed priest, who is, I believe, a most worthy man, though a priest and a brother of the Order of Jesus.

I had soon, however, affairs of my own to think about. It transpired one morning that every one on the establishment, except myself, had received notice to leave; and on inquiry I found that the concern had been sold to a limited company, of which Lord Folkestone, Mr. Pulston, M.P., a couple of local magistrates, and Mr. Grindley were the directors. The *Albion* was to be amalgamated with the *Telephone*, which perhaps was the reason why I did not receive notice to leave with the rest, as the notice was only a legal requirement of the transfer, and Mr. Grindley had shortly before asked me to take charge of the *Telephone*. This I had declined to do, not being disposed to undertake night-work, and for the same reason it became evident that my continuance on the staff was impracticable under the new arrangements.

There was some talk at this time of an evening journal being brought out by the proprietors of the *Mercury*, and I called at their office one evening to ascertain whether there was any truth in it, and, if so, whether there was any prospect of an engagement on the paper. Mr. Lovell had not arrived, and a gentleman on the sub-editorial staff told me he had not heard of the rumour and did not believe it. Mr. Lovell, on his arrival, told me there was no truth in it, at the same time expressing sympathy with me in the position in which I so unexpectedly found myself. Similar expressions of friendliness were received from Mr. Weatherall, sub-editor of the *Daily Post*.

Before I left Liverpool, however, a gleam of hope appeared in the form of a sympathetic letter from Mr. Moy Thomas, enclosing one from Mr. Charles Welsh and his reply thereto. It appeared that Mr. Welsh had been asked to recommend an editor for " a Liberal paper in an important cathedral town, a new venture, with plenty of money behind it," and had passed on the request to Mr. Moy Thomas, who had replied that the promoters " could not have a better man than Mr. Thomas Frost, the author of 'Forty Years' Recollections.'" This reply he forwarded to me, to be sent to Mr. Welsh, accompanied by my application for the appointment. I waited for the result hopefully, and not without anxiety, but I heard no more of the affair. I had some reason to believe that Chester was the "important cathedral town" in which the venture was to have been made; but the intention was not realized, and I returned to Barnsley when the snows of the waning year were whitening the adjacent moors.

CHAPTER XXVI.

The *Barnsley Independent*—Drawbacks to its success—Controversy with a correspondent—The general election—Split in the Liberal camp—Mr. C. S. Kenny—Mr. Pickard—Liberal compact with the miners—National Association of Journalists—Deterioration of journalism—Results of a career considered successful.

BEFORE I left Liverpool I received a letter from the gentleman who was then the chief reporter of the *Barnsley Times*, acquainting me with the arrangements in the office consequent on my resignation and the manner in which they had resulted. I had been succeeded by a person who absented himself on the first two days of the second week, and who, making his appearance on the third day in a semi-inebriated condition, had then been summarily dismissed. Since his departure the literary work in connection with the paper had been performed by the proprietor, with such assistance as could be rendered by the reporter in the way of sub-editing and proof-reading. How the editing had been done I had afterwards an opportunity of seeing, for I had not seen the paper since my departure from Barnsley. The original matter consisted of a leader, leaderettes on local topics, and a column of "Town Talk," the political, municipal, and social gossip of the town and district. While I was at Liverpool there had sometimes been no leader, sometimes a leader without any leaderettes, or, if these appeared, no local gossip.

A young Scotchman was installed in the editorial armchair on the Monday morning after my return to Barnsley; but on the succeeding Monday morning I received a visit from the reporter, who was commissioned by the proprietor to negotiate for my services on the paper, pending whatever arrangements for the future might be made either by him or myself. The Scotchman had proved utterly incompetent, and, having the rare faculty of discerning his incapacity, had gone straight to the railway-station after "treasury" on Saturday, and taken his passage to his home beyond the Tweed. I went down to the office, therefore, acquainted Mr. Wood with the state of my negotiations with the people who were supposed to be promoting a Liberal journal in an important cathedral town, and undertook the editorship of the *Times* pending their completion or collapse.

About a week afterwards I was made confidentially acquainted with the proprietor's intention to make a new departure in journalism. The *Times* had never been a success. It was to become extinct at the end of the year, and then, like the phoenix from its ashes, the butterfly from the chrysalis, the *Barnsley Independent*, independent in politics as in name, was to dawn upon the world, or that portion of it at least which lies between Wakefield and Rotherham. If it would suit me to undertake the editorship, I should have sole supervision of the literary department and the salary that I had lately received at Liverpool. This offer I accepted, being satisfied by this time that the opening of which I had heard through Mr. Moy Thomas had collapsed.

The new departure was not, in a commercial sense, the best that might have been made, though the proprietor had often remarked that, as a tradesman, he was bound to manage his newspaper property on strictly commercial principles. Independence of party was not a promising platform in a district where Liberalism was construed as Gladstonism, and Conservatism was translated "belief in Lord Salisbury and all his works,"—where Liberals regarded Conservatives as the natural enemies of the people, and Conservatives stigmatized Liberals as Bradlaughites, Parnellites, and Anarchists. The Liberals were so much the stronger political section of the district, in point of numbers—the chief point to be considered in these days of penny newspapers—that more of the elements of success would have been commanded by taking advantage of a weak point in the defences of the local Liberalism to introduce an organ of more advanced views than found an exponent in the *Barnsley Chronicle*.

This I saw clearly at the time; and it was seen by all the more advanced Liberals of the town when another and more decided step towards the realization of the Parliamentary reforms proposed by the People's Charter had been made in the Franchise and Redistribution Acts and the agitation began which preceded the general election of 1885. The need of a local organ of Radicalism was a frequent subject of conversation, and I was again and again told that now was the time for the appearance of such a paper. But the financial means for the purpose were not at my command, and there was not enterprise enough in the town to furnish them, though every Radical was convinced that success would be certain. The proprietor of the *Chronicle* had lost much of his inherited popularity since he had become the owner of Cockerham Hall, and he had been ousted from his seat at the municipal council-board. The growth of a more advanced Liberalism became more distinctly manifest after the formation of the local Radical Association. The *Chronicle* ignored that movement until the action of the *Independent* rendered that course injudicious, and frequently indulged in a scarcely veiled sneer at its leaders. The Radicals regarded the editor of that journal as a political jelly-fish, and acknowledged that the non-partisan *Independent* was more liberal than the professedly Liberal *Chronicle*, the moderatism of which at length caused its proprietor and editor to be suspected of coquetting with Conservatism.

But Mr. Wood was both too much a Conservative and had too much of that Yorkshire cautiousness which would deter a "Tyke" from giving a shilling for a sovereign, lest the latter should prove a counterfeit, to make a venture in Radicalism. He aimed at retaining the Conservative readers of the *Times* and gaining new readers in the ranks of Liberalism; and, to a certain extent, he was successful in both directions. Most of the Conservatives accorded to the new journal the support they had given to the defunct one, and a considerable accession of new readers was gained, who were of course drawn from the Liberal ranks. But the *Independent* was heavily handicapped from the first by its Conservative associations, to say nothing of the obstacles to a triumphant success presented by the inability of minds of average calibre to understand that a journal could support a beneficial Gladstonian measure without being Liberal in a party sense, or criticize unfavourably the foreign policy of Mr. Gladstone unless Conservative, and the force of habit, more powerful in Yorkshire than in any other part of England I have ever been in, which caused many to prefer the *Chronicle* for no better reason than their having read it all their lives, though they contemptuously described its leaders and leaderettes as "milk-and-water." Hence, while the more cultured of the Liberals took both papers, the masses rejected the *Independent*, without looking at it, as "the old Tory paper with a new name," while not a few of the Conservatives, though they read it, declared they could not make out whether it was Conservative or Radical, and that it ought to be either one or the other.

The Conservative proclivities of the proprietor caused him to lend a willing ear to the complaints of his fellow-partisans, and he now and again came into the editorial room to suggest some "good opportunity of pleasing the Conservatives." As he was never anxious to please the Liberals, I had to counteract the Conservative bias which the Radicals sometimes thought they detected by administering, as opportunity offered, homœopathic doses of philosophical Radicalism, with the natural result of earning the disapproval of the Conservatives. Though the correspondence columns were as open to one party as to another, it was intolerable to the ultras of that party that Liberalism, partisan or otherwise, should have any voice in a paper which, though announced, in the plainest terms, as being independent of party, they regarded as their organ. An attack, which looked very much like the result of a conspiracy, was made, therefore, upon the editor, whom they regarded as the cause of what seemed to them the Radical bias of the paper, if not the cause also, in some degree, of the change of front effected at the commencement of 1883.

I received from an unknown correspondent a request that I would write an account of the Manchester massacre of 1819, or, if unable to give a complete history of the affair, to state the circumstances which led to it, and whether the Whigs or the Tories were in office at the time. I responded to this request by stating, very briefly, in my answers to correspondents, the leading facts of the case, and added—" The Tories were in office at the time." Next week I received a letter from a Conservative gentleman who had been a frequent correspondent of the paper, using various *noms-de-plume*, the present being " Vindex," charging me with having made the statement as to the Tories being in office in 1819 for the purpose of " discrediting a great political party," and expressing surprise at the appearance of such a statement in the columns of a Conservative journal. I inserted this letter, and replied to it in a leaderette, stating that the *Independent* was not a Conservative organ, quoting the announcement in its first issue that it would advocate national interests, irrespective of parties, and showing the ridiculous character of his accusation by the absence of any expression of opinion in the reply I had given. Thence commenced a controversy in the paper which went on for several weeks, each letter from "Vindex" exhibiting increased violence and acrimony, to which I could not always reply with vigour and effect in my editorial capacity, without imperilling the position of the *Independent* as a non-partisan journal. Sometimes, in addition to a leaderette, I wrote a paragraph of "Town Talk," which gossiping column was signed "Asmodeus," and not acknowledged as editorial; sometimes, while defending myself in my editorial columns, I assumed the offensive in a letter, with a *nom-de-plume*. I cared little or nothing for the contention of "Vindex" that it was well known that I was "Asmodeus," and that it was inferrible from internal evidence that I was also the writer of the letters signed "A Radical," in which I showed that the views of Alison concerning the Manchester meeting and massacre were, staunch Tory though he was, at variance with those which had been put forward by "Vindex."

No one, I think, could have imagined that such a storm as assailed me could have been raised by the simple statement of an indisputable historical fact. But "Vindex," putting aside all assertions on my part to the contrary as falsehoods, persisted in maintaining that I had not been asked whether the Whigs or the Tories were in office at the time, that I had made that statement for the purpose of throwing odium on the Tory party, and that I must have had that intention because the statement was calculated to have that effect. Arguing in this manner, he launched into a long tirade on the alleged crimes of the Radicals, and denounced me as an accessory after the fact, on the ground that only a Radical would write as I had written on this subject, and that, being a Radical, I was constructively a participator in all Radical misdoings, past and present, on the principle that every one of the individual components of a mob is liable to prosecution for any riotous acts of that mob. I doubt very much whether any other journalist than myself would have allowed himself to be abused and vilified week after week in a paper edited by himself in the manner and to the extent I was by "Vindex;" but I had the satisfaction of knowing, as the controversy went on, that the sympathy of even Conservatives was veering to my side, and that I was allowing him the proverbial "rope enough" to metaphorically hang himself. When this had been sufficiently demonstrated by his being reduced to the repetition of false and abundantly refuted accusations, I pronounced the correspondence closed. It was about time. So far its sole effect had been to increase the circulation of the paper, but by this time the public were becoming tired of it. Finding himself debarred from continuing his virulent and mendacious attacks in the *Independent*, he issued a handbill, declaring himself unfairly treated, and calling upon me to resign!

The storm passed over, without any damage to myself or the paper, notwithstanding its violence, or perhaps because of its violence and the preposterous character of the ground on which the attack was made. I foresaw, however, that a more serious difficulty was likely to be raised when a general election took place under the new political conditions of uniform franchises and equal electoral districts. In the excitement of an election contest no journalist can be neutral, and support of either candidate on the ground of national interests or the common good of society is sure to be construed into support of the party represented by that candidate. At the commencement of the contest in the Barnsley division the Liberals were disunited and the Conservatives disorganized. The latter were, in consequence, unprepared with a candidate, and the former had two. The moderate section of the Liberal party selected Mr. Milnes, only son of Lord Houghton, and the Radicals invited Mr. Acland. Both gentlemen came forward, and addressed the Liberal Caucus, after which a ballot took place, with the result that Mr. Milnes had a small majority of votes over Mr. Acland, who had estranged the shopkeepers by his advocacy of co-operation. The death of Lord Houghton very soon afterwards rendered Mr. Milnes an impossible candidate, and then the Radical Association seized the opportunity to bring forward Mr. Courtney Stanhope Kenny before the Caucus, in which moderatism was then predominant.

Mr. Kenny was fortunately adopted by the Caucus, and Mr. Acland was eventually returned for the Rotherham division.

The new electoral conditions had encouraged among the miners the hope of being able to return a candidate of their own for one of the eight divisions into which the South-West division of the West Riding had been cut up under the Redistribution Act. They had organized themselves for this purpose with the machinery ready to their hand in the Yorkshire Miners' Association, and Mr. Benjamin Pickard, the corresponding secretary of that organization, was the selected candidate. There was at first an idea of contesting the Barnsley division, but this, for divers sufficient reasons, was abandoned, and a compact was entered into between the Liberal leaders and the Miners' Association, by virtue of which the miners' vote was to be given to the Liberal candidates in all the eight divisions, and Mr. Pickard was not to be opposed in the Normanton division by another Liberal candidate.

The success of Mr. Kenny was practically assured before the Conservatives had succeeded in catching a candidate. Mr. W. S. Stanhope, who had once represented South-West Yorkshire, but had been rejected in 1880, would not have been an unacceptable candidate to many of the moderate Liberals even, but he could not be prevailed upon to present himself again under conditions so greatly altered. Mr. Guy Senior, a local brewer, was induced to allow himself to be announced as the Conservative candidate; but politics constituted a region in which he was a stranger, and the terrors of its exploration, which his imagination created, induced an attack of brain-fever, which necessitated his withdrawal from the contest, and even from the scene. At the eleventh hour a scion of the house of Wentworth, a youthful lieutenant in the Guards, was nominated in the interests of the Conservative party, and fought a losing battle with considerable spirit. The result is known. Mr. Kenny was returned by a majority which astonished even his supporters, so much was it above what they had anticipated.

In the meantime the contest had weakened my position on the *Independent*, not so much by anything done by me to alienate the Conservatives, because any ground lost in that way would, in the absence of an organ of that party, have been recovered after the excitement of the election had subsided; but because the excitement had fanned the undying Conservative fire in the proprietor's soul into a flame, and it was kept alive by the repeatedly expressed wish of prominent supporters of Mr. Wentworth for a paper that should be thoroughly and distinctively Conservative. He had heralded the candidature of that gentleman with a flourish which could only have been justifiable in the case of a popular independent candidate, and met my remonstrance against this departure from the principles of the paper with the remark that he had only recommended him to the Conservatives!

A few weeks after the election I received an intimation from him that he was about to make alterations in his editorial staff which would involve his dispensing with my services. As the entire literary staff consisted of myself and a reporter, the explanation was absurd, and the grandiloquent manner in which he spoke of his editorial staff was rather amusing. The changes really made were his assumption of the editorship himself, the elevation of the reporter to a sub-editorial stool, and the addition to the staff of a second reporter. The paper then became Conservative, and the proprietor had his mental vision gladdened by the prospect of saving the difference between my salary and the second reporter's, which was quite sufficient to blind him to the further prospect of a loss of circulation. The average Yorkshireman prefers saving sixpence to earning a shilling. A farmer called at an office in Barnsley one day to receive payment for a load of straw. He had not a receipt stamp, and, on the clerk telling him he must get one, he went out and lost an hour in walking about the town endeavouring to beg one, though he was close to the post-office. He would not have minded the loss of the hour if he could have saved the penny.

The National Association of Journalists had been founded by a conference of press-men at Birmingham in the autumn of 1884, and on a branch being formed at Sheffield shortly afterwards I attended the meeting held for that purpose, and was enrolled as a member. I was actuated in this course by the hope of arresting the downward progress of the profession by working from within, as I had failed in the single-handed attempts I had made some time before from without. I had made certain suggestions to the London Press Club in the preceding spring, and in the summer I had written to Lord Houghton on the subject, and endeavoured to arouse both the profession and the public to a due sense of its importance through the medium of the *Athenæum* and the *Times*. But no reply was accorded me by Lord Houghton, and my letters to the press were not inserted. The avowed objects of the Association were "to protect the common interests of the journalistic profession," and "to advance the status of the profession, and secure those advantages which, in the case of other professions, have been found to accrue from union." The means by which these objects were to be attained were not set forth. After the preliminary business of the Sheffield branch had been disposed of, I rose, therefore, and asked the chairman, Mr. Dunbar, what it was supposed the Association could do for a journalist that he could not do for himself? The response was an evasion. It was a very large question, Mr. Dunbar observed, and he was sure that I must see that it could not be dealt with then, when the hour for dinner had arrived. So the important question of the means of realizing the objects of the Association was shelved in favour of dinner.

"I think the question may be answered in three words, Union is strength," observed a Sheffield reporter who sat on my left.

"That depends upon the use that is made of the strength," I rejoined.

That was the point which I desired to see settled, and, with a view to its ventilation, I initiated a correspondence in the *Athenæum* in which Mr. S. Bennett, of the London Press Club, and Mr. J. B. Atkinson, of the *Manchester Examiner*, who was one of the secretaries of the Association, joined. My contention was, that the programme of the Birmingham Conference provided no means for the attainment of its objects, and that to protect the common interests of the profession, advance its status, and "secure those advantages which, in the case of other professions, have been found to accrue from union," it was necessary that the same organization and machinery should be adopted as existed in other professions. The legal and medical professions had rules for maintaining their status and securing the due remuneration of their members. Journalists must have similar rules, or the objects of the Association could not be secured. To these representations it was replied that the Association was in its infancy, that the profession must be organized before such a movement as I had indicated could be attempted, and that the Birmingham Conference had resolved that "the Association does not contemplate interference in any dispute which may arise relating to the rate of payment or remuneration of any member of the profession."

The controversy in the columns of the *Athenæum* created considerable interest in the journalistic profession, and I received several letters from different towns conveying information as to the degradation of its members and the deterioration of press-work that was being brought about by the competition of newspaper proprietors, and the process of reducing expenses that was in constant operation as the result. The following came from a large manufacturing town in Yorkshire:—

"I trust that you will pardon my taking the liberty of thus writing to you; but I have followed the discussion *re* the National Association of Journalists in the *Athenæum* with considerable interest, and felt a desire to communicate with you on the subject. The same question that you have so well dealt with in that correspondence has so often occurred to myself, and more especially in the light of recent events, which I will enumerate. A few months ago the proprietor of the —— advertised for a senior reporter. I applied for the vacancy, having previously been on the staff of an evening for about three years as reporter and assistant sub-editor. I received a telegram a month after, asking me to run over from —— to ——, where I saw the proprietor. I named my terms, but these appeared to him pretty high; but I held out for 2*l*. 10*s*. and no less. He consented to consider the matter from Saturday to Monday, on which day he informed me he had decided to give me what I asked. I commenced my duties a fortnight afterwards, and, in addition to reporting, had to sub-edit all the manuscript (which was somewhat bulky), and also to superintend the reading. In the meantime he procured two juniors at 15*s*. per week, and after six weeks informed me that his finances would not bear the strain, and the consequence was I was shortly on my beam ends; and the paper is now being worked by three juniors and himself, one receiving 1*l*. and the other two 17*s*. 6*d*. per week. I have now been out of an engagement five weeks, and have answered numbers of advertisements; but, because I ask the modest salary of 2*l*. 10*s*. or 2*l*. 5*s*., I am unable to obtain a place, one gentleman having written to me that had no fewer than 100 applications from reporters willing to commence at 30*s*. per week. I would gladly become a member of any association that could assist those situated like myself; but I am utterly unable to see how the Association can do anything for a man that he cannot do himself."

This letter illustrates a process that has been widely adopted in newspaper offices. I know an evening paper in a large manufacturing town in Yorkshire on which only one reporter is employed, that position being filled at the time to which my knowledge of it refers by a young man receiving only 25s. per week. On an evening journal published in an important commercial port there were, three years ago, five reporters employed, only one of whom was over seventeen years of age. The number has since been reduced to four. On a weekly issued in another manufacturing town in Yorkshire there are two reporters, one receiving 35s., the other 18s.; and on another paper in the same town only one reporter is employed, at the munificent salary of 30s. per week. Now, what would be the operation of a journalists' association organized on lines similar to those of the National Typographical Association? A scale of salaries would be adopted conformably to the circumstances of different classes of newspapers, and youths who had not been seven years in the profession would (unless they had entered it after attaining the age of twenty-one) be treated as apprentices, the number of whom in any office would be limited by rule.

Editorial salaries are undergoing the same process. How frequently journalists who have to do editorial work are engaged by a trick as sub-editors I have before noticed, and the salaries these gentlemen receive range from 30s. to 2l. per week. "I have never paid more than 35s.," said a Yorkshire newspaper proprietor to me a few years ago; and I know that in one instance he paid only 32s. I should not like to say that 30s. is the minimum, for I have seen in the *Athenæum* an advertisement for a sub-editorship, the duties of which the advertiser announced his willingness to perform for 25s. per week.

The result of this state of things is the growing deterioration of journalistic work. The diffusion of elementary education which flooded mercantile offices with clerks whose qualifications were limited to the ability to write legibly and add up columns of figures has, for several years past, had the result of over-running the reporterial market with lads whose sole qualification for reporting is the knowledge of shorthand. As a rule these young gentlemen are ignorant of grammar, in many instances cannot spell correctly, know little or nothing of modern history, the knowledge of which is essential to a journalist, and whenever condensation is required are apt to make their sentences unintelligible. Their employers, looking for their pecuniary gains from advertisements rather than from the circulation of the paper, condone their deficiencies in consideration of their cheapness; and in time they are promoted to the editorial room, at salaries considerably less than their predecessors received, and proceed to write leaders and reviews without knowing how to construct a sentence in good literary English, or even to write grammatically. It is not surprising, then, that there should be a too numerous class of journalists who are, as an old and esteemed friend of mine, formerly well known in the press world, observed to me not very long ago, "illiterate, illogical, ill-everything."

In closing these reminiscences, a few words remain to be said in reference to a matter glanced at by the *Athenæum* reviewer of my "Forty Years' Recollections."

It was remarked that my Chartism had been useful to me in what is known as "getting on in the world," as it had helped me to become "a successful journalist." Let us see what this means, when tested by the facts. My gains from the field of labour I was supposed to have cultivated so successfully have never exceeded 100*l.* per year, and my entire income from journalistic and other literary undertakings combined have never exceeded 200*l.*, an amount which I received, in fact, for only one year, when I edited a periodical, wrote leaders and leaderettes for two newspapers, and was an occasional contributor to two or three other publications. Is this what the *Athenæum* reviewer understands as successful journalism?

My requirements, and even my desires, are of an exceedingly modest character, as the reader may suppose; but an income of 60*l.* per year, and that derived from an inheritance, and not from the accumulated savings from the earnings of former years, will be admitted to be an inadequate provision for them. Is this the position in which a hardworking *litterateur* should find himself at the close of a successful journalistic career, or, as the writer of the review of the "Recollections" in *Lloyd's Newspaper* said, of "a long life of work and of thought?" Yet, in my sixty-fifth year, it is mine. My years—not the ordinary infirmities of the sexagenarian, for as yet I have not felt them—shut me out from journalistic work in the future. Young men get the preference when the work to be done is insufficient to employ all the labourers who press into the field, and the enthusiasm of youth combines with the glamour which surrounds the literary life to tempt those upon whom the responsibilities of life have not begun to press, to accept any rate of remuneration that may be offered, as a beginning. Within the last few months I have known an able and experienced editor supplanted at the age of fifty by a younger man, the difference of years being the only ground for the preference of his successor. What chance, then, has the veteran of sixty-four?

I do not repine. I have no regrets, and should probably run the same career again could I, like Faust, renew my youth. If I have not been "a successful journalist," in the sense which the world attaches to the word "success," I have done something, according to the measure of my capacities and opportunities, to keep society moving ever onward to a higher and better phase, and the consciousness of having realized that aim will always be regarded by me as my best reward.

THE END.

www.ingramcontent.com/pod-product-compliance
Lightning Source LLC
Chambersburg PA
CBHW081216170426
43198CB00017B/2627